Lives in Transit

Why are they
here?
—neoliberclism

Neolineraliom
as market +
economic foreign
policy

+ political
   economy

+ Structurelviolence

+ neo linerciom
   ⤷ economic system
      open market
      fewer reguardton
      lazzonfere

CALIFORNIA SERIES IN PUBLIC ANTHROPOLOGY

The California Series in Public Anthropology emphasizes the anthropologist's role as an engaged intellectual. It continues anthropology's commitment to being an ethnographic witness, to describing, in human terms, how life is lived beyond the borders of many readers' experiences. But it also adds a commitment, through ethnography, to reframing the terms of public debate—transforming received, accepted understandings of social issues with new insights, new framings.

Series Editor: Robert Borofsky (Hawaii Pacific University)

Contributing Editors: Philippe Bourgois (University of Pennsylvania), Paul Farmer (Partners In Health), Alex Hinton (Rutgers University), Carolyn Nordstrom (University of Notre Dame), and Nancy Scheper-Hughes (UC Berkeley)

University of California Press Editor: Naomi Schneider

1. *Twice Dead: Organ Transplants and the Reinvention of Death,* by Margaret Lock

2. *Birthing the Nation: Strategies of Palestinian Women in Israel,* by Rhoda Ann Kanaaneh (with a foreword by Hanan Ashrawi)

3. *Annihilating Difference: The Anthropology of Genocide,* edited by Alexander Laban Hinton (with a foreword by Kenneth Roth)

4. *Pathologies of Power: Health, Human Rights, and the New War on the Poor,* by Paul Farmer (with a foreword by Amartya Sen)

5. *Buddha Is Hiding: Refugees, Citizenship, the New America,* by Aihwa Ong

6. *Chechnya: Life in a War-Torn Society,* by Valery Tishkov (with a foreword by Mikhail S. Gorbachev)

7. *Total Confinement: Madness and Reason in the Maximum Security Prison,* by Lorna A. Rhodes

8. *Paradise in Ashes: A Guatemalan Journey of Courage, Terror, and Hope,* by Beatriz Manz (with a foreword by Aryeh Neier)

9. *Laughter Out of Place: Race, Class, Violence, and Sexuality in a Rio Shantytown,* by Donna M. Goldstein

10. *Shadows of War: Violence, Power, and International Profiteering in the Twenty-First Century,* by Carolyn Nordstrom

11. *Why Did They Kill? Cambodia in the Shadow of Genocide,* by Alexander Laban Hinton (with a foreword by Robert Jay Lifton)

12. *Yanomami: The Fierce Controversy and What We Can Learn from It,* by Robert Borofsky

Lives in Transit

VIOLENCE AND INTIMACY ON
THE MIGRANT JOURNEY

Wendy A. Vogt

UNIVERSITY OF CALIFORNIA PRESS

University of California Press, one of the most distinguished university presses in the United States, enriches lives around the world by advancing scholarship in the humanities, social sciences, and natural sciences. Its activities are supported by the UC Press Foundation and by philanthropic contributions from individuals and institutions. For more information, visit www.ucpress.edu.

University of California Press
Oakland, California

Library of Congress Cataloging-in-Publication Data

Names: Vogt, Wendy A., author.
Title: Lives in transit : violence and intimacy on the migrant journey / Wendy A. Vogt.
Description: Oakland, California : University of California Press, [2018] | Series: California series in public anthropology ; 42 | Includes bibliographical references and index. |
Identifiers: LCCN 2018016212 (print) | LCCN 2018019795 (ebook) | ISBN 9780520970625 | ISBN 9780520298545 (cloth : alk. paper) | ISBN 9780520298552 (pbk. : alk. paper)
Subjects: LCSH: Immigrants—Violence against—Mexico. | Immigrants—Abuse of—Mexico. | Immigrants—Services for. | Central Americans—Mexico.

Classification: LCC HV6250.4.E75 (ebook) | LCC HV6250.4.E75 v64 2018 (print) | DDC 362.88086/9120972—dc23
LC record available at https://lccn.loc.gov/2018016212

Manufactured in the United States of America
25 24 23 22 21 20 19 18
10 9 8 7 6 5 4 3 2 1

For my family
and for migrants everywhere

Contents

Illustrations

Acknowledgments

This book is dedicated to the migrants, shelter workers, priests, activists, and local community members who shared their lives and their stories with me. It has been the privilege of my life to witness and work alongside you as you struggled to cross borders, support your families, and speak truth to power. I am particularly humbled and inspired by the work of everyday people who in big ways and small choose love over hate and justice over profit. For reasons of confidentiality I am not able to mention the people who fill these pages by their real names, but it is my hope this work contributes in some way to ongoing and collective struggles for rights and justice.

The School of Anthropology at the University of Arizona was a wonderful place to be a graduate student. In Tucson, I cultivated rich and meaningful relationships with my mentors, peers, and friends. Through her example, my advisor Linda Green taught me the power of critical and politically engaged research, and I am forever grateful for her unwavering support, guidance, and friendship. I thank Thomas Sheridan and Laura Briggs for their sharp insights and enthusiasm. I am also indebted to Linda and Laura for showing me that academic motherhood is not just possible but comes with many rewards. I also thank Ana Alonso, Diane Austin, Bill Beezley, James Greenberg, Eithne Luibhéid, Norma Mendoza-Denton,

Lydia Otero, Barnet Pavao-Zuckerman, Jennifer Roth-Gordon, and Drexel Woodson, at the University of Arizona. My fellow UA alums continue to be a wonderfully rich source of inspiration and friendship, and I love connecting with you all at conferences and visits. For their input and support on this project, I especially want to thank Brian Burke, Jacob Campbell, Daniela Diamente, Heide Castañeda, Karin Friederic, Natalia Martínez Tagüeña, Nick Rattray, Robin Reineke, Rodrigo Rentería Valencia, Andrea Rickard, Jeremy Slack, and Joanna Stone. Special thanks also to my friends Jennifer Josten, Gabrielle Civil, Nick Kawa, and the Alkov, Ricchiuto, and Rubin families. Extra special thanks to my bestie Sarah Rubin, who has been on this anthropology journey with me since our days in Kroeber Hall.

I found a second home and some of my most cherished friendships in Mexico. Thank you to Glen and Flora Strachan, Randy and Susie Hinthorn, Jayne Howell, Alder and Ryan Bartlett, the extended García family—mi familia Oaxaqueña, the amazing women at CAMINOS, all the people I crossed paths with in the shelters I call Casa Guadalupe and Albergue Nazaret, and many others I cannot name. I thank the staff of Mexico's Fulbright Commission. At the National Autonomous University of Mexico (UNAM), I thank Dra. Martha Judith Sánchez Gómez and Dra. Julia Tagüeña. At the Organización Internacional para las Migraciones (OIM), I thank Fernanda Ezeta and Juan Artola. I also thank the staff of the Instituto Nacional de Migración (INM) and the Archivo General de la Nación (AGN). At the Instituto Oaxaqueño de Atención al Migrante (IOAM), I thank Mtra. Lucía Cruz.

I am fortunate to work with a wonderful group of colleagues at Indiana University – Purdue University Indianapolis (IUPUI). Susan Hyatt has been a true champion since we first met one fateful day in Montreal, and her commitment to collaborative research and social justice continue to inspire me. I thank Paul Mullins for his mentorship and witty sarcasm, both of which have been much appreciated throughout the book-writing process. I am also grateful for the support and friendship of Holly Cusack-McVeigh, Jeanette Dickerson-Putman, Gina Sánchez Gibau, Chris Glidden, Eric Hamilton, Angie Hermann, Laura Holzman, Liz Kryder-Reid, Modupe Labode, Audrey Ricke, Michael Snodgrass, Jeremy Wilson, and Larry Zimmerman. I have been fortunate enough to have some wonderful graduate students at IUPUI, including Ryan Logan, Alessandra De

Chancie, Brian Laws, Erin Donovan, and Sean Baird. Special thanks also to the incredible and inspiring students in my 2017 Masarachia seminar, particularly Guadalupe Pimentel-Solano, Patricia Alonso-Ceron, and Umaymah Mohammad.

Over the many years of writing this book, I have benefited from the insights, comments, and editing of friends and colleagues. Karin Friederic, Brian Burke, Andrew Gardner, and Laura Holzman all provided feedback on sections of the book. Nick Rattray read several iterations of the book in the stolen hours of night after our kids went to sleep and before they awoke. Finally, my writing partner extraordinaire, Heide Castañeda, generously read and provided comments on the entire manuscript, was a constant source of support and camaraderie, and helped me through some of the most difficult stages. Thank you, Heide.

I am inspired by a larger group of scholars who demonstrate the ways ethnography and public scholarship can engage with the world in meaningful ways. Over the years, conversations, panels, and other exchanges with a number of them have been particularly influential on my thinking in writing this book. I thank Deborah Boehm, Noelle Brigden, Mario Bruzzone, Susan Coutin, Whitney Duncan, Amelia Frank-Vitale, Rebecca Galemba, Ruth Gomberg-Muñoz, Charles Hale, Lauren Heidbrink, Josiah Heyman, Sarah Horton, Jayne Howell, Christine Kovic, Krista Latham, Ellen Moodie, Anya Peterson Royce, James Quesada, Gilberto Rosas, J. C. Salyer, Lynn Stephen, and Kristin Yarris. I am grateful to the "smuggling gang," most especially Antje Missbach, Luigi Achilli, and Gabriella Sanchez. I also wish to acknowledge several people whose lives were lost too soon, but who shaped this work. Conversations about this project with the late Michael Kearney, Michael Higgins, and Sandra Morgen were more influential than they probably knew. My dear friend Flora Strachan and Alberto Donis Rodríguez supported this work and my fieldwork in Oaxaca, and for that I am forever grateful.

Generous support for the fieldwork for this project was provided by the National Science Foundation and the Fulbright-Hays Doctoral Dissertation Research Abroad program. Subsequent research and writing support was funded by the P.E.O. Sisterhood, the University of Arizona, the IUPUI Arts and Humanities Institute, the New Frontiers in Arts and Humanities Program at Indiana University, and the EMPOWER program at IUPUI. I also thank the Greater Philadelphia Latin American Studies Consortium and especially Satya Pattnayak.

It is an honor to have this work included in the California Series in Public Anthropology, and I thank my editor, Naomi Schneider, and Robert Borofsky for their commitment to public scholarship and enthusiasm for this project. At the University of California Press, I also thank Benjy Malings, Peter Dreyer, Cindy Fulton, and Chris Sosa Loomis. Thank you to Bill Nelson for creating a wonderful map. Many thanks also to Ruth Gomberg-Muñoz, James Quesada, and an anonymous reviewer for their excellent insights and suggestions in reviewing the manuscript.

Earlier versions of or excerpts from this book appeared previously in "Crossing Mexico: Structural Violence and the Commodification of Undocumented Central American Migrants," (*American Ethnologist* 40, no. 4 (2013), reproduced by permission of the American Anthropological Association; "Stuck in the Middle with You: The Intimate Labours of Mobility and Smuggling along Mexico's Migrant Route," *Geopolitics* 21, no. 2 (2016), reproduced by permission of Taylor & Francis; and "The Arterial Border: Negotiating Economies of Risk and Violence in Mexico's Security Regime," *International Journal of Migration and Border Studies* 3, nos. 2–3 (2017), DOI: 10.1504/IJMBS.2017.1000144, reproduced by permission of Inderscience Publishers. I am grateful to the publishers for permission to use this material in its present form.

I am extremely grateful for my family, who have nurtured and supported me for many years. My earliest teachers were my parents, Jim and Suzi Vogt, who encouraged me to ask questions, challenge the status quo, and find beauty in the diversity of the human experience. My sisters, Kelly and Kristina, are my best friends, and I am grateful for their unconditional love. It was a dream to celebrate the end of the book with onion pancakes, dumplings, and noodles on the streets of Hong Kong and Shanghai with you all. Thirty-seven? Many thanks to my vibrant (and growing!) extended family—the Vogt-Rattray-Lepore-Campbell-Guevara clan—I love you all, and few things make me happier than getting together with you to share in a good meal and conversation. An extra-special thank you to my in-laws, Terry and David, for being wonderful grandparents.

My greatest debts and deepest levels of love and appreciation go to the people I get to come home to every day. No one knows this project like my husband, Nick Rattray, who was there when it was just an idea on paper, by my side during crucial moments of fieldwork, and has seen it through to the end. As a scholar I am lucky to have such a brilliant partner, but more important, I am fortunate to have such a generous and loving person to share in all the other stuff in life. The greatest joy has been raising our two daughters, Iris Qia and Zaya Quin. Iris, you were with me in my belly during the fieldwork for this project, traveled with me to the farthest reaches of Oaxaca when you were a toddler, and yesterday you told me you thought it was really cool that I was writing a book, and you can't wait to read it. I love you mamoosh. To my spunky girl Zaya, you came into our lives as this book finally began to take shape and have been an endless source of joy, much needed silliness, and perspective. While it may have taken a bit longer to get this book out the door, the time spent with you and your sister instead of working was worth more than a million books. I cherish you both with all my heart. And to our new tiny surprise, I can't wait to meet you.

Preface

When I was a kid, my friends would say that if you dug a hole in the ground and kept digging you would eventually get to China. It seemed to be the most exotic and faraway place in the world. But for me, China was the place where my mom and grandparents were from. It was also the place they had left behind.

My mother was born in a small island village near Shanghai in 1949, the same year the Chinese civil war ended and the People's Republic of China was established. Not long afterward, like many Chinese citizens, my grandparents were deemed "capitalists" by the government and were forced to close the small restaurant they owned. My grandmother worked several odd jobs in the informal sector, including sewing doll clothing and making soap to sell on the streets, but it was not enough to get by. My mother remembers watching her mother cut away pieces from long gold chains—their life savings—to sell and pay for their basic necessities.

After years of unemployment, in 1957, when my mother was eight years old, my grandparents decided to flee mainland China for Hong Kong. They hired a female smuggler to pose as my mother's mother to take her across on a passenger ferry with false documents from Macau, which was then a Portuguese colony, to Hong Kong. Separately, my grandparents stowed away in the stomach-churning conditions of the bottom of fishing boats to cross the sea to Hong Kong. They were not alone. In the early 1950s, significant numbers of refugees fled mainland China to live and work in Hong Kong, which was under British Crown rule. Before 1951, it was relatively easy to cross into Hong Kong, but in 1951, increased enforcement tightened control of the island colony's borders. Between 1950 and 1980, an estimated one million Chinese mainlanders risked dangerous conditions to swim or stow away on boats in their attempts to reach Hong Kong.

Several years ago, I interviewed my mother about her experience. Although she was only a child, she remembered the journey well. She remembered visiting the village where she was born to say goodbye to her family. She recalled how scared she was when her mother handed her over to her smuggler—a complete stranger—who, for a few crucial hours, held her life in her hands. Her mother had given her a bundle of special cakes, something they normally could never afford, but she was too nervous to eat them and gave them away to other children. She told me about the profound sense of loneliness she felt during the crossing, staring at the water, not knowing whether she would see her parents again. When they disembarked at the port, she remembered the feeling of her ponytail being yanked by the border guard, and the fear that washed over her as he scrutinized her hair and clothing, treating her with suspicion, while her smuggler-mother argued with him in Cantonese, a language she did not understand. For reasons still unknown to her, he finally let them pass through. Finally, she spoke of the relief she experienced seeing her father, whom she had not seen for six months, waiting for her at the port on the other side, and a few days later when they reunited with her mother.

On the other side of the world half a century ago, my mother was an "unaccompanied minor" whose family was forced to flee conditions of economic and political uncertainty. The story of her journey from rural China to Hong Kong to Los Angeles is woven into the fabric of my family. In untold ways, it has shaped my own interests in understanding the intimate ties and embodied realities of contemporary movements of refugees and migrants around the world.

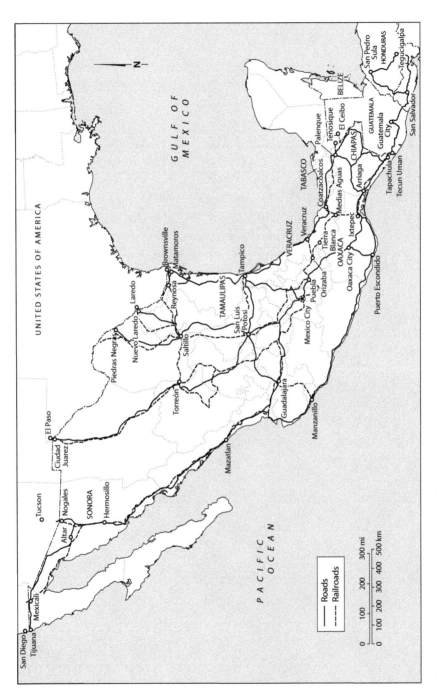

Transit routes across Mexico's "arterial border"

Introduction

On a quiet cobblestoned street near the bus station in Oaxaca, Mexico, the logics of the global economy play out on a daily basis. On one side of the street sits the loading dock behind one of Mexico's largest superstore chains, where each day trucks, machinery, and men unload boxes of vegetables, clothing, and electronics grown, sewn, and assembled in factories and farms all over the world. These disappear behind thick plastic curtains before being unveiled on the store's floor. Inside, the aisles are lined with pasta from Italy, wine from Chile, and strollers from China. Tortillas made with corn grown in Indiana are stamped out onto conveyer belts, barely resembling the thick, hand-pressed patties of fresh *masa* being cooked on hot ceramic griddles by indigenous women on the sidewalk out front.

Directly across from the loading dock, there is a heavy black metal gate set in a graffiti-marked wall bearing the painted words, "Here, no one is a foreigner." This is the front entrance to Casa Guadalupe (not its real name),[1] a small compound, where another type of global flow also arrives in daily waves. Unlike the swift, ordered movements of global cargo, however, these movements are circuitous, unpredictable, and illicit. This is a way station, a sanctuary, for clandestine flows of unauthorized migrants. People from Honduras, El Salvador, Guatemala, and beyond arrive in search of a hot meal, medical attention, or simply a safe place to rest their heads for the night. These immediate needs are welcome distractions from what they've left behind, and what they continue to sacrifice to reach their destinations.

Behind the gate, they find a temporary reprieve from their exhausting, perilous journeys. If you look quickly you might catch a glimpse of a child riding a rusty tricycle, or a small group of men and women sitting down to a bowl of warm beans, salsa, and tortillas, undoubtedly purchased in bulk from the superstore across the road.

On an almost daily basis, I observed this absurd contrast: the sanctioned free movement of goods and commodities between and across international borders and the dangerous, unauthorized movements of people who traveled on the very same roads and freight trains. It served as a reminder of the dizzyingly unequal structural conditions that brought people to the doorstep of this modest migrant shelter and helped me begin to make sense of the unimaginable stories I collected inside.

I spent a year between 2008 and 2009 working as a volunteer at Casa Guadalupe. Within its walls, I observed people break bread, share stories, tips, and even their few precious possessions. I listened as people made heartbreaking phone calls home to the children they had recently left behind. I watched strangers come together to forge social bonds. I also watched groups of traveling migrants fracture and disintegrate. Rumors, skepticism, and distrust flourished alongside compassion and solidarity. Casa Guadalupe was a rich site from which to observe the encounters, strategies, and social relations of Central Americans in transit through Mexico.

A CEMETERY WITHOUT CROSSES

In the United States, political and public discourses on migration from Latin America typically begin and end at the U.S.–Mexico border, but for many people crossing that border is but one phase of a much longer journey. Each year tens of thousands of people from Guatemala, Honduras, El Salvador, and beyond leave their homes in search of a more secure future. Before reaching the scorching, deadly deserts of Arizona or the sweeping currents of the Rio Grande/Río Bravo, migrants must first cross Mexico, a paradoxical, resource-rich, naturally and ethnically diverse land of striking economic inequality, and the center of a hemispheric war on drugs. Between Mexico's southern and northern borders, migrants spend indefinite periods of time navigating the complex physical and human terrain of the journey. Increased militarization and state enforcement by roadside checkpoints, raids, and detention centers have created borderlike conditions throughout Mexico's interior. Migrants are funneled into more clandestine and dangerous routes, where they may engage human smugglers, buy passage from the organized criminals who control transit routes, and sometimes ride on top of freight trains. They routinely encounter abuse, injury, extortion, sexual assault, and kidnapping as they become caught up in local economies that profit from their plight. In response to this violence, a diverse network of migrant shelters has been established along transit routes, offering aid and advocacy to migrants in need.

In 2006, when I first began research on Central American migration across Mexico, there was very little media or scholarly attention to the topic.[2] It was the underbelly of one of Mexico's darkest hypocrisies: the inhumane treatment of transit migrants at the southern border and simultaneous critique of U.S. immigration policy at the northern border. Yet in recent years, particularly in the wake of several highly publicized tragedies, international news outlets have become fascinated—if only temporarily—with the spectacle of Central American migration.

In 2010, the discovery of seventy-two, mostly Central American migrants found brutally murdered on a ranch in the northern state of Tamaulipas gave the world a brief glimpse into the violent realities that Central Americans face while crossing Mexico. But it was not until the summer of 2014 and the arrival of more than sixty thousand young Central Americans on the southern border of the United States that the spectacle was broadcast nightly on television screens in living rooms across the United States. While much media coverage was fueled by moral panics over a "surge" of child migrants, there were also more sympathetic accounts of a humanitarian crisis that had silently raged for years. News articles, reports, photo essays, blogs, and documentaries covering the perilous journey inundated viewers with dramatic images of desperate migrants clinging to the tops of freight trains and packed into detention centers under subhuman conditions. Rape. Kidnapping. Extortion. Dismemberment.

Murder. Massacre. Repeat. These were the headlines. And they were real and often accurate. In the words of one priest I interviewed, "Mexico is a cemetery for Central Americans; a cemetery without crosses."

The documentation of violence through public and social media is a crucial strategy in Mexico's migrants' rights movement, particularly because violence against migrants has long been invisible. Yet these stories risk becoming dangerously ordinary and one-dimensional.[3] Through the barrage of news stories and reports of the spectacular violence of kidnappings, murders, and heroic police rescues, migrants' bodies are dematerialized and transformed into what Eric Klinenberg calls "journalistic commodities," abstracted from the social causes of their demise.[4] As discussed in more depth below, proliferating stories of migrant women being raped also perpetuate gendered narratives that flatten the agency of female migrants and ignore the diversity of victims of sexual assault.

Media and politicians often attribute the violence experienced by migrants to a typical cast of "bad guys"—brutal drug cartels, human smugglers, a few "bad apple" corrupt authorities, and sometimes migrants themselves. Indeed, unauthorized migrants are treated as both criminals and victims, depending on political strategy and context. In all these cases, blame is placed on opaque extralegal entities that render states and citizens devoid of responsibility.

Inspired by a rich body of literature in the anthropology of violence, this book offers a different perspective so that the story of Central American migration does not become yet another predictable tragedy and fade into the background static of contemporary drug and border wars. It seeks to complicate the narrative of Central American migration by focusing on the deeper conditions that systematically produce and sustain violence along transit routes and in people's lives. In reality, the "bad guys" blamed for violence are actors maneuvering within the constraints of the structures of global capitalism and state enforcement where there is profit to be made from the mobility of unauthorized people.

Scholars have examined the complex and often nuanced ways in which violence operates and manifests itself in the spectacular and the ordinary in times of both conflict and peace. Nancy Scheper-Hughes and Philippe Bourgois propose a "continuum of violence" to understand the ways in which visible and invisible forms of violence—structural, symbolic, gendered, political, and direct—are mutually constitutive and reinforcing.[5] The everyday acts of direct and physical violence that migrants experience en route cannot be understood outside their deeper structural and historical contexts. A political economic framework of structural violence thus allows us to trace how misery "and inequality [are] structured and legitimated over time."[6] For example, a structural lens allows us to trace the ways in which global economies and state security projects propel migration, create the conditions for violent and clandestine crossings and manifest themselves in structural vulnerabilities once migrants arrive at their destinations.[7]

Pushing this analysis further, the question becomes not only how violence is produced, but who benefits from it? A central argument I make throughout this book is that violence and impunity are key processes in a multilayered migration industry from which diverse actors profit. In such a framework, migrant bodies, labor, and lives become valuable commodities in both global and local economies. To understand such processes, I examine the ripple effects of violence as it travels through power relations and inequalities at the local level and in social relations, what Linda Green has called the "microeconomics of difference." [8] Along these lines, the more recent concept of "poststructural violence" allows us to deepen understandings of how migrants respond to structural conditions of violence, in some cases themselves becoming perpetrators of it as a means of survival.[9]

Such an analytic of violence is also informed by the feminist concept of intersectionality to link together structural forces and inequalities based on race, ethnicity, nationality, gender, sexuality, class, legal status, and disability with people's everyday lived experiences of violence.[10] Kimberlé Crenshaw's seminal work on the ways in which violence experienced by women of color is the result of interlocking systems of oppression—namely, racism and sexism—helps us to think through the social dimensions at play along migrant routes in Mexico. The prevalence of racial profiling, sexual assault, forced labor, and kidnapping of Central Americans cannot be understood outside migrant subject positions as unauthorized, racialized, and gendered others struggling to survive in the contexts of state-sanctioned violence, transnational security politics, and an unequal global capitalist system. Taken together, such a layered approach to violence illuminates the historical and transnational threads and state policies that create the conditions for migration and violence and their ripple effects on communities, individuals, and bodies. Through these conceptual avenues, the book shifts the focus from the spectacle of violence to the less visible infrastructures and economies of mobility, violence, and intimacy that undergird spaces of transit.

TOWARD AN ANTHROPOLOGY OF TRANSIT

If a deeper understanding of the production and reproduction of violence is one goal of this book, a second goal is to develop a more nuanced, human-centered understanding of the social processes involved in clandestine transit migration. In anthropology, the topic of migration has been approached through both micro and macro levels of analysis, ranging from neoclassical economic rational actor models to dependency and world-systems theories.[11] Anthropologists have sought to bridge these approaches by looking at both people and processes, recognizing the structural and historical contexts in which individuals make choices and act.[12] The ethnographic focus has primarily centered on the dynamics of migrant sending and receiving communities. Scholars have considered the forces and impacts of out-migration in communities of origin, and how immigrant communities negotiate their lives at their destinations. In the 1990s, as scholars began investigating the fluid links, flows, and circuits between these socio-spatial zones, the field of transnationalism emerged.[13] This scholarship grew out of an attempt to reject narratives of immigrant assimilation and instead focus on the material, discursive, and ideological circulations between migrant sending and receiving communities. Such analyses challenged bounded conceptualizations of identity and locality and instead explored how flows of people, information, capital, and identities were increasingly deterritorialized.[14]

Despite the turn to studying transnational processes at multiple locations, in practice, this literature remains wedded to a conceptual framework centered on locally fixed origins and destinations and the connections between them. Moreover, migration is often treated in binary terms: people migrate or they stay home; they are mobile subjects or immobile subjects. Yet most of the world's migrants—and asylum seekers—do not simply board a jetliner or a cruise ship and arrive at their destinations a few hours or days later. On the contrary, they may live in a liminal state of transit for weeks, months, or even years as they attempt to cross land and sea borders, earn enough to live on, evade immigration controls, hire smugglers, secure shelter, feed themselves, and find protection. By not considering transient populations, the embodied realities experienced by people traversing different socio-spatial zones are overlooked. Mobility is not an abstract process; it is a material and embodied one.

It is also not a linear process. En route, the lived realities of transit are fraught with uncertainty, and movements are incremental, circuitous, and often stalled.[15] Migrants are caught up in what scholars have called "regimes of mobility" and "precarious transit zones" produced at the nexus of exclusionary state policies and increased circulation around the globe.[16] They are legally excluded, making them both visible and invisible in the eyes of the state.[17] Such legal liminality and disconnection from core familial, spatial, and social networks opens the door to new types of exploitation, and migrants become potential sites of profit in both licit and illicit markets.[18] At the same time, migrants develop strategies and social relationships with one another and with local residents in the communities they pass through to cope with the precarity of their situations.

The concept of transit migration has primarily been applied to Europe's borders, [19] but it is also a useful lens through which to study clandestine migrant routes worldwide.[20] With good reason, most scholarship on Latin American migration to the United States has historically concentrated on the U.S.–Mexico border, where one of the world's most visible displays of state power, manifest in a sophisticated enforcement infrastructure, has significant political, economic, and social consequences for both migrants and local communities.[21] There is no doubt that national borders are crucial to ongoing projects of state-making and national sovereignty in our globalized world.[22] However, scholars have moved beyond understandings of borders as fixed "lines in the sand" to reconceptualize the political geographies where borders are "enacted, materialized and performed."[23] As William Walters has argued, decentering political borders enables us to focus on other types of spatialities, particularly the geographical and infrastructural transit routes where the politics of migration are "visualized, problematized, policed and contested,"[24] and new forms of violence, intimacy, and solidarity emerge.

This book looks beyond the U.S.–Mexico border region to understand the material, political, and social infrastructures that shape clandestine migration along what I call Mexico's *arterial border.* Central American migrants have moved through Mexico in significant numbers since the 1980s, first as refugees fleeing civil war, then as "economic migrants," and now, arguably, as refugees once again, though they are not legally recognized as such.[25] Mexico, generally conceptualized as a country of origin, is also a major country of transit, geographically and geopolitically caught between Central and South America and the United States. Over the past half-century, the Mexican state has implemented various crackdowns on Central American migration—largely in response to U.S. political pressure and with U.S. funding—during periods of increased concern over immigration and hemispheric security. Roadside checkpoints, technological surveillance, vehicle patrols, police raids, and detention facilities enforce "diffused" control of clandestine Central American migrants' routes through Mexico.[26] This has most recently been embodied in Mexico's Programa Frontera Sur (Southern Border Program), a highly aggressive securitization strategy, resulting from U.S. pressure during the 2014 unaccompanied minor crisis. However, Mexico is not simply a pawn in the U.S. geopolitical agenda. The Mexican state and state actors profit considerably from border enforcement and militarization, which have increasingly come under the larger umbrella of "security" in Mexico's southern border region, and in the context of Mexico's drug war, a notable instance of the internalization of border controls.[27]

Critics of the proliferation of immigration enforcement in Mexico's interior call it a "vertical border," but the dynamics of Central American migration are not that simple. Just like a horizontal one, a vertical border still consolidates state power in a linear, ahistorical, top-down manner. In contrast, the concept of the *arterial border* presents state power in terms of the more fluid, multidirectional, and contested regimes of mobility that manifest in everyday encounters, discourses, and material infrastructures.[28] The arterial border is in constant flux, expanding and contracting as migrants, organized criminals, and local activists engage, evade, and contest the state along highways, train routes, and the network of shelters that traverse the country like arteries (see map 1). As migrants negotiate the arterial border, obstacles emerge and people's journeys slow down. Migration flows thicken and become more viscous, sticky even. In some cases, migrants become stuck in place, unable or unwilling to move on for a variety of reasons, whether abuse, injury, robbery, or opportunity. For these migrants, the initial goal of reaching the United States may be deferred. The physical immobility that people experience may be mirrored by an existential immobility, what Ghassan Hage has called "stuckedness," in which migrants must cope with the anxieties and uncertainties of waiting.[29] The transit of migrants can thus be both temporary and characterized by an extended, and in some cases semi-permanent, state of liminality.

Whether they are in transit for a few weeks or a few years, people must develop strategies, not only to move, but also to live and meet their most basic needs of sustenance and survival. In doing so, migrants alter the local communities they pass through, just as local communities impact people's migration experiences. Certain corridors become hot spots of migration-related activity, and complex social dynamics emerge around places like shelters and train yards. As people negotiate their lives in transit, they become embedded in particular localities. They look for work. They buy things. They seek medical attention. They develop relationships. An ethnography of transit cannot thus focus solely on the experiences of migrants themselves, but must also look at the complex social worlds that emerge in transit zones.

As my research developed, it became clear that this is a story, not only about violence, but also about resistance and solidarity, as individuals, families, and communities began to say, "¡Ya basta!"—"Enough already!" The migrant journey, and migrant shelters in particular, have emerged as key sites in a robust social movement around migrant rights, humanity, and justice. There are over fifty migrant shelters and *comedores* (dining halls) in Mexico. Most of them are connected through the transnational Pastoral de Movilidad Humana (Human Movement Pastorate) of the Catholic bishops of North America, Central America, and the Caribbean region.[30] In addition to Movilidad Humana, the Congregation of the Missionaries of Saint Charles, or Scalabrinians, provide sanctuary for migrants in Mexico.[31]

Much of on-the-ground organizing and aid to clandestine migrants has been led by a radical subset of Catholic priests, several of whom draw inspiration from the rich tradition of religious leaders advocating on the behalf of marginalized peoples across the Americas. One such leader was

Archbishop Óscar Arnulfo Romero who was assassinated in 1980 shortly after asking the United States to stop supplying military aid to El Salvador. Along with Romero's teachings, the Sanctuary Movement of the 1980s in the southern United States and the wider influence of liberation theology, with its emphasis on justice and giving preference in ecclesiastical social work to the poor and powerless, have been important antecedents of Mexico's migrants' rights movement.[32]

While migrant shelters are spaces of solidarity and hope, they are also fraught points of contestation as they are impacted by local economies of violence, and shelter workers, residents, and migrants must grapple with everyday insecurity. On one hand, through everyday encounters of care, shelters and local residents have challenged the othering and exclusion of migrants. On the other hand, the increased presence of outsiders perceived to be dangerous, coupled with few protections from the state, has exacerbated local tensions around the politics of safety and security. I explore these tensions, but also look beyond the public arena to some of the less visible battles that are waged as the ripple effect of violence impacts humanitarian aid shelters, neighborhoods, and family homes.

CASA GUADALUPE

It is my first day of work at Casa Guadalupe. I ring the doorbell, precariously connected to a bundle of wires on the outside gate of the walled complex. From the other side a man's voice asks, "Who is it?" Talking to the wall, I introduce myself as the new volunteer. The metal door cracks open, a pair of eyes behind tinted glasses peer out at me, and the door widens just enough to let me through. Mauricio, a man in his early thirties with spiky black hair wearing a punk band T-shirt and stonewashed jeans, is on the other side. He smiles and holds out his hand to greet me with a typical handshake, kiss on the cheek, and "Mucho gusto." Hiding behind his legs is a young girl with thick black curly hair and wide-set big brown eyes. Mauricio introduces me to Carmina, his four-year old daughter, who along with him and his wife, Flor, have lived at Casa Guadalupe since Carmina was an infant, when they came here from a rural village about three hours' drive from Oaxaca City. Now they are in charge of the shelter's daily operations. All their belongings are packed into a small room they share across from the shelter's basic kitchen. Mauricio tells me that Araceli, who is officially Casa Guadalupe's secretary, but whose role extends far beyond administrative tasks, is on her way to meet me. She would become my closest interlocutor, travel companion, and friend during my fieldwork here.

Mauricio guides me to the main living room, presided over by a large painting of Mexico's beloved Virgin of Guadalupe captioned "Maria Guadalupe, Take care of our migrants." Juxtaposed with her benevolent presence is a corkboard full of newspaper clippings and advisories. The headlines chronicle a recent wave of assaults and kidnappings of migrants in the region: "Terror in Chahuites: Federal Police abuse migrants"; "Raid on train with over 100 migrants confirmed."

A woman seated on an old brown plaid couch greets me with a warm smile and invites me to join her. She introduces herself as Sandra. Mauricio playfully jokes that Sandra doesn't need them anymore at the shelter, that she is just gracing them with her presence with a rare visit. She smiles and blushes.

Sandra is one of the regulars at the shelter. She is from Honduras, where she has four children between the ages of five and thirteen, whom she left with her ex-husband. She tells me she left home six months and five days ago, and I am impressed by her precision, but realize that this is because her departure was likely very difficult. I begin to ask for more details about her children, but I can sense that it is too much to talk about. Instead, she tells me about her journey. As I would find throughout my fieldwork, people were often quite forthcoming with the details of their journeys in Mexico and the injustices they experienced. After being robbed twice in the state of Chiapas, she decided to stay in Oaxaca to look for work. She tells me about being assaulted, but makes sure to clarify that, by the grace of God, she was not raped. Many women are raped, but not her. Still, she tells me, she had to walk for seven days between Huixtla and Arriaga in Chiapas, an area known as La Arrocera, where *rateros Mexicanos* (Mexican thieves) lie in wait for migrants seeking to bypass military and police checkpoints.

"It is a difficult life," she says, shaking her head.

In exchange for cooking and cleaning, Sandra lives with a local woman who sells *atole*, a traditional corn-based beverage, from a street stall. She has found intermittent work over the past few months, but says there are not many opportunities, especially for outsiders like her. She almost managed to get a job in a food stall at Oaxaca City's sprawling outdoor market, the Central de Abastos, but the offer was withdrawn when they found out that she was *indocumentada* (undocumented). People assume she is a prostitute, like the other Central American women who work in the strip clubs that line the road to the airport. "But even if you are from here, it is difficult to find work. Look at all the Oaxacans who are leaving," she observes. Dismissing the discrimination against her, Sandra explains that she needs to earn more anyway. Her plan is to go to Mexico City where she says they pay more. In fact, she has come to Casa Guadalupe today to borrow money for a phone card to call her uncle in the United States and ask him to wire her some money. Her uncle crossed Mexico four years ago and now lives in Virginia. To get there from Honduras, he had to pay a smuggler U.S.$6,000. Sandra tells me that she doesn't have a smuggler for the whole journey but did meet a *coyote* on the train in the Isthmus of Tehuantepec, near Albergue Nazaret.[33] She plans to meet him in Nuevo Laredo and pay him U.S.$1,500 to get her across the U.S.–Mexico border. For now, she just needs 360 pesos to pay for her bus ticket to Mexico City.

As we are talking, a group of four people—three men and one woman—enter the room and sit down at the dining table. Flor, whom I briefly meet, comes out of the kitchen with some reheated beans and tortillas. Sandra is busy working on logistics with Mauricio, so I sit down with the group. One of the men, who appears to be in his mid-forties, tells me that he has lived in the United States for nineteen years but was recently deported back to Guatemala. He is extremely talkative and speaks with me in Spanish and English. He is traveling with his younger cousin and his cousin's wife, who look to be in their late teens or early twenties. The young woman is visibly nervous. The older man explains that they have just had a traumatic experience. In the same region where Sandra was robbed, they were held up by four armed men. These men made the young woman take all her clothing off but only asked the men to remove their belts and shoes. As they checked the young woman's clothing for valuables, one of the men held a machete up to the girl's neck. He says they didn't do anything else to the girl, but that she hadn't been the same since. He tells me about the last town they visited before getting to Oaxaca City. A local man had offered them breakfast there, but the young couple refused to enter his house. He says they don't trust anyone, so I am somewhat surprised that he is so forthcoming with me about the intimate details of the robbery. Perhaps he feels safe sharing these details because we are inside the shelter. Yet I note that neither of his companions speak or even make eye contact with me at all. I later wonder if the man is in fact their cousin, or perhaps their smuggler.

The fourth man, Efrain, tells us he is not from Central America; he is Mexican. He just arrived that morning and hasn't eaten a full meal for several days. He also appears to be distraught, but he speaks quickly, so fast that it is difficult to make out what he is saying. From what I gather, he was recently deported from the United States and is trying to make his way back home to his community in Mexico's most southern state, Chiapas. On his journey south, he had sought help from a local church, where they had recommended he come to Casa Guadalupe. Efrain has no money and claims that the police are still after him. When I ask what his plan is, Efrain turns his head toward the ground and simply says, "I don't know."

I spend the afternoon assembling toiletry kits with Flor. When I arranged my volunteer/research position with a Maryknoll missionary who helped found the shelter, I asked if there was anything I could bring from the United States. "Travel-size toiletries," she told me, because migrants always need them when they arrive. Flor was excited when I showed her the two large bags of travel-size shampoos, mini soaps, and razors I had brought with me.

As we pack the plastic baggies, the doorbell rings. Just as he did when I arrived, Mauricio approaches the front door and cracks it open. From the couch I can see him through the window talking to a man and woman on the other side, asking them questions and searching their backpacks. I later learn that Mauricio checks the belongings of all migrants who pass through to check for weapons. He opens the door and the couple, Elena and Miguel, come inside and greet us. Mauricio invites me along when he goes to show them the separate men and women's dormitories. The women's dormitory is located inside the main building, adjacent to the living room and close to the kitchen and Mauricio's family's bedroom, providing a bit more security. The sparse room is dark and dank; there is not much air circulation, but the bunk beds are tidy. Mauricio tells Elena she can choose whichever open bed she wants. There is just one other woman currently staying at the shelter. We walk outside where Mauricio leads us to another small building, where the bathrooms and men's dormitory are located. Several of these beds are occupied, and Mauricio suggests a lower bunk for Miguel. He tells them both to get some rest before their obligatory intake interviews.

Later that afternoon, as we prepare canned sardines and beans for the evening meal, I have a chance to speak in more depth with Elena, who has volunteered to help. I am surprised when she tells me they are from Nicaragua, since most migrants who pass through are from Honduras, Guatemala, or El Salvador. They have been on the road for just over two weeks, and Elena tells me a bit about who she calls the "devils" and "angels" they have encountered so far: the bandits who robbed them at gunpoint; a man who bought them bottles of cold soda; the local woman who took pity on them and allowed them to sleep on the floor of her home. "I was so grateful to sleep at that woman's house," she says. "I was so tired!"

But this was just the beginning. Elena tells me about their narrow escape from organized criminals who had nearly kidnapped them. She explains that along the route, there are many people who pretend to be your friends, but in reality, they are trying to pry information out of you to see if you are a good candidate for kidnapping. They look for people with family members in the United States from whom they can extort large ransoms.

During their stay at Albergue Nazaret (another shelter in the Isthmus of Tehuantepec, which would also become a secondary field site for my research), Elena and Miguel were befriended by a young migrant looking for some traveling companions, whom they guessed was around sixteen years old. But when he persuaded them to leave the shelter extra early to catch the next train, Elena sensed that something was wrong. They met up with three other men, and Elena overheard their companion describing the clothing and features of two women also staying at the shelter. They were being set up. "These were not migrants, they were Los Zetas," Elena said. This was the first I had heard about the Zetas, the notoriously brutal organized criminal group that has come to control the migrant routes. One of the men suggested that Elena and her husband split up before they jumped the train. She knew then that they needed to get out of there. Not knowing what else to do, Elena decided to feign sudden stomach pains. She started wailing, drawing attention to herself. She told Miguel to hail a taxi, claiming that she needed to go to the hospital immediately. Luckily, there was a taxi nearby, and they were able to quickly jump in. They told the driver to take them directly back to the shelter; they had to warn the women. Padre José, the priest in charge of Albergue Nazaret, advised them not to continue on the train. The train route through Veracruz was quickly becoming the epicenter of mass kidnappings and violence. As he would do time and time again for migrants over the next year, Padre José helped pay for their bus tickets to Casa Guadalupe. First, he sent Elena and Miguel there. The next day, he would send the two women. We were all relieved the following day when the doorbell rang and the two young women appeared outside. The journey was brutal, but local people were responding, and this organic network of assistance continued to take shape.

In less than twenty-four hours, I had already met people from four different countries who had been in transit for different periods of time and were moving in different directions. I heard tales of danger, deception, and violence. Of journeys begun, journeys stalled, and journeys coming to an end. Through their words and gestures, people hinted at solidarity and sacrifice, suspicion and tension. Each person was motivated by her or his own histories and dreams. Yet what I was most struck by—and it would take months for me fully to grasp this—was that the shelter itself was a space of intimacy. Within its walls, people shared stories about the most intimate aspects of their lives—their children, their aspirations for the future—and their harrowing experiences en route. Shelter workers, many of them women, shared in testimonies, prayer, and everyday forms of carework. In a context of social exclusion, a warm embrace, even a handshake, could be a profound act of human connection, one of myriad intimate encounters, social relationships, and embodied realities.

THE INTIMATE ECONOMIES OF MOBILITY

Inspired by a rich body of feminist scholarship on the linkages between global, state, and structural processes, on the one hand, and the intimacies of people's everyday lives,[34] on the other, this book focuses on the intimate, intersectional and embodied dimensions of life in transit. Rather than seeing them as separate realms, feminist scholars have examined the ways in which the global and the intimate constitute each other and are important sites for understanding the reproduction of power and social inequalities, as well as forms of resistance.[35] For example, migration scholars have focused on how state immigration policies impact relations of gender, kinship, care, and identity within transnational and mixed-status families.[36] Through border enforcement, forced removals, and the more general condition of deportability, (im)migrant families grapple with the hardships of family separation, loss, and life in the shadows.[37] At the same time, despite new forms of inequality, (im)migrant families are able to create meaningful relationships across borders and generations.[38] Scholars have sought to construct a framework of intimacies that goes beyond state-recognized family relations in order to understand the other types of meaningful affective ties, social relations, arrangements, and household strategies that may emerge in (im)migrant worlds.[39]

For example, the concept of "intimate labors" interrogates the ways intimate relations are linked to transnational processes of exchange, labor, and cash economies through practices like transnational adoption, sex tourism, and even the intimate labor of nail salons.[40] Critical feminist geographers have examined the intimate economies that pervade migrants' detention and deportation.[41] Inspired by this collective work, I examine how migrants' journeys have emerged as important spaces to study intimate relations and the intersections between intimate and economic life in the contemporary world, often viewed as separate realms.[42] I investigate how intimacy is created, managed, and negotiated in relation to immigration enforcement, the smuggling and kidnapping industries, and networks of care. The complexities of these emerging relations, encounters, and configurations are what I call *the intimate economies of mobility*.[43] Such a framework rejects top-down notions of global forces "penetrating" intimate life and instead focuses on the dialectics between global intimate relations and individual strategies at the local level.[44]

I use "intimacy" here less as a term for private, personal, or sexual relations than as a flexible analytical concept, emphasizing what Ara Wilson calls "relational life," and what Lieba Faier describes as the "intimate encounters" arising from everyday interactions between and among migrant and resident populations.[45] Within a context of transience, the

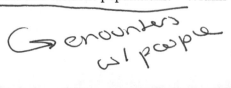

intimacies of transit are often temporary, serendipitous and constituted between strangers. Despite the traditional placement of intimacy within the private realms of homes and bedrooms, the intimate economies of mobility are often forged between social actors in the public, exposed and everyday zones of transit, such as migrant shelters, free clinics, or even the tops of moving freight trains. These public spaces have also become crucial to the feminist-inspired politics of much of the migrants' rights movement in Mexico.

Looking at intimacy focuses attention on the contours of reciprocity that can develop between mobile—and sometimes temporarily immobile—subjects. By highlighting agency and their strategies for survival, this approach challenges gendered constructions as either victims or criminals, not only of migrants, but also of smugglers, shelter workers, and local people. At the same time, relationships of mobility and care may both depend on and reproduce social inequalities. Care, trust, and profit can thus not easily be separated along the migration route. Intimate labors involve relations where inequities based on race, class, ethnicity, and gender are both maintained and resisted.

A NOTE ON GENDERED VIOLENCE

After I returned from the field, I was interviewed for a national radio program doing a feature story on female migrants. The host asked me to relay some of the most harrowing stories of sexual assault and violence experienced by women. She also wanted to know exactly how many Central American migrant women are raped during their journeys. Statistics floating around claim that between 60 and 80 percent of migrant women are sexually assaulted during their journeys. However, I found her request to boil these experiences down to soundbites and numbers problematic. On one hand, making violence against women legible is a key task of the migrants' rights movement. We cannot address a problem until we recognize that it exists. Yet it seemed to me that there was so much sensationalized discourse around violence against women that it had become almost normalized. Women being raped was the status quo. When shelter workers wanted to stress how dire the situation of gendered violence had become, they would talk—in hushed voices—about sexual violence against migrating *men*. Like assaults on LGBTQ migrants, this is also a reality of Central Americans' clandestine migration through Mexico, and one that does not get much attention, but it almost seemed as if the rape of a man was being constructed as somehow worse than the rape of a woman. The transgression of heteronormative boundaries seemed to exacerbate the vileness of the crime exponentially.

I was also hesitant because I found that while some people were willing to talk openly about their own experiences of sexual assault, many preferred to talk through euphemisms, or focus on other people's stories. This is something that feminist scholars who study sexual violence have noted in other contexts as well. For example, in her work on state-sponsored rape in Guatemala, Julie Hastings found that public and legal testimonies of sexual violence are not always in the best interests of women seeking political asylum. She argues that the lack of survivors' accounts of rape was less likely due to shame or stigma, and more due to the fact that the construction of people as "gendered victims" in testimonies potentially compromised the more important claim of being a political victim, which was crucial to being determined to be a legitimate refugee.[46] Kimberly Theidon speaks of moving from frameworks of "break the silence" to respecting certain silences.[47] Can silence be a form of agency?

I suspect that many migrants did not talk to me openly about rape because the threat of it was very much still present throughout their journey. An assault could take place anywhere, at any moment, during encounters with state agents, criminals, smugglers, other migrants, or even shelter workers. Silence was a survival strategy for these women and men. The narratives they constructed for me were not of victimization, but of resilience, of strength, and of faith that they would arrive. Students, researchers, and activists working on these issues should perhaps take their cue from these women and men and resist the temptation simply to reproduce statistics and spectacles of violence, and instead focus on deeper, more critical analyses of the underlying conditions that produce gendered violence.[48] Might we not, for example, see sexual violence as a product of militarization or racial and patriarchal power?[49]

This is not to say that the book does not include stories of gendered and sexual violence. On the contrary, almost every chapter of this book includes stories of gendered violence, because nearly every dimension of migrants' journeys—from the decisions people make to leave home to their encounters with state agents, the suffering they experience, the social relations they forge, the care they give, and the transnational solidarities that evolve—are imbued with gendered dynamics and intimate relations. Individual stories are important to put a human face on suffering, but as a political project, it is crucial that we contextualize the lived and embodied forms of gendered and sexual violence experienced by migrants in transit. Gendered violence, like much of the violence experienced along the journey, is not just the work of bad individuals, but rather produced at the nexus of state and structural forms of violence that permeate the lives of migrants at home, during their journeys, and once they reach their destinations.

[handwritten annotation: Violence produced? How.]

ETHNOGRAPHY AT THE DEPOT

Inside the coin purse of my wallet I carry a single folded bill worth two lempiras, the national currency of Honduras, which was given to me by Jimmy and Melsy, a Honduran couple and parents of two young children. I met Jimmy and Melsy early on in my fieldwork and learned quite a bit about their lives in a short period of time. Since they both suffered from various health problems, I spent several days accompanying them to the local clinic. I was particularly interested in their decision to migrate together, as opposed to one of them staying behind in Honduras with their children. The rationale was that if they both worked in the United States, they would be able to return to Honduras and be reunited in half the time it would take if only one of them migrated. For the past twenty-five days, Melsy and Jimmy had traveled from their home in Honduras to Oaxaca, where they were robbed of everything they had except a cheap cell phone and the two lempiras.

"This is all they left us with," Melsy said as she held out the bill for me to see. When I tried to hand it back to her she said, "No, you keep it. We have no use for it now. And besides, now you will have something to remember us by." They left in the late afternoon, planning to take an overnight bus north to Mexico City. Several days later I received a hurried phone call from them stating they had arrived safely in San Luis Potosí, in central

Mexico, and would call again later. This was the last I would hear from them. Back from the field in the United States, I am transported back to the shelter and to my memory of Melsy and Jimmy whenever I open my wallet to pay for a latte or a parking place and see the two-lempira bill. What happened to them after that last phone call? Did they make it to the U.S.–Mexico border? If so, were they able to cross over? Where are they now? Did they ever make good on their promise to return home to their children?

Ethnography with people in transit often yields more questions than answers. It also challenges traditional concepts of fieldwork. Anthropologists have advocated for multi-sited ethnography as a way to study the links, networks, and processes of a globalized, transnational world.[50] Others have deconstructed travel and the dichotomy between "home" and "field" in ethnographic fieldwork.[51] "Anthropology potentially includes a cast of diverse dwellers and travelers whose displacement or travel in 'fieldwork' differs from the traditional spatial practice of the field," James Clifford writes.[52] Yet the emphasis on "diasporic scholars" is still focused primarily on the movement of the researcher and not the research subjects. How, as anthropologists, do we resolve the tensions around the transience of our interlocutors and the ethnographic authority attached to "being there" in the field? Where, exactly, is "there" when we are talking about such fluid, transient populations?[53]

As mentioned above, there is a rich body of literature on transnational migrants and communities that employ ethnographic methods primarily in sending and receiving communities. Beyond this, some scholars have collected powerful narratives of the strategies and lived experiences of journeys and border crossings, including compelling accounts by Central American migrants who had arrived at their destinations.[54] Several recent ethnographies exemplify innovative approaches to the possibilities of multi-sited fieldwork with migrants in transit. For instance, Seth Holmes took a multi-sited approach in his commitment to "follow the people" in ethnographic research with Triqui migrant farmworkers between rural Oaxaca and the berry fields of Washington State, including crossing the border with them.[55] Ruben Andersson traveled to key sites in the Euro-African borderlands and documents the experiences of clandestine migrants within what he calls the "illegality industry."[56] Jason De León brings together ethnographic and archaeological analyses in multiple locales to examine the violent consequences of U.S. state policies on the border-crossing experience and the ripple effects on migrant families.[57]

Initially, I had envisaged fieldwork "on the move," accompanying migrants from Guatemala to the U.S.–Mexico border. I was first drawn to the topic of Central American migration in 2005 during a conversation with Macario, a Mixtec street vendor living on the U.S.–Mexico border. I was doing research for my Master's thesis on indigenous transnational migrants, and Macario and I were talking about discrimination against migrants in Mexico. "If you want to know who is really screwed in Mexico, you have to go to the southern border and see what is happening to Central Americans," he told me. The next year I made my first trip to the Mexico-Guatemala border region, where I visited shelters on both sides. The following summer I made my way north, visiting shelters and transit sites in the Mexican states of Oaxaca and Veracruz. These early ethnographic encounters, several of which are discussed in this book, were crucial in exposing me to the diversity and complexity of the migrant journey across different spaces. And while primarily focused on the experiences of migrants themselves, I also became fascinated by the work being done in migrant shelters. I realized that studying migration did not require me to be constantly on the move. On the contrary, vital insights could be gained by establishing myself in one or more of these fixed locations in order to more deeply observe the logics and logistics of transit flows for both migrants and the communities they move through. Migrant shelters were ideal locations to safely access this largely invisible population. Close daily interactions would enable me to witness the quotidian aspects of transit and humanitarian aid and do my small part for migrants' rights on a daily basis.

I was particularly intrigued by the work being done in Oaxaca, where the two shelters I visited had recently been established in response to increased flows of migrants. Albergue Nazaret, which had been established just a few months earlier by Padre José, consisted of little more than an open-air chapel and kitchen on a dirt lot along the railroad tracks, with a few folding plastic tables and chairs. Migrants frequently entered and exited the shelter as they waited for the next train to depart (fig. 1).

In contrast, Casa Guadalupe, founded by Padre Luis, with the assistance of two lay missionaries from the United States, was located in urban

Figure 1. Migrants take a break from washing clothes at Albergue Nazaret to watch the train go by. Photo by author.

Oaxaca City, on a parcel of land donated by the previous governor. While Padre Luis cynically called the donation not much more than a photo-op, I found it remarkable that the shelter was sanctioned by the state, while also in many ways working against state practices. Casa Guadalupe was not located directly on the train route, which at that time was the means of transport favored by migrants heading north, but on an increasingly popular alternate route. Migrants who sought to bypass one of the most feared sections of the train route, between Oaxaca and Veracruz states, traveled instead by bus to Casa Guadalupe on their way to Mexico City. Shelter workers at Albergue Nazaret sent the most vulnerable migrants to Casa Guadalupe—women, children, and recent victims of crimes like kidnapping. The diverse cross section of people who passed through the two shelters made them particularly rich locations in which to explore issues of (im)mobility, violence, and intimacy in the lives of clandestine migrants.

My fieldwork was thus both multi-sited and grounded in what I came to conceptualize as a depot where a highly fluid population of people constantly arrived and departed. Between 2008 and 2009, I spent a year working as a full-time volunteer at Casa Guadalupe, with regular trips to

Albergue Nazaret and visits to other shelters throughout southern Mexico. I also spent the summers of 2010 and 2013 conducting follow-up research. By establishing myself as a volunteer at Casa Guadalupe, I was able to observe the daily experiences, movements, and obstacles that migrants face and capture the raw emotions, thoughts, concerns, and strategies of people in the midst of an uncertain and dangerous process. This shelter served as a nexus from which to explore transit spaces so as to understand the diversity of contexts and landscapes of migrants' journeys. I also attended local, regional, and national training sessions and conferences for the network of shelters across Mexico. My daily tasks included intake interviews for newly arrived migrants, accompanying people to the local health clinic, helping with shopping and cooking, and leading orientations on the risks of the journey. During downtime at the shelter, I both informally interviewed hundreds of migrants and taped formal, semi-structured interviews with sixty people, primarily migrants and shelter workers I had come to know well.

This research strategy was not without challenges, the most obvious being that in some cases, I had only a few days or even hours to spend with some of my interlocutors. The example of Melsy and Jimmy that opens this section was typical. I was able to spend several intense days with people, only to watch them depart as quickly as they had arrived, and would generally never hear from them again. As a female student from the United States and a resident of Tucson, Arizona, then the most popular U.S.-Mexico border-crossing location, I found myself able to build rapport with migrants over a fairly short period of time. When people learned that I was from Tucson, they would ask me everything from joking requests to help arrange a smuggler to questions about the likelihood of encountering a snake or what types of shoes to wear crossing the Sonoran desert. Even so, these encounters were fleeting, and I was often left with partial, unresolved stories. I worried that this might detract from my ability to uncover the deeper levels of social processes and relations, but I believe that the element of fluidity and the rawness of the migrants' perspectives I recorded sets this study apart from other work on migration.[58] Moreover, as circumstances dictated, I was able to establish longer-term relationships and rapport with migrants who temporarily settled in Oaxaca, like Sandra, and with my co-workers at the shelter.

Personal safety was another concern that shaped my decision to conduct research from within the structure of migrant shelters. Early encounters with individuals participating in illicit activities along the tracks, and the concern of my PhD committee and family members, influenced this decision. After several trips alone, I decided it was more prudent to travel with a companion, which usually meant my co-worker and closest confidant at Casa Guadalupe, Araceli, or when possible, my husband, Nick, who joined me intermittently during my fieldwork.

With the clarity of hindsight, I now see that the shelter offered a lens through which to study one slice of a longer journey, and with it, the depth of understanding that can only come from situated, long-term fieldwork observing everyday realities. Shelters are not spaces where migrants simply languish, but places where people form connections, make art, eat, play games, pray, and laugh together. Within shelters people often let their guard down a little to reflect on their experiences, bounce ideas off one another, and plan their next steps. Conversations in shelter dormitories, hospital waiting rooms, and at kitchen tables thus reveal the layers of meaning and emotion that imbue clandestine crossings. From the vantage point of humanitarian aid shelters, I was also able to capture the complex and contradictory interworkings of solidarity, charity, and ethical demands in a context of cascading forms of violence. The intimate spaces constituted by shelters, and the social dimensions in which they are embedded, serve as points of departure for understanding the political, moral, and affective economics of transit life. Through the "infinite repetition of the present," ethnographic research is able to gain access to the everyday, while also maintaining the distance necessary to put the taken-for-granted in a larger context.[59]

Ultimately, the transient presence of migrants parallels the transience of ethnography itself as a subjective and unfinished practice.[60] As ethnographers, we do our best to capture and connect lived experience to larger historical trajectories. Yet the realities of our contexts remain in flux. Policies change, social relations diminish, infrastructures crumble, and the occupants of seats of power are replaced. Our interlocutors, friends, and colleagues get on with their lives after our fieldwork has ended. Since returning from the field, I have grappled with the unease of not "being there," as if one more stint of fieldwork or series of interviews would bring closure. But ethnography inevitably remains unfinished, a process more than project. As such, this book captures a moment in history made up of people, places, and processes that are infinitely layered, interconnected, and changing. I hope that by documenting my experiences and analyses, this work contributes to deepening our understanding of the veiled complexities of life in transit.

THE STRUCTURE OF THE BOOK

Each chapter of this book illuminates different dimensions of violence and intimacy along Central American migration routes in Mexico. Chapter 1 situates lived experiences of violence in the deeper temporal and spatial context of violence across the Americas. Structural forms of violence, including the legacies of civil war, neoliberal securitization, and everyday insecurity, propel migration from Central America. I suggest a historical continuum where the violence people experience along the journey is not conceptualized as new or unique, but rather a continuation of processes they have known all their lives.

In Chapter 2, I turn to the ways in which the discourse and practices of state securitization projects cross borders along with migrants. I trace the development and implementation of Mexico's arterial border from the 1980s to the present through stories of abuse and extortion, with an emphasis on sexual violence, as migrants encounter state agents along the journey. This chapter also introduces the shifting dynamics and novel strategies migrants develop as they are funneled into more clandestine transit routes. In doing so, the chapter highlights the disjuncture between discourses of security and the lived realities of human (in)security.

Chapter 3 delves into the ways the journey across Mexico has become a site of intense violence and exploitation in what may be conceptualized as an industry. Through migrant testimonies, it traces how Central American migrants' bodies, labor, and lives are transformed into commodities in economies of smuggling, extortion, and kidnapping. I examine how such processes depend on dehumanizing state, legal, and social practices that construct migrants as unwanted criminals and racialized and gendered others. The commodification of migrants also coincides with the transformation of local spaces into new sites of insecurity.

Chapter 4 shifts the focus to the visible and less visible embodied realities of transit migration. Through analysis of injury, illness, and sexual violence, the chapter explores meanings of deservingness as related to migrants' health and well-being.

Chapter 5 examines the diverse social relations and economies of intimacy in which migrants engage en route. It aims to complicate normative understandings of human mobility and human smuggling by focusing on the intimate social relationships and forms of care that develop along migrant journeys, as well as the contradictions they produce.

Beyond the effects of migration on migrants themselves, an ethnography of transit must also examine the ways such movement impacts the communities they pass through. Chapter 6 examines some of the complexities around economies of compassion and the politics of security in local spaces. On one hand, the emergence of migrant shelters shows how local actors challenge the state and advocate for migrants' rights through the creation of spaces of refuge. On the other hand, however, migrants are often feared by local people, causing them to contest humanitarian aid shelters. The dynamics between priests, shelter workers, and local residents throw into relief the ways in which the moral imaginaries of charity, inclusion, and justice are shaped by everyday economic and social realities of safety and security.

Chapter 7 examines the gendered dimensions of solidarity, care, and activism in multiple contexts along the migrant journey. It links together the highly visible labors of a caravan of mothers of disappeared migrants with the less visible, yet no less important, labor of the local women who sustain migrant shelters on a daily basis. In doing so, I seek to shed light on the transnational feminist politics and forms of solidarity that undergird these local and transnational economies of compassion and social justice.

.   .   .   .   .

A mural at Casa Guadalupe depicts scenes from the journey between Central America and the United States: a mother and child looking northward, people clinging to the tops of freight trains, and masked gunmen robbing them as they pass through military checkpoints before arriving at

Figure 2. A mural at Casa Guadalupe. Photo by author.

a wall of graves along the U.S.–Mexico border. But there are also scenes of hope: churches, migrant aid shelters, women throwing food to migrants, and protestors demanding "Justice for Migrants" in the United States. The legend beneath a series of interconnected faces in different shades of brown reads: "El migrante no es una estadística, tiene rostro y dignidad" (The migrant is a not a statistic, [he] has a face and dignity" (fig. 2).

This book aspires to make these faces and this humanity visible. As the mural so beautifully depicts, Central American migration north is a complex journey involving a myriad of social actors, connected between and across borders. Their stories are often told through the brutality of violence, but this violence does not come without struggle. This is a book about that struggle and about the people whose everyday labors of hope, solidarity, and care animate it.

1 Circulations of Violence

"May I please go to the internet café?" Elio asked in a playful, pouty voice.

"Yes, of course, go ahead," Araceli, the coordinator at Casa Guadalupe, replied.

Elio jumped up. "Thanks, I'll only be gone for thirty minutes!" he exclaimed as he rushed to the men's dormitory to get ready. Araceli smiled and shook her head, giving me a knowing look. Going to the internet café down the street was one of the activities Elio depended on to distract him from the monotony of life at the shelter. "I'm so bored here!" Elio would lament with a big sigh as we sat in the shade and watched the rabbits and chickens putter about the yard. Indeed, Casa Guadalupe was not the most exciting place for a fourteen-year-old kid.

While most of the migrants who arrived to the shelter in the summer of 2013 stayed for just a few days waiting for their money orders to arrive, Elio had been there for weeks stuck in limbo. With no money, he could not hire a smuggler. He was unable to get in contact with his family back home and felt ambiguous about his future. Sometimes he said he wanted to continue on to the United States, at other times he said he'd rather return home to be with his mother. Since he was officially classified as an unaccompanied minor, shelter staff carefully considered what that meant in terms of his rights and protections in Mexico, as well as their obligations in supporting him.

Elio was born in San Pedro Sula, Honduras, a city with one of the highest murder rates in the world. He left home two years earlier at the age of twelve. He hoped to find work and send money home to his mother. Elio had four siblings in Honduras, including two older brothers. And while many adolescent boys look up to their older brothers, Elio feared his. "They do drugs. They have guns. I'm scared of my own brothers. I'm scared to be in my own country.

"You fear returning home?" I asked. Elio replied: "Yes: my country, it takes your smile away."

While we sat in the yard watching my then three-year-old daughter chase rabbits on the uneven pavement in the back patio, Elio told me about the first time he witnessed death. He was hanging out with a group of friends from his neighborhood near his house "just messing around." Seemingly out of nowhere he heard two of their names called out. He looked up and saw two men in a car holding guns fitted with silencers. Four silent shots and the two named boys dropped to the ground in front of him. Elio explained further: "It's not just MS [Mara Salvatrucha]. It's Barrio 18, Vatos Locos, all the gangs are there." For many young boys entering adolescence in urban Honduras, El Salvador, and Guatemala, gang violence had become an inescapable reality. The violence he experienced was not chaos swirling around the margins; it was knocking at his front door.

Soon after witnessing these murders, Elio's stepfather told the family he was going north. Elio begged to go along. He saw migration as an alternate path to a future in gang life that had consumed many of his friends and brothers around him. They traveled across Mexico's southern border with Guatemala by raft in broad daylight and made their way by foot around military checkpoints. In Chiapas, they were robbed by armed gunmen who took their money before releasing them. Instead of continuing on La Bestia (The Beast), the dangerous freight train that carries unauthorized migrants through the complex physical and human terrain of Mexico's migrant routes, they decided to continue along the Pacific and look for work in one of the coastal cities. They settled in Puerto Escondido, a picturesque port town on the coast of Oaxaca.

A few months after their arrival, Elio's stepfather disappeared after befriending a woman. Elio speculated that the two had continued on without him, perhaps to the northern border. While this would be the point at which many twelve-year-olds would return home, Elio was determined to make good on his promise to his mother. He decided to stay in Mexico. He rented a small room and found intermittent work at the port. He was able occasionally to wire money home to his mother and younger siblings, but it was not much. Two years passed. Life was difficult, and while he never talked to me directly about the details of what he did, rumors of drugs and other illicit transactions for money swirled among the other migrants when Elio's name came up.

"He's young, but he's seen a lot of things in his life," commented one of the men in the same dormitory. It was difficult to reconcile these rumors with the sweet, fresh-faced, playful young man I had come to know.

Life in Puerto Escondido caught up with him. When he heard about a priest in the Isthmus of Tehuantepec who helped Central Americans, he decided to buy a one-way bus ticket to Albergue Nazaret, where he met Padre José. As he did with many of the most vulnerable migrants, Padre José paid for Elio's bus ticket and sent him to stay at Casa Guadalupe, which offered a more stable, enclosed environment, safer for a young man like Elio.

Not accustomed to having an unaccompanied minor at Casa Guadalupe, shelter staff reached out to Mexican social service and child-protection agencies to assist in his situation. It was unclear whether Elio, a Honduran citizen, was eligible to receive the benefits and services covered by Mexico's family welfare agency. There was a DIF (National System for Integral Family Development) shelter in the Yucatán that was floated as a possible landing place for Elio, but the logistics of sending him there were complicated, and the staff were uncertain whether it would be a good place for him. Word had started to spread between the shelters that there was an unaccompanied minor at Casa Guadalupe.

CNN México wanted an interview with him. "CNN called again," Araceli told Elio one afternoon. He rolled his eyes and repeated, "I still don't want to talk to them." Elio was reluctant to share his story. He did not want any more attention.

. . . . .

While we did not know it at the time, the next summer would be filled with stories of Central American youth like Elio attempting to make their way to the United States. Indeed, as the spectacle of the unaccompanied minor crisis unfolded, I often thought of Elio. Much of the coverage in the U.S. media around the "surge" of unaccompanied youth focused on the U.S.–Mexico border region, as if this was where the problem originated. There were reports about border apprehensions, the poor conditions of detention centers, and the protests by border residents who feared a tidal wave of outsiders that would siphon off public resources and spread disease. One U.S. congressman, Rep. Phil Gingrey MD (R-GA), penned a letter to the Centers for Disease Control and Prevention calling on them to address the health risks posed by undocumented children, who, he claimed, potentially carried deadly diseases like swine flu and Ebola and lacked the proper vaccinations. The construction of children as dangerous threats reflects a longer history of "othering" migrants along the U.S.–Mexico border.[1] When Central American youth were not constructed as threats, they were constructed as victims—of gangs, of smugglers, and of their own parents. At the height of the crisis President Barack Obama made this plea to parents in Central America, "Our message absolutely is don't send your children unaccompanied, on trains or through a bunch of smugglers. . . . If they do make it, they'll get sent back. More importantly, they may not make it." Such discourses fail to recognize the agency of unaccompanied youth who must balance the risk of migration against the risks of staying home. Moreover, they obscure the immediate and structural contexts within Central America that propel people to migrate in the first place. Even at the height of arrivals, minors made up only 30 percent of all Central Americans apprehended at the border. Central Americans—children and adults—have been fleeing their homes for decades.

So why do Central American migrants risk such a violent journey to reach the United States? Why would people intentionally put themselves or their children at risk of rape, kidnapping, or murder? Are they unaware of the risks before they embark on their journeys or do they simply have faith that they will beat the odds, where others have not? Are the pulls of a job or family reunification really worth it? In other words, how do Central Americans assess risk and reward as they negotiate violent landscapes?

Such questions are important and speak to the agency of individuals, yet they frame migration as an act of rational choice and with a purposeful orientation toward the future. In contrast, many of my interlocutors framed their migration in relation, not only to the future, but also to the past; *if you want to know why we risk this brutal journey, where we are raped, violated, robbed, and abused, you must understand where we come from.*

Most of my interlocutors saw migration as the best option to escape the everyday insecurity and violence that defined their lives. While there is a perception that all Central Americans are in search of the American Dream and thus cross through Mexico to get to the United States, I came across a number who simply wanted to reach Mexico. Their mobility was framed more in terms of fleeing Central America—whether it was from the hand of an abusive spouse, the barrel of a loaded weapon, or the daily grind of crushing poverty—rather than the pull of a job or new flat-screen TV. Migration is a response to violence, a strategy of survival.

Through the stories of migrants like Elio, this chapter situates contemporary migrations and violence within a deeper historical context and framework of structural violence.[2] A comprehensive history of violence in Central America is well beyond the scope of this book, but Central American migrants' own explanations of why they left home shed light on the entangled webs of power, capital, and violence that have shaped the movements of Central Americans over the past half-century. The supporting role of the United States in state-sponsored repression during the Central American civil wars, the deportation of thousands of gang members from Southern California in the early 1990s, and the continued dispossession of the poor through neoliberal economic policies that displace people from their lands and livelihoods, are all deeply intertwined with contemporary mobilities. There is no one "root cause" to explain migration from Central America; rather, we must interrogate the layered factors that produce everyday insecurities. Analysis of these intersecting dynamics enables us to see how pluralities of violence shape people's lives across time and space.[3] Such a framework conceptualizes violence, not only as relative and layered, but also as cumulative in understanding what may initially seem to be a paradox—but turns out to be no paradox at all—of why people would insert themselves into such a path of near certain suffering. More than this, a historical perspective works against efforts to "silence the past" in contemporary debates about violence and migration in Central America.[4] Contemporary migration stems from decades—and arguably centuries—of exploitation and violence suffered by people in Central America.[5] It is only with this history, and recognition of the role of the United States in the political and economic instability of life in Central America, that we can understand everyday conditions so dire that a teenage boy like Elio, so full of wit and life, has no other way to describe his home than as a place "that takes your smile away."

COLD WAR KIDS

The idea that violence is relative and cumulative is illustrated by two of my closest interlocutors, Ever and Carmen. While many of the migrants I met I only knew for a few days or perhaps weeks as they passed through the shelter, I was able to establish a longer-term relationship with Ever and Carmen as they ended up settling in Oaxaca for the duration of my field-work. I first met them after a late evening meeting at Casa Guadalupe. Most migrants had retreated to the dormitories, but I noticed a couple who lingered in the living room. Ever appeared to be nervous or agitated, fidgeting as he waited to speak with one of the staff members. When I approached him, he started speaking rapidly, "We know the policy is that people can only stay here for three days, but my woman, she is pregnant, and we are hoping we can stay longer". He went on, "Our dream is not to reach the United States, but to stay here in Oaxaca." I told him that I would speak with the staff and see if we could work something out. The next morning everyone agreed that because Carmen was pregnant, they should be allowed to stay. When they came into the office, Araceli gave them the news and I could see the relief wash over their faces.

Over the course of the next year, I would come to know Ever and Carmen quite well during downtime at the shelter and during visits to the clinic for Carmen's prenatal appointments. Several months into their stay, Carmen's older sister, Mari, decided that she wanted to come to Oaxaca to support her sister and help with the baby. The sisters often came into the office to make phone calls back to their family who lived on the outskirts of San Salvador, an area riddled with gang violence. There was one espe-cially distressing call when they learned that their youngest sister, who was only fifteen, was being pursued by a well-known gang member to be his "girlfriend." Such relationships were coercive and dangerous they explained; everyone in the family was worried.

But for this trio, violence was not new. "For us there has never been a time without violence," said Mari one afternoon sitting on the bottom bunk in the men's dormitory along with Carmen and Ever. They had grown up in 1980s El Salvador during the civil war.[6] Indeed, many of the Central Americans crossing Mexico in the mid 2000s lived through or were born soon after the years of civil war and state repression in Guatemala, El Salvador, Nicaragua, and Honduras. Mari shared a mem-ory from her childhood:

> I remember when I was six years old, inside the patio where we lived, right there in the corridor there were dead people. They were in the trees, there were people hanging there who had had their skin stripped off their bodies. The neighbors said they didn't see anything, but there they were at dawn, tied to the trees without their skin. This is what I remember of my childhood.

Ever nodded his head in agreement. While it would be years before he met Mari and Carmen, his childhood was also marked by what seemed to be senseless violence and injustice:

> It was the soldiers who were killing. They killed a guy where I lived, and they killed him unjustly. He was defending his brothers who were being recruited by the soldiers. His brothers didn't want to go with the soldiers, and their older brother went to defend them. One of the soldiers pushed their mother and he said, "Why did you push my mom?" and he shoved him. The soldier just went up to him and put a bullet here, in the middle of his chest. And then he shot his brother too. He shot a lot of people. That's it. That is all I remember.

While these are only snapshots into Mari and Ever's childhoods, they offer a glimpse into the types of stories that are seared into people's memories. For Mari, the family patio would forever be associated with those dead hanging bodies. Ever's early encounter with the brutality of the military would become crystalized as a permanent distrust and fear of the state, even as his country transitioned into a period of democracy. Such events laid the foundation for a life in which violence was normalized and perhaps even seen as inevitable. As Michelle Bellino argues, war not only leaves its marks on bodies and landscapes, but also shapes the subjectivities of the next generation.[7]

While not always explicit, these conflicts were also often Central Americans' first encounters with the United States. While the geopolitical tension of the Cold War is often perceived to have focused primarily on Eurasia, significant battles were also being fought in Central America. During the Cold War, the United States saw Central America as a crucial site to fight the spread and influence of Soviet communism.[8] Largely during the presidency of Ronald Reagan, the United States supplied weapons, financial assistance, and military training to Central American military governments, and in the case of Nicaragua, right-wing counterrevolutionary forces known as the Contras. An estimated $9.7 billion (2013 constant dollar values) was spent bankrolling the Central American wars in the 1980s.[9] The United States systematically trained tens of thousands of Central American soldiers, including some of the most notorious dictators, at the School of the Americas, teaching counterinsurgency techniques, psychological warfare, and military intelligence and interrogation tactics, including torture.[10]

Taken together, it is estimated that a quarter of a million people died during these conflicts. Tens of thousands were "disappeared"—victims of state terror likely tortured or killed—and millions more were displaced from their homes. Since the end of the civil wars, truth commissions have determined that U.S.–backed government forces were largely responsible for a host of human rights abuses.[11] In 1995 the *Baltimore Sun* exposed the atrocities committed by the U.S.–backed Honduran death squad called Battalion 316.[12] According to the report, which was based upon newly unclassified government documents, the Reagan administration purposely misled and minimized the violence to the American public and to Congress to maintain the flow of congressional funding to Honduras.[13] In 2013, José Efraín Ríos Montt, the former dictator of Guatemala, a man President Reagan openly praised, was convicted of genocide and crimes against humanity. Through death squads, massacres, torture and disappearances, Central America became in Greg Grandin's words, the "Cold War's last killing fields."[14]

Like Mari and Ever, a thirty-year-old mother from El Salvador named Blanca described how the rippling effects of war on her family growing up directly influenced her decision to migrate. When she was eleven, members of the Salvadoran military killed her father. She described how her father's death triggered a new cycle of violence and abuse in her family. After the war and her father's death, the family struggled financially. Her mother eventually remarried, but to an openly abusive man. When Blanca discovered that her stepfather had been sexually assaulting her older sister, she feared she would be next. At the age of fourteen, Blanca decided to move out of the family home and move into a neighbor's house. She explained that she never had the opportunity to have a proper childhood. She became pregnant at fifteen. Now that her own daughter was almost fifteen, all she wanted, she said, was to be able to throw her a *quinceañera* (girl's fifteenth birthday celebration) and pay for her to continue her studies:

> I am a single mother, and I want my daughter to be able to study. I don't want her to grow up like I did. There were nine of us and my father was killed in the civil war in '89. We were left without a father, and really without a mother, because without him, well, there just wasn't enough money for all of us. And that is why I decided to leave El Salvador. I do not want my daughter to go through what I had to go through or live like I had to live. I want her to go to school, be a professional, learn how to defend herself on her own. I don't want her to have to have a husband in order for her to be alright. I want her to have the profession that she wants. That is why I left.

The war and her father's death were defining moments in her childhood that would shape the trajectory of her life. Blanca saw migration as a way to break the cycle of violence and poverty within which she was embedded. When I met her, she had already been deported from Mexico five times. The farthest she had ever reached was Lechería, a well-known railroad junction area on the outskirts of Mexico City. Despite her failed attempts, when I spoke with her she was gathering resources to try again. Blanca was determined to give her daughter what she had not had.

For most of the people I interviewed, the subject of the civil wars conjured up painful memories and suffering. These were stories that I had come to expect. Yet for one of my interlocutors, Hector, wartime Guatemala marked a period of stability and purpose. Hector's life story captures some of the historical contradictions that underpin contemporary migration from Central America.

Hector

On a late winter afternoon a few weeks before Christmas, I entered the living room of Casa Guadalupe where I found Hector reading a small pocket-sized bible. The bible was one of the few possessions he carried with him from his home in Quetzaltenango, Guatemala. Hector identified himself as an indigenous speaker of Mam, a Mayan language spoken in parts of Guatemala and Mexico, though he clarified that he was the only one in his family to still speak the language. Even though we were inside, Hector wore a bright blue rain jacket, which stood out against his dark polyester pants, T-shirt, and midnight black hair. The deep wrinkles around his eyes hinted at a lifetime of hard work. He had a large black mole on his right cheek, a silver-plated top right incisor and a severely chipped left top incisor. I had become accustomed to noticing moles, birthmarks, tattoos, plated teeth, and other distinguishing features on people's faces and bodies. We recorded these details on our intake forms for each person who passed through, because they could become crucial markers in helping to locate a missing person or identify a recovered body.

This was Hector's third time crossing Mexico. Forty-five years old, and the father of five children, he was traveling with his eighteen-year-old son Federico and his wife's nineteen-year-old niece, Delmy. His three youngest children remained in Guatemala with his wife, and his eldest daughter lived in South Carolina. He took out a crumpled plastic baggy from his pocket and unwrapped a small brown wallet. He unfolded it to show me four passport-sized photographs tucked into the plastic wallet inserts. The photos were of his wife and three of his children, two daughters and one son, all with serious expressions on their faces. The older daughter's photo looked to be from her high school graduation and was the only one printed in color. Aside from the photos, Hector's wallet was empty; no ID card, no credit card, no cash.

As he put away his wallet and put his bible to his side on the couch, he shared his story with me. When he was twenty-two, he had been recruited into the Guatemalan military. He served between 1985 to 1996, during some of the most brutal years at the end of Guatemala's civil war.

The Guatemalan civil war, which was the bloodiest of all the wars in Central America, officially lasted from 1960 until 1996, when Peace Accords were signed. Throughout the conflict, the United States had a heavy hand in the violence. In 1954, the CIA orchestrated a coup to oust the democratically elected president of Guatemala, Jacobo Árbenz, which put the anti-communist military party in power. During the 1960s and 1970s, the Guatemalan military modernized its weaponry, use of intelligence, paramilitary groups, and torture techniques. In the early 1980s, in response to a rise in the insurgency movement and the formation of the Guatemalan National Revolutionary Unity (UNRG), the Guatemalan army stepped up its counterinsurgency tactics and warfare. Throughout Ríos Montt's de facto presidency (1982–83), the Guatemalan army initiated one of the most deadly periods during the thirty-six-year conflict, a "scorched earth" counterinsurgency that committed genocide, torture, rape, and disappearances of men, women, and children. Many of the victims were indigenous Maya who lived in the rural highlands. The campaign ultimately killed two hundred thousand people and disappeared tens of thousands of others.

Knowing this history, I was somewhat taken aback as Hector began to invoke alarmist language about the threat of communism and his sense of urgency in fighting the guerillas as if we were still in the midst of the Cold War. Most of the people I encountered lamented the war years and were not sympathetic to the Guatemalan military or any of the U.S.-backed military governments in Central America. For Hector, however, these had been the good years, years of stability and purpose. In the military, Hector's job was to train soldiers how to use various weapons. He became more animated as he systematically recited names of all the artillery he knew how to operate.

Yet as we continued to speak, Hector went on to discuss his dismay at the end of the war and his personal downward spiral after the military was downsized and he was let go. Hector found himself with few economic opportunities. He explained that the economic situation had become nearly impossible in the postwar period, since food and oil prices continued to rise:

> When the gas prices rose so did everything in the *canasta basica* [basic basket of consumer goods], everything went up, and now we can't survive. Everywhere in Guatemala, the prices went up, but the salaries remained the

same, and the companies, they exploit the workers. They don't pay fair salaries, and in the factories where we worked, we didn't have any labor benefits. These are the conditions in which we come, craving the American dream. That is what we are looking for. We are here not because we want to be here, but we are looking toward the future, to do something in life so that later our children can have a better life.

Hector had been deported from the United States before and knew that if he were caught again by Immigration and Customs Enforcement (ICE), he would face lengthy imprisonment under 8 USC 1326, "Re-entry of Removed Aliens."[15] Like Blanca, however, he decided that it was still worth the risk to try crossing, because he wanted his younger children to continue their studies in Guatemala.

The contours of Hector's life and decisions reveal how present-day migration from Central America is deeply embedded in transnational histories of violence, economic insecurity and militarization. Hector was a member of a U.S.-backed military in a war that killed an estimated two hundred thousand people, many of them other indigenous people. He had no support from his military or current government, which he saw as largely corrupt and responsible for the economic crises and rise of violence and organized criminals in his community. As Hector tried for the third time to reach the United States to make a better life for his children, he was considered to be illegal, an alien, and his act of migration, criminal. If he was caught, he risked spending years in a prison run by the government that indirectly supported him and his family twenty-five years earlier.

The violence of the civil wars in Central America did not end with the signing of the Peace Accords. On the contrary, the postwar period marked a new phase in violence and economic insecurity, which as I discuss next, are inextricably interlinked.

POSTWAR VIOLENCE, NEOLIBERALISM, AND INSECURITY

> El Salvador is like a prison. The only way to gain liberty is to escape.
>
> —Ever

The legacies of political violence in Guatemala, El Salvador, Nicaragua, and Honduras, coupled with growing economic inequality created the conditions for an intensification of violence—and social struggle—to emerge in postwar Central America.[16] Since the early 2000s, El Salvador, Honduras, and Guatemala have consistently had some of the highest homicide rates in the world.[17] They also have some of the highest rates of feminicide, where violence against women is tied both directly and indirectly to the state.[18] Like the killing of the two boys described by Elio, many of my interlocutors described violence as immediate and visible. It permeated the landscapes of their everyday lives.

Some migrants talked about the violence in the postwar period as similar to or even worse than during the war, a sentiment captured by scholars working in the region.[19] Just as the death squads left their signatures on the murdered bodies of victims during the civil wars, in contemporary Central America, decapitated heads and body parts are put on display in public spaces. One migrant who lived in San Salvador, the capital of El Salvador, explained how the local MS gangs kill people and display their corpses as warnings: "They don't just sell human organs, but take them just to show them off to the people. They throw them in the streets, there are parts of arms and hands, there are human body parts. They don't even sell them, but just waste them."

Such acts reinforce fear and insecurity even when one's life is not in immediate danger. Whereas the violence of war could be explained and legitimated by state involvement, for many of my interlocutors, the violence of the postwar period was more nebulous, irrational, and uncertain. Naya, a female migrant from El Salvador, described the shift to me during our interview: "The violence is different now because before it was between governments and political parties that were fighting. But now, it is between the people. It is harder now because this is something that has come from nothing, the gangs are something from nothing."

But is this violence really from nothing? Violence for the sake of violence? Scholars of Central America have dedicated significant attention to understanding the nature of violence in the postwar period of democracy.[20] For instance, Elana Zilberg has written about the reappearance of death squads in El Salvador, Jennifer Burrell has documented a new wave of vigilantism and lynchings in postwar Guatemala, and Cecilia Menjívar and Shannon Walsh have analyzed the rise of feminicide in Honduras after the 2009 coup.[21] Across Latin America, there is a prevalence of what Enrique Arias and Daniel Goldstein call the "violent pluralism" of state and nonstate actors, often working together in civil society.[22] Rather than seeing violence as evidence of failed states, Arias and Goldstein argue, these pluralities of violence co-exist with the aspirations of neoliberal democracy in Latin America.[23]

In addition to the ideological interests of U.S. involvement in Central America, the wars also opened the region to a new phase in a U.S.–driven economic agenda based on principles of free-market capitalism known as neoliberalism. Building on decades of foreign investment in various industries, such as the foreign-owned banana industry,[24] neoliberalism in Central America prevailed during the "transition to democracy" in the late 1980s and 1990s.[25] For example, in El Salvador, the United States began attaching neoliberal economic conditions in exchange for its financial and military support of counterinsurgency policies.[26] Similar processes unfolded in Guatemala as the Peace Accords signed in 1996 ushered in a new phase of neoliberal capitalism.[27] Ellen Moodie argues that neoliberalism in El Salvador represents a clear example of what Naomi Klein calls the "shock doctrine" model of "disaster capitalism" where societies reeling from shocks like war or a natural disaster are reengineered under a neoliberal mode.[28] Indeed, as Greg Grandin has argued, the type of absolute free market capitalism supported in this model was only possible through state repression.[29]

Reforms such as deregulation, elimination of tariffs, free trade, privatization, and reduction in public expenditures were intended to pave the way for foreign investment and bring Central American countries into the global economy.[30] However, neoliberal policies and practices displaced people from their traditional livelihood strategies, weakened the social safety net, minimized worker protections, and forced many into the informal sector or to migrate. For example, much as in Mexico after the implementation of the North American Free Trade Agreement (NAFTA), the opening of agricultural markets in Guatemala undermined both economic and cultural ways of life for many Maya farmers, who could not compete with cheap food imported from the United States.[31] No longer able to feed their families, people moved to work as migrant wage laborers in foreign-owned factories called *maquiladoras* located on the edges of cities as the region became a hotbed for foreign capital in extractive industries and manufacturing.[32] However, for many, work in the factories was highly exploitative and increasingly dangerous, because local criminal networks began to extort wages from workers. It was also unstable. Beatrice, a mother of three from Honduras described the hardship she faced when the clothing factory where she worked closed its doors to relocate to Asia. After months of unemployment, Beatrice decided the only way to provide for her kids was to migrate north.

Accompanying neoliberal economic policies was the expansion of state and transnational security initiatives, what Elana Zilberg calls a "neoliberal securityscape" linking flows of people, policies, and capital across the Americas. Everyday violence and insecurity are seen as the product of criminal actors—gangs, deportees, and delinquents—rather than of neoliberal states. By describing violence as criminal and not political, the state is able to legitimize increased securitization in the name of public or citizen security. For example, in response to this rise in gangs over the past decade, El Salvador, Guatemala, and Honduras have all implemented harsh "zero-tolerance" policing strategies. As Susan Coutin describes it, "public concerns about crime and increased stigmatization of gang members in particular authorized the reintroduction, under color of law, of measures that resembled certain tactics used during the war."[33] Such heavy-handed tactics have generally proved counterproductive in their attempts to curb violence.[34] State security policies become a way to address the insecurities produced by neoliberalism, yet ultimately reproduce more insecurity and violence. As people become increasingly disillusioned by the state and its ability to protect the populace, security itself is privatized through the employment of private security firms, neighborhood watch groups, and, in extreme examples, vigilantism.[35]

The disarticulation of wartime political violence from postwar criminality is a strategy used by states to shift accountability from the state to other groups, most notably gangs and other unsavory actors generally referred to as *delincuentes* (delinquents).[36] Moral and individualized discourses are used to blame gangs for violence, obscuring the historical and structural roots of their formation.[37] Transnational gangs like the Mara Salvatrucha (MS) and Barrio 18 (18th Street Gang) originated, not in San

Salvador, or San Pedro Sula but in Los Angeles, among youths recruited from the Central American refugee population. In the mid-1990s, during aggressive deportation campaigns in the United States, many were then "exported" back to Central America. They arrived back in countries like El Salvador, which had just recently signed Peace Accords in 1992, with very little political or social infrastructure to reintegrate this population. Young men hardened on the streets of LA and in the U.S. prison system were thrust back into a life, not only outside of prison, but in a completely different country. A weak political system also allowed criminal groups to take root in local neighborhoods, cities, and eventually entire countries. It is estimated that in El Salvador alone, a country with only six million people, there are currently over sixty thousand active gang members and close to half a million people who are economically dependent on them.[38]

Many of the young adults I interviewed specifically cited fear and pressure to join local gangs as factors motivating them to migrate. As Jon Wolseth uncovered during his research among Honduran male youth, transnational migration is considered the only way to escape not only physical but social death—the feeling that many young people had that there was no place for them in society.[39] This was exemplified by Ever's rationale for leaving his home in El Salvador. Despite his attempts to remain unaffiliated, Ever became implicated in the activities of the Mara Salvatrucha gang in his neighborhood. He spent several months in prison, and when he was released he started receiving death threats and feared for the safety of his family and Carmen. In his words,

> I left my country because of the delinquency. I was scared that they were going to kill me. I don't want to be a victim. Right now, we are looking to move forward, even though everything is really dangerous . . . I want a normal life without the threat of being killed. And many of us are looking for the same thing, to arrive at a place, a better place where we can achieve something and have things that in our countries we cannot obtain. This is what we are all looking for, even though on the journey we suffer a lot. We fall into the hands of criminals and kidnappers, rapists, people who steal whatever you have. These are the things that we have all experienced.

In addition to direct threats and fear of recruitment, across Central America gangs and criminal organizations have wreaked havoc in their neighborhoods by taking control of economic markets, businesses, and individual livelihoods through systematic extortion schemes. Gangs demand what is called *la renta* (the rent) from local people on a weekly or monthly basis in exchange for immunity from violence. Blanca, whom I introduced earlier in this chapter, described the impact of the rise of gangs,

> Around 1990, after the war was over and the peace accords, that was when the gangs arrived. The gangs that are in El Salvador leave backpacks in the parks with people's heads. There are arms and legs in the streets. This is normal there. If you have a little business the gangs come by to demand your money and you have to give it to them. If you don't, they plunder every-thing—they will take everything from your house. If you go out to work and you leave your house empty, when you come back you won't find anything because they have taken it all.

Another female migrant from El Salvador describes a similar dynamic with local gangs, extortion and violence:

> You can't walk alone, nor can you own your own business or anything. If they see that you have a business and are working peacefully, they put a tax on you. They make you pay *la renta*. The gangs put a quota on you that you have to pay to them on the day they demand. If you don't pay them, they start with your family. With your son or with your mother. They kill them. There was a case near my home. On the corner where I had my shop, there was another little shop. The woman who works there sells sodas and water and they demanded a rent of two thousand dollars. Two thousand dollars. The woman could not pay it, and they kidnapped her son. For these reasons, we have to leave our own country, for the good of our families and for our children.

Similar descriptions were used to describe gangs and extortion in Guatemala. I interviewed Eduardo, a man in his mid-forties from Chiquimulilla, Guatemala, who could not continue to support his family as a farmer or even find local work as a construction worker. He said that he could have tried to move to a town with a *maquila* (factory) or to the capital, where he might earn more, but that money would likely be taken by gangs as *la renta*. In his words,

> I am migrating for work. In Guatemala, what there is, is very little. The work is hard, it takes a lot out of you, and they pay you very little. Work in con-struction, or in the fields, the beans and corn that they cultivate. There is more work farther, like in the *maquilas* [factories] where you can earn

more, but there is a lot of extortion by *los mareros* [gang members], they put a tax on you and you have to pay them monthly. If you don't pay them, they kill you. *Maras* [gangs] from Barrio 18 or MS, the Mara Salvatruchas. If you go to the capital, you have to give them half of your salary. If you don't give them half of your salary then they threaten to kill you. They give you two opportunities, and the third one, well that's it. They stab you or shoot you with bullets. There is a lot of disorder in Guatemala.

Through these narratives we see the double-bind of economics and insecurity that many migrants expressed. For ordinary people, the incentives to move to capital cities and work in the maquiladoras, where wages are higher, are lessened by the proliferation of extortion and ultimately the state's failure to protect its citizenry. In this case, criminal actors feed off of the market openings fueled by neoliberal policies that open trade and move business abroad. Factory workers and people who own small businesses, perhaps selling tortillas, bread, or sodas, are regularly targeted in local extortion rings.

Thus, aside from the immediate threat of violence, everyday people find themselves economically strangled by a criminal-state system motivated, not by human security, but rather by profit. *La renta* has become a significant source of income in Central America over the past decade and in some cases gangs use it to support imprisoned gang members and their families (Zilberg 2011). Moreover, as Ainhoa Montoya observes regarding the proliferation of extortion rackets and private security in El Salvador in the 2000s, "Extortion and security are mutually complementary and self-reinforcing in ways that produce private profit from violence."[40] As I discuss in more depth in chapter 6, state securitization creates apertures for private profit, and in some cases the privatization of security itself in communities and shelters that do not feel protected by the state.

Neoliberal democratization and securitization produce the conditions for violence to flourish and ultimately profit from conditions of insecurity in ways that blur the lines between political violence and criminal violence.[41] Organized criminals and gangs often collude with state authorities, operating with impunity. The idea that violence comes from "nothing" or "nowhere" erases the historical threads to the legacies of wartime violence, neoliberal economic policies, and role of external actors, namely, the United States, in manufacturing a state of ubiquitous insecurity.

BETWEEN CRIMINALS AND THE STATE

> El Salvador is a war zone. It is not a war like Iraq with lots of
> explosions, but a silent war, where people cannot speak. Here
> in Mexico, the police still dominate the gangs. In El Salvador,
> the gangs control the police.
> —Salvadoran migrant

This statement captures the pervasive sense of fear, insecurity, and disillusionment many migrants expressed in relationship to the state and justice systems in their home countries. Many people felt that government officials had not only abandoned their duty to protect the citizenry, but were complicit in and sometimes active perpetrators of criminal violence. A profound mistrust of state agents and official institutions persisted during their journeys in Mexico. Maribel illustrated the Salvadoran state's impotence in the face of violent crime using an example from her own family's experience:

> The government does not do anything. They do not do anything with respect to crime. Especially the police, they are afraid of the criminals. When there is a problem, like someone is robbed or someone is killed, the police show up two hours later. I know this well, in my family we had a case, two robbers entered my house and they had us all on the ground with guns pointed at our heads. One of my sisters was lucky and was able to jump out of a window and leave through the other side onto the neighbor's property. She left and advised the rest of the family, anyone who was close to leave because the robbers were there and they had guns and so everyone left. They left and called the police but they never appeared. My nephew arrived and he did not realize they were armed. He tried to take them down and the robber put his gun right here [to the chest], and this is where he shot him. The robbers fled and my family chased after them but did not catch them. I returned to my nephew because he was still there sitting in his own blood. I carried him and everyone thought that I was the one who was shot because I was covered in blood. My nephew was in the hospital and three hours later the police showed up asking, "What happened here?" And can you imagine, I was so upset that I told them to leave right now, that I didn't want anything to do with them. They said, "But look, Miss, you have to file a claim." But no, because if we do, tomorrow they are going to come after all of us. It is better that we don't speak. One cannot speak. And this is what happened to us at my home. [In] the majority of the homes in all of El Salvador and in Honduras, it is like this, this is how we live.

Maribel's description reveals the violence and terror experienced by many ordinary Central Americans and the failure of the state to respond and protect its citizens. The police in this case were more concerned with filing a claim than with seeking justice. Yet it is not just that the state has failed to protect citizens and prosecute perpetrators. Many people described officials as being directly involved or complicit in the violence itself. Alejandra chimed in during a group interview to tell me about the situation in Honduras:

> My brother has a little business there in Honduras, and the gangs began to demand *la renta*. And when the first demand arrived, they said that if he did not pay by the date, they would feel very sorry for his daughters. It has always been like this; it is just more difficult now, because now more people are left without work. Employment is really scarce. And the government does not do anything; they are corrupt and sometimes they are even involved. Yes, they are part of the organized gangs. Just like here with Los Zetas, who kidnap people. It's like that in Honduras, the only difference is that Los Zetas are interested in fast cash, and not there, there, you have to keep paying them for weeks, weeks, weeks.

The security situation in Honduras quickly deteriorated after a military coup that ousted democratically elected President Manuel Zelaya in 2009. In the months following the coup, the numbers of Honduran migrants arriving to shelters in Mexico increased substantially and many people petitioned to stay in Mexico on humanitarian grounds. Following the coup, Honduras emerged as the world leader in homicide rates, a title it has shared with El Salvador ever since.

The narratives of Central American migrants like Ever and Alejandra show that violence in Central America is not simply perpetrated by uncontrolled delinquents. Rather, it is embedded in institutions and practices that deny people safety, justice, and rights and historically linked across societies. Celestino, a young man from Honduras makes these linkages clear:

> In Honduras, the violence is really bad. At times one thinks it is better to leave the country. . . . Maybe one has a job or their own business, but what little you have, they will take it from you for your life. For a bicycle or a cell phone. They take it from you and if you are reluctant, they kill you. For a cell phone they kill you, for any fucking little thing you have. Many of my friends have fallen like this. And others, well, they do what they have to in order to

leave their countries. There are many of us who leave our countries, not necessarily to improve our lives, but because we are fleeing, fleeing the justice system of our country. But many here end up failing anyway, because migration gets them. Even if they are able to pass through here, ultimately they just get locked up.

Framing Central American migration as flight forces us to rethink the distinctions we often make between economic migrants and asylum-seekers/refugees. Many of my interlocutors' narratives did not fit the traditional or legal definitions of either category, raising questions about the cogency of such terms and the need for broader analytical categories of mobility and violence as spatially and temporally deep. Moreover, migrants' narratives bespeak the historical entanglements connecting Central America and the United States. The insecurities produced through a history of neoliberalism, criminal-state violence and securitization continue to undermine people's ability to live with safety and justice. Through migration people both spatially express collective histories of violence as well as enact their determination for a better future for themselves and their families. The violence people experience along the journey echoes both the violence and the struggle for dignity that in many cases have shaped their entire lives.

BOY GONE

In listening to the stories of Central American youths like Elio, with whom I began this chapter, I am reminded of James Quesada's poignant case study of a young Nicaraguan boy named Daniel. Quesada illustrates how boys like Daniel teach us about the ways children grapple with chronic "normal abnormality" in conditions of war, scarcity, and destruction. Children both endure and embody the legacies of war and chronic forms of social suffering. Daniel viewed death as one outcome, one way to help others to live.[42]

Ever, Elio, and others like them know that migration has enabled others to live, but they know, too, in migrating, that their own journeys may lead to death. In the end, they have only one goal: to survive. Their stories teach us that despite discourses of victimization, young people like Elio are also agents of their own futures.

The last time I saw Elio was on his fifteenth birthday. The summer was coming to an end, and I was returning to the United States to prepare for my fall courses. Mauricio and Flor told me about the small party they were going to have in Elio's honor. I arrived with my daughter, promising her cake. Everyone was gathered in the kitchen, but Elio was nowhere to be seen. "He's still getting ready," one of the other migrants explained. When he finally walked in, everyone whistled and teased him. He had borrowed a crisp black *guayabera* (Mexican dress shirt) from Mauricio, and his dark hair was combed back with gel. He blushed at our teasing, his dimples like bookends to his wide smile. He opened his presents: a jumbo bag of peanut M&Ms and a soccer ball. He was particularly pleased with the soccer ball, which he kicked around the dirt yard for hours. Finally, something to pass the time with! When it was time for cake, we sang the traditional birthday song, "Las Mañanitas." "And now in English!" someone yelled. "Happy birthday, dear Elio, happy birthday to you." He paused an extra moment before blowing out his candles.

A few months after my return to the United States, I spoke to Araceli on the phone. She told me that they had finally tracked down and contacted Elio's mother in Honduras. On the phone, Elio's mother had seemed ambivalent about his return, because she worried about his safety. She saw what was happening to the other young men in the community. Since his departure, Honduras had become even more dangerous. That year, San Pedro Sula, Elio's hometown, surpassed Ciudad Juarez as the murder capital of the world, with a documented 187 homicides for every 100,000 people. The following year, calculations showed that on an average day fourteen people were murdered in Honduras. But in the end, Elio decided to return home. The residents at Casa Guadalupe took up a collection to pay for his bus ticket back. They put him on the bus, waving goodbye. He was gone. As with so many others who passed through Casa Guadalupe, we would never know what happened to him. What we do know is that the next year more than sixty thousand unaccompanied minors and close to two hundred thousand adults moved in the opposite direction, fleeing to the north.

2 The Arterial Border

In July 2006, I made my first trip to the border between Mexico and Guatemala. I disembarked from a long, stomach-churning bus ride in the city of Tapachula, located in the southernmost Mexican state of Chiapas. Even though I had spent time in the highlands near Chiapas's old capital, San Cristóbal de Las Casas, I was taken aback by the thick air and sweltering heat of the Soconusco region, situated between the Sierra Madre de Chiapas mountain range and the Pacific coast. The bus station buzzed with the usual hustle and bustle of arrivals and departures. Women carried bundles of fresh bread and colorful tote bags and teenagers slurped instant noodles from white Styrofoam containers. The World Cup was in full swing, and a bright green soccer pitch lit up the TV screen in the main hall. At first glance, the station looked like any other bus station in southern Mexico. Then I saw the rows of pictures and mismatched homemade flyers plastered along the bus station's whitewashed walls.

When I looked more closely I realized that these were flyers asking about missing persons. *Have you seen my daughter? Do you have any information on this person? Missing.* Most flyers had photographs accompanied by a short description of the last known location, clothing worn, and date of disappearance. Daughters and sons, mothers and fathers. At the bottom of each sheet of paper were long phone numbers with the country and area codes for Guatemala, Honduras, and El Salvador. People walked by the flyers without a glance. Pictures of missing migrants were ordinary sights in this transit town. Welcome to the southern border.

Several days after my arrival to Tapachula I set off to visit a migrant shelter in the city of Tecún Umán, located on the other side of the border. Mexico's southern border with Guatemala and Belize spans over 1,100 kilometers. It has been called *la otra frontera* (the other border) or *la frontera olvidada* (the forgotten border) because of the limited attention it receives from politicians, journalists, and academics, as compared to Mexico's northern border with the United States.[1]

I took a 45-minute *combi* (minivan) ride, the most common form of transportation in the region, to the small border city of Ciudad Hidalgo, a place once described to me as a lawless frontier. The *combi* was packed with people; children sat on their parents' laps. A little boy sucked on a lollipop and when he was finished, casually tossed the foil wrapper and tiny white stick out the open window. People got on and others got off before we reached the final stop. The driver of the *combi* directed me toward the *puente* Dr. Rodolfo Robles. This is the bridge that connects Mexico to Guatemala, named for a Guatemalan physician who first linked parasitic worms to onchocerciasis, otherwise known as "river blindness." With my passport ready, I passed through the turnstiles at the official immigration checkpoint. During our phone conversation the day before, the priest that runs the shelter in Tecún Umán warned me that Guatemalan officials would try to charge me an "entrance fee" of what amounted to U.S.$1–2, even though there is no official tax. He explained that this was basically a form of everyday institutionalized extortion and said I should refuse to pay. He told me to tell them I was a visitor to the shelter. I was prepared. Sure enough when I reached the grumpy-looking border guard, he demanded I pay the fee. I attempted to explain that I was visiting the shelter and the priest had told me there was no fee, but the guard was unimpressed. I was already an hour late so I paid the fee and passed through to board one of the ubiquitous bici-taxis waiting on the other side, whose drivers were also known for ripping off unsuspecting foreigners.

When I reached the shelter in Tecún Umán, the first thing the priest asked me was if I had paid the guard. Embarrassed, I told him yes. "But I told you!" he gently berated me. This encounter, my first encounter with state officials along the Mexico-Guatemala border, opened my eyes to the power of intimidation, the power of everyday state agents over individuals. Given that I was a passport-holding U.S. citizen, I can only imagine what a paperless Guatemalan or Honduran woman might feel in such an encounter.

After spending the day visiting the shelter and interviewing the priest and several migrants, I returned to the border crossing. The bridge runs over the expansive and muddy brown Suchiate River. This was one of the areas most hardly hit by Hurricane Stan the year before. Abandoned homes near the river's edge were still filled with thick mud that nearly reached the ceilings. While we did not understand the extent of it at the time, the devastation caused by Hurricane Stan in the region and along the transportation infrastructure specifically would have ripple effects on the journeys of migrants for years to come.

As I looked down from the border crossing, I watched hundreds of people cross the border between Guatemala and Mexico on makeshift rafts made up of large black inner tubes and wooden planks. People stacked boxes, backpacks, and groceries to make the crossing. As one migrant told me, passengers are treated like cargo too. Some are going to work in Mexico, some are going shopping, and some are on their way to the United States. Locals told me that even though they have the proper papers to enter Mexico, it is just easier to hire one of the rafts to take you across. The border guards, who have front-row seats, don't seem particularly bothered. The bridge, the physical marker of the boundary between the two neighboring nations represented sovereign state power, but its guardians were deliberately blind to the illicit flows of people and merchandise below. While the ceaseless churning of people crossing the river was utterly quotidian, it was also a critical juncture in the lives of many migrants.

In many ways, Mexico's southern border is a visible marker of one of the most perplexing paradoxes that undergird this research. The physical border is porous and relatively easy to cross; in some places there is not even a symbolic show of enforcement by the state. Yet as Aurelio, a migrant from Honduras explained to me, "Mexico is where the American Dream begins. It is there, as soon as you cross the river between Guatemala and Mexico." It is also there that Central Americans are transformed from legal to illegal

subjects. Since the signing of the Convenio Centroamericano de libre movi-
lidad (Central America–4 Border Control Agreement) in 2006, citizens of
Honduras, El Salvador, Nicaragua, and Guatemala can move freely across
the borders of these countries without inspection. But Mexico is where the
regional integration of Central America ends. "Mexicans have it easy,"
Aurelio went on. "They *only* have to cross the northern border. We Central
Americans have to cross Mexico. This is where our journey *really* begins."
This idea is hard to fathom considering how very deadly the U.S.–Mexico
border crossing is, but from Aurelio's perspective that was just one segment
of a much longer and more dangerous trajectory.[2]

After Central Americans cross into Mexico, they run a risky, dangerous
gauntlet of violence. In Mexico's interior, the state, which may have turned
a blind eye at the border, now becomes enemy number one. "Once you
reach the other side, the soldiers are waiting for you," Aurelio explained.
And things only get worse the deeper you go into Mexico. As soon as you
begin moving north, you enter a militarized zone of intense surveillance
and racialized policing along the highways, with checkpoints, guns, camouflage and police dogs. This is what activists have called the vertical border—though what I conceptualize rather as a nonlinear arterial border—
the layers of enforcement that permeate highways, roads, and railways,
spreading like arteries throughout Mexico's interior.

The concept of an arterial border allows us to reimagine state bordering practices across a vast and complex migration infrastructure that
spans frontiers, transportation routes and local communities.[3] Unlike the
relatively bounded spaces of state enforcement along national borders, the
arterial border is ever-changing; it expands and contracts across space
and over time, depending on local, national, and transnational sociopoliti-
cal contexts.[4] As state presence intensifies, migrants seek more clandestine routes, and the arterial border splinters and follows them. New arteries are created along remote roads, railways, near migrant shelters, and in
other areas where migrants move.

Yet this is not a simple game of hunter and prey between migrants and
the state, about protecting the nation or asserting state sovereignty. The
arterial border is not fixed or static. Rather, it must be understood as continuously *performed* by officials, politicians, migrants, smugglers, criminals, local residents, and activists constructing, engaging in, evading, and

arterial border [handwritten margin note]

contesting a dynamic mix of everyday practices, material infrastructures, discourses, and encounters.[5] Such a framework allows us to see how transit routes become spaces where economies of exploitation, violence, and profit emerge and are contested by migrants who develop new strategies of mobility and survival.

I began to visualize the dynamism of the arterial border during an encounter one morning at Casa Guadalupe. I was talking to a migrant named Mario, who had lived in Miami for sixteen years and spoke near perfect English. He had traveled back to his hometown in Honduras to help his mother sort things out after his father's passing, but was now on his way back to his life in Florida. Unlike most of the people I met, who traveled in groups, Mario was on his own. He did not trust anyone. We were sitting on the steps outside the office at Casa Guadalupe chatting about the journey, during which he had been extorted twice by police, when he asked if he could show me something.

Mario pulled out a square of neatly folded paper from the pocket of his jeans. "I've been documenting everything," he said, handing the paper to me. I carefully unfolded it to reveal a swirl of handwritten notes, numbers, and symbols plotted onto points on the page. As I looked closer, I could see that this was in fact a map, a detailed map of Mario's journey thus far (fig. 3). It did not begin in Honduras, but near the Mexico-Guatemala border in Tapachula. It then wound up along the main highway in the state of Chiapas, where he had recorded information on distances and specific details about every town and major landmark he passed. There were details about which *combis* to take, where to get on and off, and even what to tell the driver. He included instructions on areas where it was better to walk, where the checkpoints were located, and which state agency controlled each checkpoint. He explained that the journey had changed a lot since his first trip sixteen years earlier, and he wanted to be prepared if he was deported, though it was not lost on me that the map could also be given—or sold—to someone else. This was valuable information.

Perhaps the most fascinating aspect of the map was not just his documentation of the checkpoints, but also the details of places to stop along the journey. He included the names and addresses of various hotels and migrant shelters—indeed, the final point on the map was the scribbled address of Casa Guadalupe. These spaces of refuge had become inextricably intertwined

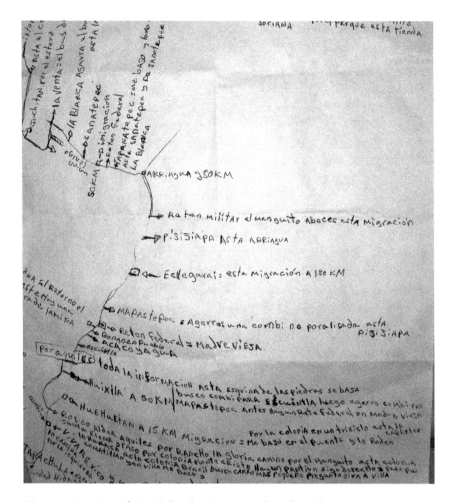

Figure 3. A portion of Mario's handwritten map. Photo by author.

and critical to both individual strategies of mobility and survival within the larger landscape of transit. Shelters are at once responses to the violence of bordering practices but, as I would learn, in turn also influence state practices and presence, tethered together within the arterial border.

This idea was made clearer to me by another set of maps. After my return from fieldwork, looking at a map of Mexico's migrant detention facilities—called *estaciónes migratorias*—produced by the Geneva-based Global Detention Project,[6] I was instantly reminded of the map that hangs

Figure 4. A map in Casa Guadalupe showing the locations of migrant shelters. Photo by author.

in the living room in Casa Guadalupe identifying the more than fifty migrant shelters across Mexico with tiny colorful tabs and stars (fig. 4). In fact, when I juxtaposed the two maps, they looked almost identical. Shelters are established in spaces where migrants are most vulnerable, spaces where the state and, increasingly, organized criminal groups have the most presence. But the presence of shelters also encourages migrants to follow similar routes, which makes them more identifiable and thus easier to target. A hand-painted map on the wall of a migrant shelter or a pamphlet that lists the names and addresses of all migrant shelters across the country become codified road maps of information that was once quietly shared between individuals. This means, of course, that such information is available, not only to migrants, but to the state-criminal nexus as well. As such, we might understand the infrastructures of state enforcement, organized crime, and humanitarianism as intimately related, comprising a larger constellation of violence, security, and care.

Decentering political borders as the sole site of analysis of enforcement practices sheds light on the ways in which border securitization begets violence. We also see how state and nonstate actors construct and reimagine borders and security in spaces far from the edges of the nation. Mario's map perfectly represented this dynamic. While it revolved around state checkpoints, the checkpoints were just one aspect of a larger mobility regime comprised of transportation routes, strategies, and shelters. And yet the map was only a snapshot of the arterial border at a particular moment in time; a month or two later, its form and directions might have changed. The arterial border is always shifting, as it has been for at least the past half-century.

SECURING THE SOUTH: FROM REFUGEES TO "CONTINENTAL" SECURITY

"The Guatemalan border with Chiapas is now our southern border," the U.S. Department of Homeland Security's assistant secretary of international affairs and chief diplomatic officer, Alan Bersin, said in 2012, referring to the need to expand U.S. immigration efforts further south.[7] In 2017, a *New York Times* article proclaimed, "Trump Wants a Wall? Mexico Is It," referring to the fact that in 2015, implementing the Southern Border Program in response to the "flood" of unaccompanied minors reaching the U.S.–Mexico border, Mexico deported more Central Americans than the United States.[8] While Mexico plays a key role in a U.S.–led transnational border enforcement strategy, this is not a recent development. Since the 1980s, Mexico has been a crucial player in the bordering of North America through various efforts to "secure the south" and curb the flows of Central Americans moving north.

State-sponsored crackdowns on Central Americans have historically intensified in relation to U.S. political pressure during periods of heightened concern over immigration, national/hemispheric security, and terrorism. For much of its history, Mexico had no formal policy with regard to foreign nationals. It was not until the mid-1970s when increasing numbers of Central Americans began entering Mexico as refugees that the Mexican state began to implement more restrictive immigration policies and categorize and criminalize noncitizens. In 1974, under the Ley General de la Población (General Law of the Population), the unauthorized entry of a noncitizen into Mexico was considered a criminal act, carrying with it the possibility of a prison sentence and monetary fine. In the 1980s, Mexico began to militarize its southern border and regulate the flow of Central American refugees.[9] Yet as the Central American civil wars escalated, pressures for asylum increased, and Mexico had to reconsider its position toward refugees. While Mexico's General Population Law did not officially recognize "refugees" as a legal category, it offered protection and assistance to some Guatemalan refugees by establishing camps in the states of Chiapas, Campeche, and Quintana Roo.[10] At the same time, Mexico faced pressure by the United States to stem the flow of asylum seekers crossing Mexican territory. In a coordinated effort with Mexican and Central American governments, in February 1989, the U.S. Immigration and Naturalization Service (INS) implemented Operation Hold-the-Line, a program intended to stop Central Americans from reaching U.S. soil, thus precluding them from applying for U.S. asylum.[11] Operation Hold-the-Line supported U.S. training of Mexican personnel, predictive intelligence sharing, the establishment of transit checkpoints and the deportation of intercepted Central Americans.[12] During the administration of President Carlos Salinas de Gortari (1988–94), roadblocks were set up throughout the country, officially to interdict drugs but unofficially to search Central Americans. The operation was deemed a "success" in the United States; in Mexico, the number of Central Americans deported in 1989 marked a 500 percent increase over the number deported in 1988. In 1990, the numbers of Salvadorans, Guatemalans, and Hondurans apprehended at the U.S.–Mexico border dropped by 20 percent.[13] Yet it could be argued that the "success" of Operation Hold-the-Line was measured less in the drop of Central Americans reaching U.S. soil and more in terms of the precedent it set for Mexico's cooperation with a U.S. immigration and security agenda. In the 1990s and 2000s, Mexico expanded its enforcement infrastructure along interior transit routes through various apprehension, deportation, and drug interdiction efforts.[14] In 1990, Mexico's Instituto Nacional de Migración (National Migration Institute; INM), established Grupo Beta, the unarmed "humanitarian" branch of the INM intended to protect migrants' rights. The first

Grupo Beta unit was established in Tijuana in 1990, and in 1996 Grupo Beta began operating along the southern border, though migrants described its presence there as minimal. The focus on "securing the south" was formalized in 2001 with the announcement of Plan Sur, under the leadership of President Vicente Fox, who emphasized the need for a "continental security" approach. Mexico began to expand its enforcement infrastructure rapidly. Between 2000 and 2008, Mexico more than doubled the number of its detention facilities, and the numbers of Central Americans deported reached peak levels in 2005, when the INM recorded over two hundred thousand deportation events. In addition to increased raids and checkpoints, Central Americans were no longer simply dropped off across the border in Guatemala, but were shuttled back to their countries of origin on buses.[15] The intensification of such practices coincided with the events of 9/11 in the United States, which largely contributed to the reframing of migration through a lens of national security in both the United States and Mexico. Not unlike the U.S. reorganization of immigration agencies under the Department of Homeland Security, in May 2005, the INM was formally designated as part of Mexico's National Security Council.

Yet perhaps nothing has been more significant in the acceleration of policing migrants than the folding of Mexico's immigration strategy into the larger crusade against drug trafficking. In the late 1980s, drug trafficking became an issue of national security in Mexico, sparking an increase in state involvement and the militarization of police forces. This period saw the rise of what Peter Andreas calls "narco-corruption" among Mexican authorities who profited from the militarization of the drug war.[16] The drug industry is a significant employer and source of capital in Mexico's fragile economy, which inhibits the success of anti-corruption initiatives among Mexico's elite. Mexico has historically been an important producer and supplier of cannabis to the United States, but its role shifted in the wake of the aggressive U.S. anti-narcotics campaign known as Plan Colombia. Established in the late 1990s, the initiative aimed to root out cartels and growers in Colombia and redirected drug flows from the Caribbean corridor through land routes in Central America and Mexico. Central America and Mexico emerged as the center of a multi-billion-dollar drug trafficking industry between the global South and the global North.[17] This shift empowered drug cartels in Mexico and Central America, which continued to traffic cocaine to consumers in the United States with no disruption.

Even so, for decades the Mexican state took a hands-off approach to the drug cartels. Politicians not only tolerated Mexican drug-trafficking organizations but actively protected them under a "blanket of impunity."[18] Yet with the controversial election of Felipe Calderón of the National Action Party (PAN) as Mexico's president in 2006, a dramatic new approach to the cartels began. Less than two weeks after he took office, President Calderón sent four thousand Federal police and army soldiers to the northern state of Michoacán, marking the beginning of a new era in Mexico's war against drugs and drug cartels.

Since 2006, efforts in Mexico to root out drug trafficking and organized crime have become imbricated with immigration control measures, and both are supported by U.S. securitization assistance. Under the Mérida Initiative signed in 2008, the United States has given U.S.$2.5 billion in equipment, training, and intelligence to Mexico to combat drug trafficking and money-laundering. The United States has also allocated millions of dollars to similar security measures in Central America through the Central American Regional Security Initiative (CARSI). As the drug war intensifies, the cycle has continued as the United States expands its multi-billion-dollar security industry, including the Mérida Initiative and CARSI to train, fund, and equip military and police units in Mexico and Central America. The United States justifies such spending through discourses that fuel fears of violence spilling over across the borders. An epigraph on the U.S. State Department's CARSI web page quotes Assistant Secretary William R. Brownfield saying: "If we ignore these threats, these problems, and these crises in Central America today, we will address them on our own front porches tomorrow." Such discourses and policies firmly place Mexico and Central America within a U.S.-led hemispheric security agenda, reflecting what Elana Zilberg has called a neoliberal "security-scape" in which immigration, criminality, security, and neoliberal economics become increasingly intertwined across transnational spaces.[19] And yet this type of militarized security strategy has yet to prove effective in stopping crime or enhancing citizens' security in Central America or Mexico.

ENCOUNTERING THE STATE-CRIMINAL NEXUS:
THE ROAD TO CASA GUADALUPE

The transnational forces that undergird state enforcement have significantly reshaped local contexts of mobility in Mexico's interior. As the
Mexican state legitimizes the implementation of regulatory and repressive
policies—framed as "securitization"—new forms of violence that affect
migrants flourish. Such forms of violence have known precedents. Lynn
Stephen writes of the ways indigenous peoples are transformed into per-
petual suspects in the context of militarization in southern Mexico where
"dominant representations of the dangerous, the subversive, the worth-
less, the marginal, and the unimportant become linked to making particular groups of people susceptible to violent abuses that allow them to be
treated with less than human respect and dignity."[20] Akin to these "indigenous suspects," Central American migrants experience similar processes
of racialized othering and suspicion by Mexican military, police, and local
residents who control the checkpoints and roads that migrants pass
through. Christine Kovic has characterized these processes as the "violence of security," the ways in which migrants are equated with drugs,
weapons, terrorists, and gangs, thus becoming targets of state violence.[21]
Such processes are particularly acute in the southern border state of
Chiapas, which Rebecca Galemba has described as a site of low-intensity
warfare and militarization since the 1990s as the state selectively repressed
both Guatemalan refugees and indigenous peoples associated with the
Zapatistas.[22]

The violence of security must be understood as historically produced in
relation to bordering practices. Above I referenced Operation Hold-the-
Line, which was implemented in the late 1980s to curb the flows of Central
American refugees across Mexico. In 1991, the U.S. Committee for
Refugees produced a report documenting the abuses suffered by Central
American refugees at the hands of U.S.–supported Mexican police and
other authorities. The author of the report, Bill Frelick, stated, "Few of the
Central Americans we interviewed had any idea who apprehended them.
Some officials, such as the federal judicial police, operate in plainclothes."[23]
The testimonies produced in the report were strikingly similar to the sto-
ries I collected during my fieldwork. I documented the widespread occur-

rence of Mexican authorities conducting unlawful immigration checks, using excessive force, and extorting migrants in transit. Under Mexican law, only certain immigration and federal agents are legally permitted to ask for documentation of citizenship. However, migrants reported a wide range of authorities who demanded to see their papers, including local, state and federal police, military soldiers, marines, and intelligence forces, as well as armed men they assumed were police or military dressed in civilian clothing. Those who could not produce proof of Mexican citizenship were threatened with deportation, shaken down, or physically abused. Particularly disturbing, as I detail below, is the way the arterial border becomes a vehicle for "state sexual violence" that is produced in the context of state security projects and preexisting social hierarches of racial and patriarchal power.[24]

The spatially diffuse architecture of the arterial border meant that violent encounters often took place in out-of-the-way locations with little oversight or accountability. Moreover, the interactions migrants had with militarized forces were not professional, orderly, or in most cases legal. Rather, they were marked by chaos, confusion, and uncertainty. The regularity with which they occurred speak to the fact that violence against migrants is not random, anomalous, or an unintended consequence of militarization. On the contrary, violence is routinized and central to state security and enforcement practices. Because migrants harbored significant distrust of authorities, and in some cases believed they deserved to be treated poorly, because they were the ones breaking the law, state authorities operated with near-complete impunity.

These dynamics are further complicated in drug war Mexico where masculine military control is glorified and increasingly difficult to separate from narco-military culture and operatives.[25] It is often difficult to tell if perpetrators of violence are state agents, organized criminals, or a combination of both. This is so prevalent that it actually seems to be a strategy used by perpetrators of violence—by blurring the lines between state violence and criminal violence, they effectively sow their own pastures of impunity with uncertainty and silence.

In what follows, I travel to several different locations on the journey between the Mexico-Guatemala border and Casa Guadalupe in Oaxaca as migrants negotiate their movements on foot, by bus, and by train. My goal is to illuminate the on-the-ground realities as migrants encounter the state-organized criminal nexus in Mexico's interior, as well as the strategies migrants and shelter workers devise to bypass and/or negotiate the ever-changing local realities of the arterial border.

La Arrocera

During my conversation with Mario, he pointed to an area on the map just past Huixtla. "Here," he said. "This is La Arrocera."

La Arrocera, it was a name that I had heard countless times. *My group was robbed in La Arrocera. Soldiers stripped searched me in La Arrocera. I saw a woman raped in front of her husband in La Arrocera. I met a Salvadoreña at the shelter who lost her baby in La Arrocera.*

La Arrocera, which gets its name from an old rice cellar in the area, refers to what is arguably the most notorious checkpoint along the stretch of the journey between the Mexico-Guatemala border and the town of Arriaga, 230 kilometers to the north. The train used to start in Tapachula, but in 2005 Hurricane Stan destroyed much of the transportation infrastructure, including the train tracks, throughout the region. For years this had been the primary route for migrants traveling north. Yet after Hurricane Stan, migrants had to devise new strategies for reaching Arriaga where they would board the train. The problem was that the highway that connects the two cities had become one of the most militarized regions in Mexico in response to the dual threats of migration and the Zapatistas.[26] Migrants described the highway peppered with about a dozen police, immigration, and military checkpoints and detention centers (fig. 5). To avoid detection and deportation, migrants engage a complex strategy using minivan *combis* that drop them off before checkpoints so that they can circumnavigate them on foot. *Combi* drivers charge an extra "migrant tax" for the service. Migrants then must walk through dense, isolated brush on the sides of the road before being picked up again by the next *combi*. This strategy, while it successfully maneuvers around checkpoints, has come at a high cost. Gangs and thieves infiltrated the region, preying on vulnerable migrants in isolated areas.

I first heard about La Arrocera early on in my fieldwork during an interview with two young men from Guatemala. One of the men, nineteen-

Figure 5. A typical military checkpoint on a Oaxacan highway. Photo by author.

year-old Eddy, on his way to Tamaulipas in search of an older brother who had disappeared, told me their story of crossing La Arrocera.

Before arriving to Ixcuintla there is a checkpoint called Arrocera. That is where they assaulted us the first time we came. We had come by *combi* and they had told us to get off before the checkpoint and walk until we found the train tracks. They told us to walk on the tracks until we got around the checkpoint. We did what they told us to, but when we got to the tracks we were met by the thieves. There were four of them. They carried heavy weapons. I recognized a shotgun and a revolver and an AK47. They stole $2,500 pesos (U.S.$150) from us. They made us take off all our clothes and they threw them into a nearby swamp. They threatened us saying that if we didn't give them all our money they would kill us. They had us there for twenty or twenty-five minutes. Then they took our clothes out of the mud and said if we didn't disappear in five seconds, they would kill us. We grabbed as much of the clothes as we could and ran off. When we got to the shelter I heard the story of this girl who had come with her cousin and two other girls and another guy. There were five of them and in the exact same

place where they assaulted us, they assaulted them. They raped all three of
the girls. They took advantage of them. They took the money from the guys
and told them that if they tried to get involved they would kill them. They
raped the three girls right in front of them.

I recorded numerous cases of men and women being strip-searched,
assaulted, extorted, and raped by both criminals and by state officials
along this stretch of the journey. It is not that the state simply turned a
blind eye to this violence—in many cases, officials themselves committed
abuses or worked in collusion with bandits, taking a cut of whatever cash
or valuables they stole.

Incidents like this were the norm in La Arrocera, which came to mean
more than this particular checkpoint. As one shelter worker explained to
me, "It is all of Chiapas, not just La Arrocera. There are many Arroceras,
many places where they do this." Indeed, as I would observe over the
course of my fieldwork, La Arrocera was emblematic of this entire stretch
of the journey between Tapachula and Arriaga, where abuse, extortion,
and sexual violence prevail. Along the arterial border, a place-name can
serve as a metaphor for the crimes perpetrated there. La Arrocera captures the paradoxical logic of security in Mexico. Militarization funnels
migrants into more dangerous routes creating the conditions for multiple
actors, including state officials, to prey on Central Americans. Lawlessness
and violence have become status quo in militarized Mexico.

La Bestia

The rumbling and screeching sound travels through the thick air, disrupt-
ing the quiet stagnation of the afternoon. It sounds like a bear waking
from a winter's hibernation, growling and moaning, stretching muscles
that have been long asleep. This is a bear of another sort, the freight train,
or La Bestia, as it is called with a mix of disdain and awe, gearing up for its
next journey, carrying goods inside it and migrants perched precariously
on top (fig. 6). I am sitting near the tracks and see people begin to collect
their few belongings, packing their bags with bottles of water and bags of
bread. As if on cue, a state police vehicle circles nearby, making their presence known, but does not stop. A group of men have gathered in front of
me, watching as the beast lurches forward and back again, the telltale sign

Figure 6. Migrants hop a moving freight train. Photo by author.

of its imminent departure. I recognize several of the men from the shelter, they are hoping to make it to Mexico City and then the border with Texas. Unlike many of the others who pass through, this is their first time hopping the train. A more experienced migrant takes them down to the tracks to give them a few pointers. He runs alongside the train telling them they need both speed and strength to jump on. "You need a firm grasp, don't hesitate, jump up with one uninterrupted motion. If you aren't aggressive and strong, the train will suck you underneath." The train is now moving slowly and he jumps on and off demonstrating for them. The men take turns of their own, smiling from the thrill of movement. The next adventure will soon begin.

Once migrants reach Arriaga, they may breathe a sigh of relief, but the feeling is short-lived, because this is where many of them first encounter La Bestia. In the 1990s and early 2000s, Central Americans responded to increased enforcement along highways and bus routes by hopping onto freight trains traveling north to Mexico City and from there to cities close to the border with Texas, Arizona, or California. The primary starting points were Tapachula and, after Hurricane Stan in 2005, Arriaga on the Pacific Coast and Tenosique in the state of Tabasco near the Petén jungle corridor. The name La Bestia initially derived from the fact that the physical journey itself is extremely dangerous. The train schedules are notoriously unpredictable, and migrants, who are often exhausted and undernourished, are ill prepared for single stretches of train travel that can take over twelve hours. There are risks of dehydration and sunstroke—the trains pass through brutally hot as well as frigid conditions. One of the biggest fears is dozing off to sleep because of the risk of falling and being sucked below. Migrants create makeshift seatbelts with ropes that they strap onto rails or look for wagons that are more secure. They drink coffee to stay alert. They are told to never stand up or put their arms out. A low hanging tree limb can easily knock you down. As more migrants began riding the trains, however, more accidents began to occur. Images of migrants clinging to the tops of the train or dismembered in train accidents have become associated with the migrant journey.

Beyond the immediate dangers of this type of train travel, the meanings of La Bestia changed over time. During my fieldwork, La Bestia was most feared because of the human elements associated with it. Train routes became strategic locations for immigration raids to intercept and deport migrants. Migrants' rights defenders regularly denounced Mexican immigration and federal police for conducting raids on moving trains, and particularly trains running at night. For example, in early 2011, they decried one raid near the town of Chahuites, where authorities approached a moving train, causing widespread panic, in which a 25-year-old man from Guatemala fell off the train, severing his right foot. The authorities did not even help the man, but left him along the side of the tracks. A local rancher found him there and transported him to a hospital.[27] As raids increased, power was abused and profits were reaped on the trains. One migrant said of the years when the train still started at the Mexico-Guatemala border:

> Before, when the train started in Ciudad Hidalgo [in Chiapas], things were really ugly. There I paid $500 pesos to the *garroteros* [brakemen], the men who wear blue uniforms and carry a club, I think they are from the state, I'm not sure. But to them I paid $500 pesos just to let me get on the train, and

then I paid $300 more pesos to let me stay in one of the train cars near the motor so I could sleep. In addition to that, I had to pay another $200 pesos to stay on the inside of the car so I would not fall out the side.

While the train is technically "free," there are unofficial forms of payment to gatekeepers who put a premium on people's physical security. The more you can pay a corrupt official, the better your chance of survival. As discussed in more depth in the next chapter, a similar dynamic emerged as the train routes became increasingly controlled by criminal groups, most notably Los Zetas.

Forms of sexual violence are standard practice during immigration raids. Blanca, whom we met in chapter 1, whose father was killed during the civil war in El Salvador, told me about her experience during a raid on the train:

> Everyone was there, migrants, the army, the Federal Police. I was the only woman who had come on the train they touched and groped me until I urinated on myself. I urinated because I was scared that they were going to rape me because there were only men to check and see if I had weapons or tattoos. I don't have any tattoos I told them, I'm a mother with a family and I don't have any nor do I have weapons, much less weapons, but it did not matter to them. They checked me everywhere, they took everything off me, they took away my clothes . . . I say they didn't rape me because we did not have sex, but they touched me everywhere to see if I was carrying drugs in my genitals. . . . A woman should have been the one to do it, not the man who did among so many soldiers and police. And immigration was there, the ones with blue uniforms and green also, we call them *zotacos* [shorties] or *garroteros* [brakemen or security guards] and immigration.

Blanca's experience of being strip-searched exemplifies what Jennifer Goett calls state sexual violence, where through state security practices, sexual violence is carried out based on preexisting social hierarchies like gender and racial inequality.[28] Begoña Aretxaga, who worked with female political prisoners in Northern Ireland, calls strip-searching "the convergence of fantasy and technology in inscribing the body (of politically rebellious women) with the meanings of sexual subjugation through a form of violence that phantasmatically replicates the scenario of rape. For the body of violence, the body of the state as well as the body of its subjects is not a neutral body, but a body already invested with the meanings of sexual difference and ethnic domination."[29] The strip-searching of migrant women's and men's bodies has become a routine, everyday form of subjugation along Mexico's arterial border.

The connection between militarization, migration, and state sexual violence is not new. The prevalence of sexual assault, rape, and humiliation of both female and male migrants along transit routes in Mexico mirrors what Sylvanna Falcón has termed "militarized border rape" along the U.S.–Mexico border, saying that "warlike conditions . . . agent impunity and the absence of accountability contribute to a border climate in which rape occurs with little consequence."[30] In Mexico, these conditions expand throughout the interior of the country, where, as Lynn Stephen argues, military and narco-military violence against women increasingly overlap.[31] Stephen argues that the Mexican state has created a discourse that glorifies masculine control and justifies violence against women and others through the promotion of military men as the keepers of order and the intimidation of women through sexual assault.[32] A 2006 study at a Mexican detention facility documented that over 50 percent of sexual assaults against migrant women were at the hands of state agents.[33] Hypermasculinity is legitimized along the arterial border, and instead of security, we see the production of everyday insecurity for both migrants and local residents.

The insecurity produced by security agents illuminates the paradox of protection for migrants and particularly migrant women. Many migrant women signaled that they preferred not to report the violence they experienced at the hands of state authorities or criminals, who were often difficult to distinguish. As Wendy Brown has argued, "to be 'protected' by the very power whose violation one fears perpetuates the specific modality of dependence and powerlessness marking much of women's experience across widely diverse cultures and epochs."[34] Appealing to the Mexican state to protect women becomes seen as futile, indicating the pernicious ways power and gender inequality operate in everyday spaces along the arterial border. Without access to protection or justice, the cycle of violence continues and impunity reigns.

Mountain Road

As the train routes became more securitized and thus more dangerous in the 2000s, migrants and shelter workers devised new strategies and alternative routes in attempts to evade state and criminal actors. The route between Albergue Nazaret and Casa Guadalupe became an important alternate route to bypass the segment of the train that passes through the state of Veracruz, which in 2008 had become the epicenter of mass kidnappings of migrants, a subject addressed in the next chapter. This alternate route requires migrants to travel by bus through one of the most remote areas in the state, called the Sierra Mixe. The Mixe are an indigenous group in Oaxaca, and the Sierra Mixe comprises one section of the Sierra Norte, one of the seven regions of the state. The trip between Albergue Nazaret and Casa Guadalupe normally takes about five and a half hours on the main highways connecting the Isthmus of Tehuantepec to the capital. But the route through the Mixe region is a two-day trek. Migrants bypass the main highway because of the permanent checkpoints. Instead, they take second-class buses on a circuitous route along winding mountain roads. Padre José and Padre Luis formed an arrangement with another priest, affectionately known as Padre Mixe, who has a church in one of the pueblos. Padre Mixe warmly offers migrants a meal and place to sleep. Migrants typically spend the night and catch a bus the next day to Oaxaca City.

One day when I was at Albergue Nazaret, Padre José asked if I would be willing to join him for his Saturday morning radio show. On the drive he told me that it was fine to discuss Casa Guadalupe, but that I should not explain in detail the alternate route through the Sierra and to Padre Mixe's church. He wanted to keep that route under the radar for as long as possible. He knew that just as this alternate route was a response to the arterial border, that border was equally mobile and dynamic. It was not long before the authorities caught on. During intake interviews at Casa Guadalupe, my colleagues and I began to hear nearly identical stories of police profiling, intimidation, and extortion along this route, the mountain road leading to Padre Mixe's church. Efrain, a migrant from Honduras described his experience:

> We were on the bus for maybe forty-five minutes when we were pulled over. Police dressed in civilian clothing boarded the bus. I imagine the bus driver must have already told them what we were wearing, and told them that we were traveling as a couple [so they could identify us]. They approached us and told us to give them our papers. We didn't have papers. They told us to

get off the bus. "Quickly, quickly!" they demanded. We were the only ones to get off and they took us behind the bus where no one could see us. We told them we were from Honduras. They took all of our money. But then they let us get back on.

Cindy and her brother Beto had a similar experience. What is interesting in Cindy's case is that after migrating from El Salvador, she had lived and worked in Chiapas near the Guatemalan border for several years and secured an FM3 visa to live in Mexico legally.[35] But because Beto did not have legal documents, they had to take a more clandestine path. She explained what happened to them while they were riding the bus through this same route:

> They stopped us, and told us to get off the bus, and I took the time to get my papers in order, but they didn't care, all they wanted was money. They threatened anyone who did not get off the bus. I said to them, "Sir, I am trying to get my papers in order," and he said "No, get down, do you hear what I am telling you." And so I got off that very moment because he was pointing his finger in my face and he said, "You are *polleros*." We are not *polleros*, and I told him, "He is my brother." I told them, but they still demanded $300 pesos from each of us. We didn't have that much money. We only had $450 pesos all together and we asked if that would be enough to let us go, because I was scared. I was not scared because they accused me of being a *pollera*, because I am not a *pollera*. We are not *polleros*, but I was scared because there we were all alone, it was really deserted, there were no houses, just mountains, and for that reason, we gave them the money. They were armed and these men did not wear uniforms or badges, they drove a regular car, and that scared me, that they were Zetas or others who were going to kidnap us and kill us, and all the things that we have been told about in the migrant shelters. So I asked him if we gave them the money that after they would let us go. They had already told the bus driver to leave us, which he did. They did let us go, and we ran so hard to catch another bus. Can you imagine? Having your FM3, being legal, but to them it does not matter, all they want is money.

After documenting multiple reports of this particular extortion racket, staff from Albergue Nazaret sent several people undercover to ride this bus route. Corroborating the migrants' account, local police who were known in the region, but dressed in regular clothing, pulled over and stopped the bus and boarded it plucking migrants from their seats. The shelter workers took photographs of them and publicly denounced them by posting the pictures on social media sites.

In this remote area, far from official migration checkpoints or the external border with Guatemala, systematic profiling and extortion were incorporated into the everyday routines of both the bus driver and the police, who worked in collusion with one another. Cindy's story highlights the fear of violence for Central Americans in Mexico, even for people who are traveling legally. These armed men used a tactic of fear to accuse them of being smugglers as part of their intimidation and extortion strategy. After extortion, many state agents let migrants continue on their journeys. Migrants often describe this type of coercion as the price they must pay for illegally crossing Mexico and actually factor extortion into their financial decision making. A key strategy for migrants is periodically to receive money orders throughout their journeys, knowing that they are likely to be robbed or shaken down multiple times along the way.

At the end of his description of being extorted by police on the road between shelters, Efrain made a final point: "And Mexicans, they don't say or do anything." The fact that none of the other passengers on the bus protested, even though they were Mexican citizens, speaks to the normalization of violence along the arterial border. On one hand this illustrates embedded social inequalities, where Central Americans are constructed as gendered and racialized others who do not enjoy the same rights as citizens. But beyond this, we must also recognize that in contemporary Mexico, local residents also live in daily fear of organized criminals and state authorities. In southern Mexico—particularly in the states of Chiapas and Oaxaca, where social unrest has resulted in increased state repression—checkpoints, heavily armed police, and inspections of ordinary citizens are standard.[36] On multiple occasions, I have been asked to show my passport and have had my luggage searched by Mexican authorities at checkpoints during bus journeys. In these cases, people rarely protest; such acts of intimidation and policing are normalized.

SOMOS LOS PIRATAS!

In the dog days of summer at Casa Guadalupe I met two charismatic young men from Nicaragua: Charley and Romulo. They stood out among the other migrants staying at the shelter. They were gregarious, constantly joking. Charley had dark skin and bleached blond curls. Both of them dressed in what might be considered a young surfer style. When I interviewed them, they described the journey as an adventure.

Romulo had a cousin who was a Mexican citizen, who lived in the Mexican municipality of Ocosingo, located close to the border with Guatemala in the state of Chiapas. When they first crossed the border they met up with her, and she helped to get them fake *cédulas de identidad*, Mexican CURP identity cards that assign each person a unique eighteen-character ID code based on his or her name and birth date. With their CURP cards, they felt free to travel within Mexico and had heard about the state of Quintana Roo in the Yucatán Peninsula. The friends traveled to the Yucatán and ended up finding work at a local restaurant chain. "It was called *Pollo Pirata* (Pirate Chicken), but in fact, *somos los piratas*, we were the real pirates with our pirated papers!" exclaimed Romulo.

During their time in the Yucatán no one, not even their bosses, ever confronted them about their nationality. They worked and saved money. They bought a TV, bicycles, a DVD player. Charley described the Yucatán as "paradise," but in reality they were not making enough money to send home to help their families or build any savings. Ultimately, the pair decided that they wanted to continue on their original mission to reach the United States, and they sold their belongings and set off on a first-class bus to Mexico City. Hours before reaching Mexico City, near Puebla, their bus was stopped and searched by immigration officials. They took the two young men off the bus and started asking questions. They showed the officials their CURP cards, and one of them asked Romulo the year he was born, but his answer did not match the date on the card. This tipped off the authorities that the cards were falsified.

They started quizzing the two men on different aspects of Mexican history and trivia, things that all Mexicans should know. "We got some right, but we got some wrong," Charley said. This is a common tactic used by migration officials to determine if travelers are indeed Mexican or Central American. Many migrants know this, and develop strategies to "pass" as Mexican in their attempts to evade authorities and criminal groups, part of a larger strategy that Noelle Brigden has called "improvised transnationalism."[37] At shelters migrants often practiced their strategies of performing *Mexicanidad* by learning Mexican slang words, memorizing facts about

Mexican history, and even creating Mexican aliases. People adopted more Mexican-sounding names, such as José, Fernando, or Maria, particularly when purchasing bus tickets (which requires names), so as to not tip off the bus drivers, who, migrants assumed, were in cahoots with police. People develop a personal narrative about where they are from, memorizing the names of towns, the governor's name, what types of food are commonly eaten in the region. In anticipation of encountering authorities, migrants and smugglers create "cheat sheets" for migrants to memorize. A friend who worked at the Tucson Medical Examiner's office later showed me a cheat sheet recovered with the belongings of a migrant who perished while crossing the U.S.–Mexico border. This cheat sheet is oriented for a person from Guatemala and includes comparisons of verbiage and even the main verses of the Mexican national anthem. Attempting to pass as Mexican was obviously more challenging for some migrants, particularly those of Afro-Caribbean descent, but some migrants used their ethnic identity to their advantage. Indigenous Guatemalan migrants, for example, would often claim to be from indigenous communities in Chiapas.

This was actually what Charley and Romulo attempted to do; they claimed that they were from Ocosingo, where Romulo's cousin lived. But the officials did not buy it. They accused the men of being *polleros*. "Trust me, if I was a *pollero* I would not be paying for a first-class bus," Charley said. Finally, they told them that they were in fact Guatemalan, also not true, but they were hoping at this point to just be deported back to Guatemala and not Nicaragua. They spent the night in a detention facility in Puebla and then several nights in the national detention facility in Mexico City. "There are people of all races there," Charley said. "Cubans, Africans, Chinese, Koreans, Brazilians, Ecuadorians, people from everywhere. There was a Turkish guy there—he tried to cross through Mexico just like us!" They said they treated them well at the national center; there were mattresses and sheets and decent food. The conditions were far better than at the facility in Tapachula, where they were sent next. "I slept better on the rocks on the train tracks than on the floor in the Tapachula detention center," Romulo said. Even so, they said that they were never physically mistreated at the detention centers, and were thankful for that. "Immigration officials treat you well, it is the police that hurt you," he said. Still working on their Guatemalan narrative, the two were deported just across the border to Guatemala. But the officials in Guatemala also quizzed the men about where they were from in Guatemala. Less prepared with answers, they were soon found out. The officials told them they were sending them back to Mexico so that they could be deported to Nicaragua. Charley pleaded with them on the spot, and then offered them $500 pesos. It worked. They were released and crossed back into Mexico again that very same day. This time, however, they did not have their fake CURP cards to travel with. They had to take the same route as other migrants, which meant traveling through La Arrocera. "This second trip is different," Romulo explained. "This time we are going little by little, from town to town, from shelter to shelter. We figured out how to get around the checkpoints." They reached Arriaga without incident, but their luck was short-lived once they boarded the train. As Charley explained,

> Everyone was on the last wagons of the train, because the middle wagons you could not sit on. Six assailants arrived with shotguns, rifles, machetes. First, they robbed us, took all the money from our wallets. But then they took us and split us into groups, between men and women. There were about eight women and the rest of us men. They made us get down on the ground and then they told us to take off all our clothes until we just had our underwear on. They even made us take our socks off. They left us looking like Adam, as we say. They told us to put our stomachs and mouths to the ground and so we all put our mouths to the ground. And where I was there was an anthill there and the ants were biting me and the other guys with us, some Salvadorans, but what could we do? We couldn't get up or even move, they had their guns pointed at us.

Charley showed me the inseam of his jeans where the robbers had cut open and taken the last remaining pesos he had hidden tucked inside (fig. 7). One strategy that migrants utilized to protect themselves in the likelihood of a robbery was to hide their money, valuables, and family phone numbers in the inseams of their pants, shirts, or shoes. Unfortunately, this was such a common practice that authorities and thieves knew to check for such secret hiding places during strip searches. Some migrants memorized important phone numbers of family members in the United States, but the majority of people I met had phone numbers scrawled out on tiny pieces of paper or written on the inside of small Bibles or notebooks. A migrant showed me the inside of his Bible with a note written to

Figure 7. Charley points to the inseams of his jeans where his hidden cash was discovered by robbers. Photo by author.

him by his brother, reading, "Goodbye brother and see you soon." On a piece of tape are the names and phone numbers of family members in the United States (fig. 8).

After they were robbed, they said, everyone on the train was distraught. The assault took place early in the morning, and they still had a long ride ahead of them. Because everyone had their backpacks and things taken from them, no one had food or water. They said one guy almost passed out and fell off the train. The train stopped in a town where usually migrants get down to buy food and drinks. But even in this area, which was known to be friendly to migrants, a local man tried to swindle them by luring them down the tracks with the promise of a free Coca-Cola. "I was so upset and even more thirsty because they made me run down there!"

They finally reached Albergue Nazaret, where they had their first meal in two days. "They treated us so well. Super well. We don't have any complaints about the shelter." And from there, they were off to Casa Guadalupe.

Figure 8. A migrant keeps important U.S phone numbers of family members in his Bible. Photo by author.

A NEW APPROACH? PROGRAMA FRONTERA SUR

Up until 2010, the violence experienced by Central Americans in Mexico was largely invisible in state policies and discourses. Most laws were still based on the 1974 General Population Law, though the Mexican government did formally decriminalize unauthorized entry in Mexico in 2008. It was not until the public outcry around what was to be known as the Tamaulipas massacre in 2010, where seventy-two mostly Central American migrants were brutally executed, that the Mexican state was forced to deal with its own immigration problem. In 2011, the Mexican Congress unanimously passed a new Migration Law replete with the language of migrant and human rights and outlined social services and protections for migrants in transit. The 2011 law streamlined the process for migrants in transit to obtain humanitarian visas, but the overall implementation of the law has been uneven, particularly in light of renewed pressure by the United States to curb the flow of Central Americans north.

In the wake of the 2014 unaccompanied minor crisis, under pressure by the United States, President Enrique Peña Nieto announced his new Programa Frontera Sur (Southern Border Program). The stated goals of the program are to protect the human rights of migrants in transit in Mexico and manage international border crossings to increase development and security in the region. Yet despite the discourse of rights and development, the Programa Frontera Sur—which is largely funded through the Mérida Initiative—has continued to expand the violent web of enforcement and bordering practices in southern Mexico. Mobile kiosks have been set up at checkpoints to collect biometric and biographical data of people transiting through Mexico. The rates of deportation have skyrocketed, but perhaps most unprecedented has been the crackdown on migrants riding freight trains.[38] As discussed, before 2014, the Mexican government largely turned a blind eye to unauthorized migrants on trains, and it was common to see trains with hundreds of migrants on top. My colleagues at the shelters described their shock when they saw trains running empty in the months after the Programa Frontera Sur was implemented. The government had brokered deals with train companies to increase their speed to deter migrants from riding, blocked migrants from boarding trains, and conducted raids in bars, restaurants, and hotels frequented by Central Americans. In March 2015, Ardelio Vargas, the commissioner of Mexico's National Migration Institute, framed the crackdown on migrants in humanitarian terms: he stated that it would be irresponsible to allow migrants to continue risking their lives on freight trains.

The Mexican state justifies the increase in raids on migrants with promises to protect migrant lives, which falls in line with the humanitarian orientation codified in the 2011 law. Despite such justifications, on the ground, we see that such policies only funnel people into more dangerous routes. To avoid raids, migrants must traverse more remote areas, located further from the network of humanitarian aid shelters, making them even more vulnerable to violence and exploitation. As discussed in the following chapters, in recent years, those with financial resources have been paying higher prices to smugglers to help them navigate the journey. Some activists argue that the new program has formalized the hunting of migrants in the state-criminal nexus. This hunting includes unaccompanied children and families fleeing direct forms of violence who have largely not been recognized as deserving of asylum by the United States or Mexico. In 2015, Mexico apprehended more than twenty thousand unaccompanied minors, of whom half had good cases for asylum, according to the Office of the United Nations High Commissioner for Refugees. Nonetheless, the Comisión Mexicana de Ayuda a Refugiados (COMAR; Mexican Commission for Refugee Assistance), afforded protection to just fifty-seven of them, less than 1 percent of the total number. Human rights organizations argue that the discrepancy between the number of minors with plausible claims and the number who receive asylum is due to the fact that immigration officials are focused primarily on detention and deportation rather than the protection needs or human rights of children.[39] Much of the burden to assist asylum-seekers falls to migrant shelters rather than state agencies. In 2017, I interviewed the director of a shelter located near the Mexico-Guatemala border in Tenosique who told me that a significant percentage of arrivals at the shelter these days are families and unaccompanied children who are not seeking to reach the United States, but to apply for asylum in Mexico. "This is no longer a migrant shelter," he said. "This is a refugee camp."

By de-centering national frontiers and focusing on interior transit routes and state practices along these routes, we see how local regimes of mobility are produced and operate. Treating border regions as exceptional obscures the larger hemispheric regimes that police the boundaries of citizenship and security across and between national borders. The interior spaces *between* borders and between "home" and destination"—are crucial sites for understanding local, state, and transnational migration infrastructures. More than this, Mexico's arterial border is not solely the product of Mexican state policies, but the result of transnational pressures and partnerships under the pretext of security and a hemispheric war against drug trafficking. The implementation of security programs like the Programa Frontera Sur illustrates the changing nature of the arterial border in Mexico and the ways diverse actors respond to shifting conditions.

As the stories in this chapter demonstrate, security regimes are at the very center of the gauntlet of violence that migrants must navigate while crossing Mexico. Beyond violence, we also see how power is produced, embodied and contested by state and nonstate actors alike—migrants, police, shelter workers, priests, migration authorities, criminals, and residents. We also begin to see how everyday actors like *combi* and bus drivers and local police reimagine transit journeys as sites of profit, particularly as migration flows are redirected along the arterial border. Such a framework elucidates the dynamic relationship between migration strategies, state bordering practices and localized economies of mobility. By moving beyond the traditional opposition of migrants and the state, and by rethinking our understanding of borders themselves, this chapter sets the stage for understanding the ripple effects of state enforcement on the production and maintenance of what I explore more deeply in the next chapter, the *cachuco* industry.

3 The Migrant Industry

It was a warm summer morning in early August 2010. Hugo and Osmin were in the office at Casa Guadalupe making phone calls home to their families in El Salvador and Guatemala. I was back in Oaxaca for the summer, and that morning I had my infant daughter at the office with me. When the men were done with their calls, we sat around to chat about life in El Salvador and Guatemala and the economic uncertainty and everyday violence and extortion that had driven them to flee their hometowns. As they took turns holding my daughter, conversation turned from the past to the future. One of the men was expecting a money wire that afternoon, which meant they would be able to buy bus tickets to continue their journey north.

They had already decided to bypass the most dangerous section of the freight train route through the state of Veracruz, which had become a hotbed of violence and kidnappings. The recent implementation of the discriminatory immigration law SB1070 in Arizona and the sweltering summer temperatures in the Sonoran desert made the duo second-guess their initial plan to cross along the Arizona border. A map on the wall of the shelter studded with tiny red dots depicting migrant deaths in the Tucson sector alone was enough to solidify their decision. Instead, they would head for McAllen, Texas, which in recent months had become a more popular route. "Look how much closer it is to cross here," one of the men said and pointed to the map of Texas. This passage would be quicker, they argued, and safer than crossing through the desert.

Two weeks later, on August 24, 2010, in the northern state of Tamaulipas, the lifeless bodies of seventy-two migrants, mostly from Honduras, Guatemala, and El Salvador were found on a recently abandoned ranch in one of the most highly contested areas of Mexico's drug war. The migrants—fifty-eight men and fourteen women, one of whom was pregnant—were found with their hands bound together and had been shot execution-style. Declassified reports published in the U.S. National Security Archive later revealed that the migrants were pulled from commercial buses traveling to the border and killed as part of an explosive turf war between Los Zetas and their former ally the Gulf Cartel. But still questions remained. Why were these specific people kidnapped in the first place? Were they being held for ransom or sought after to smuggle drugs across the border? And at what point did these seventy-two individuals go from being valuable to being so useless that they were disposed of in such a brutal and inhumane manner?

The gruesome photos of the migrants' bloodied and bloated bodies circulated through the media. I could not help but study each and every photo I could find, looking for any trace of Hugo or Osmin. If all had gone according to their plan, they would have been traveling by bus through Tamaulipas that very week. While the Tamaulipas massacre captured headlines across the globe—Central Americans are being targeted by organized criminals for kidnapping in Mexico—those on the ground working in the shelters knew this was only the tip of the iceberg.

Over the past decade Mexico has emerged as the Bermuda triangle of Latin America. In Mexico when people go missing, they can vanish with little trace. Mexico's Interior Ministry reported over twenty-seven thousand official disappearances in Mexico between 2007 and 2016. The actual number is believed to be higher. In the first four months of 2016, it was estimated that at least ten people were kidnapped in Mexico each day.[1] Families of the missing, frustrated by inept officials and the lack of justice, have formed organizations across the country. Some have even taken it upon themselves to search for and dig for the remains of their loved ones in suspected mass grave sites. The 2014 forced disappearance of forty-three students from the Ayotzinapa Rural Teachers' College in the town of Iguala, Guerrero, thought to be ordered and carried out by a mix of local government officials, municipal police, and organized criminals, has come to symbolize the age of mass disappearances in Mexico. The failure to find the remains of the missing students, and the cover-ups revealed in the process, point to the culture of impunity that reigns throughout the country. What does it mean that forty-three young people can disappear without a trace and without justice?

In a context where a country's own citizens vanish, how can we begin to understand the extent of the problem with regard to missing migrants? While there have been no long-term systematic efforts to track the numbers of noncitizens who go missing or perish in Mexico, there are indications that they are high. In 2010, Mexico's Human Rights Commission documented over eleven thousand cases of individual kidnappings and two hundred and fourteen cases of mass kidnappings of Central American migrants over a period of six months. The Mexico City–based advocacy group Movimiento Migrante Mesoamericano, a leading voice on Central American migration, estimates that more than seventy thousand Central Americans have disappeared since President Felipe Calderón's drug war began in 2006. The testimonies collected during my fieldwork, which overlapped with the early years of the drug war, offer a glimpse of the evolution of migrant kidnapping, which, although we did not know it at the time, would become widespread across transit routes between Mexico's southern and northern borders.

COMMODIFICATION AND THE *CACHUCO* INDUSTRY

In this chapter, I shed light on these developments by locating migrant kidnapping in a larger political-economic framework. These disappearances are not simply the result of Central Americans being caught in the crosshairs of drug-related violence. Rather, they are central to a thriving larger industry that transforms migrants into valuable commodities. As Padre José described it to me:

This is the *cachuco* industry. When I say *cachuco* you know that is a derogatory name for a Central American. It means pig, dirty pig, dirty Central
American pig. It is derogatory and discriminatory. So, within the *cachuco*
industry, the goal is to make the most money, to maximize the profits from
the costs of migrants themselves—dead or alive, whole or in parts, through
kidnapping.

Padre José intentionally uses the derogatory term *cachuco* to make a
point about the ways the exploitation of migrants is contingent upon
existing systems of social inequality and oppression. That is, the violence
experienced by Central American men and women cannot be understood
outside racism, nationalism, and patriarchy. The *cachuco* industry is part
of a global economic system fueled by cheap, exploitable migrant labor
and exclusionary state policies that construct migrants as illegal, racialized, gendered others.

The conceptualization of migration as an industry is not new.[2] Such a
framework is useful in understanding immigration politics and labor
markets in host and reception sites, and how people migrate across space
and place, as well as the value of the migrants themselves.[3] In the United
States, Tanya Golash-Boza examines what she calls the immigration
industrial complex, where politicians, the media, and corporations profit
from a culture of fear and immigration enforcement laws.[4] Not unlike the
prison industrial complex or the military industrial complex, the criminalization of supposedly dangerous others benefits both state and nonstate participants financially and politically. In his gripping ethnography
of what he calls Europe's illegality industry, Ruben Andersson argues that
immigration enforcement is not just about repressive border controls, but
rather about the *productivity* of such controls. According to Andersson,
the enforcement produces the very thing that it is meant to eliminate—
illegality, which ultimately renders itself highly profitable.[5] In the Euro-
African borderlands, the reception, detention, surveillance, care, and even
study of unauthorized migrants is a lucrative business for defense contrac-
tors, aid workers, academics, and smugglers alike.[6] Moreover, as scholars
like Peter Andreas and Rebecca Galemba have argued, punitive immigration enforcement and security strategies increase demand for more clandestine economies to move people, weapons, and drugs.[7] Across multiple

scales, the production of illegality, and thus deportability, is crucial to migrant value in both licit and illicit economies.[8]

So how exactly do these industries play out along Mexico's migrant routes to generate new forms of exploitation, violence, and profit? Particularly crucial to Mexico's migration industry is the way it has developed in relation to a hemispheric war on drug trafficking. The early years of Mexico's drug war and the rise of specific organized criminal groups significantly reshaped the everyday realities of the journey. Migrants were exploitable, and not just as human cargo to smuggle across borders. Their bodies, labor, and their lives were transformed into valuable commodities. As Lesley Sharp notes, "commodification insists upon objectification in some form, transforming persons and their bodies from a human category into objects of economic desire."[9] While in transit to become productive laborers abroad, migrants may be valued, in various combinations, as cargo to smuggle, bodies to prostitute, labor to exploit, organs to traffic, or lives to exchange for cash. Yet, as I demonstrate in this chapter, the value of migrant life, and in some cases migrant death, is always shifting.[10] Migrants may both gain and lose value during their journeys in material and embodied ways through their dismemberment, disappearance, and death.

While under conditions of capitalism, migrant labor has already been transformed into "a commodity like any other," I suggest the journey itself represents a new phase in commodification.[11] The systematization of kidnapping, smuggling, and extortion underpins the *cachuco* industry, where violence becomes the central mechanism through which vulnerabilities are produced and profits are derived. Often it is the fear of violence and concerns for individual and collective safety that fuel economic demands. What emerges is a seemingly highly sophisticated and entrenched structure of networks, payoffs, and impunity. At the same time, transactions within the industry can be opportunistic, happenstance, and poorly executed.

KIDNAPPING

I began to hear whispers about Los Zetas and the ways they were transforming migrant routes early on in my fieldwork in 2008. Manuel, a migrant who was deported to El Salvador after being detained for speeding and driving without a license in Oregon, described the way the journey has changed since the first time he crossed the border nearly two decades earlier,

> Before on the journey, there were robbers and everyone knew that they would steal whatever you had on you, but then they would leave you in peace. But now, with these groups that are kidnapping, well it's a whole other level, now they are organized together with the police and they carry weapons, heavy artillery. The same police that denounce them are the ones who protect them. It's the same group that you see on the news, the ones who kidnapped the thirty-two [migrants held captive in Puebla in 2008]. They have not been around long, I think it was just this year that it all began, or maybe two years. Imagine, they kidnap twenty, or ten or even five people and they ask for $5,000 dollars for each one. They know that their families will send money even if they cannot afford to.

One of the by-products of Mexico's intensified war on drugs was the reshuffling of power among organized criminal groups and drug cartels. During my initial exploratory trips interviewing migrants I often heard stories about *maras* (gangs) along the route. But when I began my year of fieldwork in 2008, something had shifted. Now people spoke more specifically about one group in particular: Los Zetas. Los Zetas were originally military commandos who left their posts to become the enforcement branch of the long-standing, powerful Gulf cartel. In the late 2000s, Los Zetas broke off on their own, quickly becoming one of the most notorious and feared criminal organizations, known for their brutality and for seizing control of territory throughout Mexico through military-style tactics. The reach of Los Zetas spanned across the border into Guatemala, where they allegedly formed alliances with former Kaibiles, elite Guatemalan military forces trained in counterinsurgency tactics. By 2007, the Zetas began to use Central America, primarily Guatemala, as the base from which to import cocaine and methamphetamine chemicals through Mexico, controlling most of Guatemala's 550-mile border with Mexico.[12]

But Los Zetas were never just a drug cartel. Early on, they diversified their illicit operations to include other types of trafficking, extortion, and taxation rackets. In the late 2000s, they began to capitalize on increasing flows of Central American migrants in Mexico. Los Zetas sought to control the routes and thus the movements of drugs, weapons, and people. Migrants and smugglers began reporting the changing conditions along the trains. Los Zetas began raiding trains in attacks coordinated with train conductors and often local authorities. No longer did migrants just need to pay off corrupt authorities. Los Zetas, or those who claimed to be Zetas, were now demanding they pay a "tax" or fee to cross their territory and ride the train.[13] Where migrants once spoke of assault and robbery by gangs or bandits, they now feared that everyone was connected in some way to Los Zetas, whose tactics proved more systematic and the consequences more deadly. Those who did not pay the tax were pushed off the trains, coerced to work for them, kidnapped, or murdered.

While it is challenging to collect the testimonies of kidnapping victims, during my fieldwork I did interview several migrants who had witnessed mass kidnappings, and a handful of people who had actually managed to escape their kidnappers. In what follows I include the stories and testimonies of two separate kidnapping incidents as detailed to me by four men who escaped. The narratives illustrate several important characteristics of migrant kidnappings: the blurred lines between criminals and police, the high levels of distrust between and among migrants, local residents, and state agents, and the fear and uncertainty migrants experience both during and after these encounters.

Sergio and Erik

I knocked on the front door of the house, but there was no answer. I had the key and so tentatively opened the door, calling out a few times to see if anyone was there. I finally heard a response, "Yes, we are here in the back, *pásale*." I walked through the house to one of the back bedrooms, where I saw Sergio and Erik both still tucked under the covers of their twin beds with the shades drawn. I asked if they wanted me to come back later, but they said, no, they were getting up. It was 4 p.m., but they were exhausted.

This was my first visit to the safe house where Sergio and Erik were staying, though I had met both men the week before at Albergue Nazaret, and they seemed happy now to see a familiar face. After one night at Casa Guadalupe, the staff thought it would be more prudent to set up a separate house for them. They were still shaken up and convinced the Zetas were after them. They were suspicious of all the other migrants staying at the shelter, even Eduardo, an elderly Guatemalan man with poor hearing, who had been living at the shelter for weeks. "You cannot trust anyone, you do not know who is connected to whom," Erik told me. A sister organization that owned the house had agreed to let them stay there until their paperwork came through.

As the men tidied their beds, we talked about their plans. Sergio said he just needed to get back to Tacoma, Washington, where he had spent the past sixteen years working two jobs; early mornings slicing meat at a butcher shop and evenings cooking behind hot smoky woks in the kitchen of a Chinese restaurant. But more important, Tacoma was where Frida lived. He opened his wallet and pulled out a photograph of a sweet-looking toddler. He told me that things had not worked out between him and Frida's mother, a Mexican American U.S. citizen, but he wanted to be there for his daughter. He tried to call her regularly on the phone, but, he said, it was not enough to fill the hole he felt inside.

Unlike Erik, who said he would not return to the United States, because he had a criminal record and did not want to risk going to federal prison, Sergio still aspired to live and work in the United States and be close to his daughter. The first time he crossed, he had walked through the desert for eight days and nearly died, he said. But for now, both men planned on staying in Mexico. They were waiting to get their temporary visas, the papers that would authorize their presence in Mexico. Erik and Sergio were promised visas in exchange for their testimonies about the November 5 kidnapping of twelve Central American women. They agreed to recount the story to me as well.

I turned the recorder on.

For Sergio, the journey from El Salvador had begun over a month ago. Things were different than he remembered from the first time he crossed into Mexico. On this trip he was apprehended and deported almost immediately by INM agents who stopped the *combi* he was on at a checkpoint just north of the city of Tapachula. It was a setback, but he crossed the Guatemala-Mexico border again the very same day. This time he knew to get off the *combi* before reaching the checkpoints and walk around through the thick brush. He reached Arriaga, the new departure point for the Chiapas-Mayeb route, without incident and was relieved to find a migrant shelter there. At the shelter, he met Erik, who is from Honduras and had also lived for many years in the United States, and another young couple. The four of them decided to travel together.

The next morning, on November 5, 2008, Sergio, Erik and the couple boarded a freight train. They heard warnings that there might be a migration raid along the route. But like the other three hundred or so people who boarded the train that day, they decided to risk it, since this would be the quickest way to cross the Isthmus of Tehuantepec. Before leaving the shelter, they prayed for an uneventful journey.

When the train reached the town of Las Anonas, Sergio spotted a suspicious looking vehicle, a white pickup truck carrying four men. He had a bad feeling, but the train kept going. They passed a cemetery near the village of 20 de Noviembre right before the train stopped. People began getting off the train and purchasing bottles of water in the town. Others bought apples and sliced watermelon doused in *limón y chile*. After people had recharged, the train started up again, but not for long this time. Minutes after leaving, the train stopped abruptly and Sergio heard people shouting from the cars behind him, "Soldados! Soldados! [Soldiers! Soldiers!]"

They were referring to the men in the white pickup truck that he had spotted earlier. Armed men, some with uniforms on and others in civilian clothing surrounded the train cars. Sergio specifically remembers one man wearing camouflage pants and a Cruz Azul soccer jersey. Without thinking, Sergio jumped down to the ground and starting running. Erik also jumped down, but ran in the other direction. The couple was right behind him, but from the corner of his eye, Sergio saw one of the armed men grab them. Another one screamed at him, "Stop, *cabrón*!" The man grabbed hold of his shirt and threw him into a fence. But Sergio managed to get up and kept on running. He heard gunshots behind him. He thinks one of the bullets must have just missed him because he temporarily lost hearing in his right ear. "I just kept running, running, running."

He finally reached an open field where he was able to stop and look back at the scene unfolding. From where he stood he could see a convoy with two trucks and several armed men. It was a chaotic scene with people fleeing in every direction. He saw a woman being dragged by her long hair and another woman being thrown into the back of one of the vehicles.

Because of the warnings at the shelter, Sergio first assumed this must have been a migration raid, because the men seemed highly trained. But the more he thought about it, the less sense that made. Migration officials do not have the authority to shoot at people. Moreover, the vehicles they were driving were unmarked. These were not the authorities, or at least not authorities acting within their legal limits. "They could have been criminals, paramilitaries, or they could have been soldiers, it is difficult to know," he said.

With no sign of Erik or the couple, Sergio found himself with a group of ten other migrants who had also escaped the raid and kidnappers. They decided not to return to the train, but to walk and look for shelter. They arrived at a small town, where they met a local priest who allowed them to stay at his church for two days. Four of the people in his group decided at that point to end their journeys and return home.

The remaining six decided to continue on. Their goal was to reach Albergue Nazaret, having heard rumors of a priest there dedicated to helping migrants. They left at dawn on the third day, now traveling on foot. They walked close to the tracks all day, passing through several tiny villages. When they could walk no further, they stopped in a town and once again sought out the church and local priest for help. This time, however, they were not given a warm reception. The person at the church treated them with suspicion. He asked if they were from around there, and they said no. He then said the priest was not there, and he could not help them. They needed to look elsewhere. They found a woman in town who reluctantly allowed them to sleep on the concrete patio adjacent to her house if they promised to leave first thing in the morning. "We slept there in the cold. It was a fierce type of cold that night. The winds were strong," Sergio recollected.

The next morning, the group flagged down a small bus traveling in the direction of the shelter. They arrived at Albergue Nazaret later that evening. Sergio was anxious to see if his traveling companions were there. A flood of relief came over him as he saw Erik, who came over to give him an embrace. But there was no sign of the couple. He had no way of knowing whether they had escaped the raid or if they were among the disappeared.

Erik, who ended up getting back on the train after the convoy left, saw one of the armed men talking to and handing over what he presumed to be a payoff to the train conductor for stopping the train. He also saw two smugglers hand over cash to one of the armed men. While we did not know it yet, this would become a routine practice along the journey, smugglers paying fees or "taxes" to organized criminals in exchange for the passage of their human cargo. As people reeled from the news, it had also become apparent that not only were migrants facing a new gauntlet of risk, but that female migrants were particularly vulnerable—and particularly valuable. A total of twelve women disappeared from the train that day.

Sergio and Erik were among about a dozen people who had witnessed the kidnapping and made it to Albergue Nazaret. Their testimony sheds light on the threats to Central American migrants crossing Mexico in the early years of Mexico's drug war. As landscapes and centers of power shifted, state and nonstate actors and interests collided and colluded in exploiting migrants. Violence was becoming more systematic and inescapable. No longer were migrants just reporting stories of individual assaults and everyday extortion by corrupt police. These were highly coordinated operations carried out by a range of actors, some of who appeared to be affiliated with Mexican police and military.

The week following the November 5 kidnapping, I was at Albergue Nazaret helping Geovany, a young Guatemalan migrant who had recently become Padre José's assistant, collect some of the official testimonies of the witnesses and prepare a report to file with Mexico's Human Rights Commission. Geovany had taken video testimonies from eyewitnesses of the kidnapping, nearly all of them describing scenes identical to those described by Erik and Sergio. Because there was significant fear on behalf of the witnesses and Padre José of some type of retribution by the kidnappers, he decided to keep them at the modest house he rented on the other side of the tracks. Padre José called a meeting at his residence for shelter workers and local volunteers one evening to debrief on the kidnapping. I walked into the front room and was met by a group of about ten people, including Sergio and Erik, lying in hammocks strung up across an otherwise bare room. As I walked toward the backyard where people gathered for the meeting, I passed Padre José's room, bare except for a mat on the ground with a few items of clothing. We began the meeting with a prayer and a reading from a book about globalization. Part of Padre José's goal was to teach local residents about some of the root causes of migration. He then provided updates on several corrupt authorities the shelter had been monitoring and the kidnapping eyewitnesses. At the end of the meeting we passed around images of the young women who had been kidnapped. The shelter in Arriaga was able to track down several family members of the missing, who sent us their photographs. Padre José talked about the value of migrant women to sex work and pornography industries as he speculated on their fate. As the images circulated, I thought back to that wall of missing flyers inside the Tapachula bus station. Would these photos be made into missing persons flyers and pinned up on the walls of bus stations too?

Ramon and Israel

Whereas Sergio and Erik were eyewitnesses to the brutal kidnapping of twelve women, I also recorded the testimony of Ramon and Israel, who had recently escaped a mass kidnapping in the state of Veracruz and had made it to Casa Guadalupe, where they were recovering from the experience. At this interview I was accompanied by Antonio, a lawyer from Movilidad Humana, who was also interested in their testimony, since he was preparing a formal complaint. Before we began the interview, we reassured Ramon and Israel that we would not make their identities or locations public to the media. They had reason to be cautious: two other escapees, including Ramon's cousin, had been interviewed and their photographs were published in newspapers and online media. Ramon and Israel did not want their identities known. Like Sergio and Erik, they feared that the kidnappers might track them down.

The men had left El Salvador about a month earlier, along with Ramon's cousin and uncle. They had had a fairly uneventful trip across the Mexico-Guatemala border and even through La Arrocera. Since bandits control the mountainous regions around the checkpoints where most migrants walk, their strategy was to walk fairly close to the checkpoints. Like Sergio and Erik, they boarded the train in Arriaga, but unlike the other two, they were able to make it all the way to Medias Aguas, Veracruz. In Medias Aguas, they waited for the next train in a fairly deserted section of the tracks. From their location, they could see another group of migrants resting in some shade a few hundred feet down from where they sat.

ANTONIO: Did anyone see you? Any vendors? We have heard reports that the vendors tip off the criminals.

RAMON: Yes, we were right there at the intersection. In the morning, a woman arrived and she was with a man. Supposedly they were a couple, that is what they said. He was a big guy and he said he was going to stay where we were sitting because he was tired from walking up and down the tracks so he stayed while she continued on selling . . . she sold food, she sold coffee to the migrants, and I think breakfast also. When she came back we told her that if the train had not come yet, we would buy lunch from her. She said she would go and check for us because they knew which trains were the right ones and which were not. Soon after she left was when the guys arrived, the kidnappers. We are not certain that she was connected to them, but she might have been. It was even more suspicious because some soldiers also arrived. They didn't come exactly where we were, they stayed back, like a block and half away. But they were able to see us, that we were migrants. And then they turned around.

ANTONIO: How many soldiers were there?

RAMON: They were driving a pickup truck. There were eight of them, eight *militares*. The kidnappers arrived right after the soldiers left. They had phones, they all had phones.

ANTONIO: So how did the kidnappers approach you?

RAMON: They got us through their lies. They told us not to go anywhere because they were looking for some kidnappers—that is what they said. They said not to run because someone was going to arrive who would be able to identify if the suspect was among any of the groups around here. Then they started putting the groups together. There were six of us, and then they brought over the four Salvadorans and seven Hondurans who were resting nearby.

ISRAEL: At first they said they were like us, migrants. They lifted up their shirts and said, "Look, we don't have any weapons, we are looking for a girl who has been kidnapped and we are trying to find the person who kidnapped her." They were looking for the suspect among us. They said that if we ran it meant we had something to hide. And if we ran they would shoot at us. So we said that we have nothing to do with the girl and we did not run. They told us to take our shoes off so that we would not run. They led us to a field where there are two huge trees and that is where they held us. They held us there for hours until it started to get dark.

RAMON: Yeah, they detained us for hours. We could hear them communicating with others. They were telling them that they needed the Suburban. But night came and the hours passed and the Suburban never appeared and they were getting really mad. Then we saw the head-lights of some cars come, a truck that had other kidnappers, a red truck like a Chevrolet. We had to walk a little further across a bridge and then they threw us into the back of another truck really quickly.

WENDY: What were you thinking during these hours?

RAMON: We thought about the things that they were telling us. For me, I was sure they were going to kill me. I don't have any money. They were talking about how they were going to torture us to get phone numbers from us and that they were going to take our money. It was awful.

WENDY: The kidnappers were saying these things?

ISRAEL: Yes. They were talking about organs. They said that they tortured peo-ple, that they took all the organs out of people.

RAMON: I definitely thought they would kill us.

ISRAEL: They said that if you cooperated with them nothing will happen to you, you will go on to the United States, you will arrive they said, nothing will happen but you have to cooperate. When they rested I also rested thinking about what I should do.

WENDY: And these were Mexicans? Zetas?

RAMON: There were some Hondurans and Salvadorans but Mexicans also. They always have Central Americans with them. They recruit them pre-cisely for this, to make the first contact with migrants to gain their trust when they first approach them. To deceive them.

ANTONIO: So within the group that you were with that had been captured, was there anyone that you noted that seemed off, or different, someone who talked a lot or a little?

RAMON: Just the woman. She acted like she had nothing to lose. She spoke with them. She stayed calm. And even the kidnappers were like, "Güera, how is it that you aren't scared? I like you because you aren't scared," they told her.

WENDY: There was just one woman?

ISRAEL: No, there were two women, but the other woman was crying.

RAMON: It is because she had already been kidnapped before. And she told them that she had been kidnapped and they had released her. They asked her why she had been released and she said because they found no use for her, but they said that they would find something.

ISRAEL: The girl was crying.

WENDY: So there were seventeen of you?

RAMON: Yes, seventeen of us, we were the first that they put into the truck. It was night, around 9 p.m.

ANTONIO: The truck was covered?

RAMON: Yes, it had a blue cover and was white with yellow. It was a big truck, the type you use to carry cargo, to carry grain, animals, fruit. The other truck was following us and because I am tall I could see outside. I wanted to escape but I was afraid the guys following us would shoot at me.

ANTONIO: Were any of the kidnappers with you inside the truck?

RAMON: No, they put us in alone.

ISRAEL: And that is how we were able to escape. We were able to escape through the space between the truck and the canvas. The canvas didn't cover the whole thing. So when the truck following us came up and passed us, the truck we were in, that was when we had the chance to jump, to escape.

WENDY: And only the two of you escaped?

RAMON: Apparently my cousin and his friend also escaped, that is what it said in the newspaper article. My cousin was already deported.

ISRAEL: The truck was going eighty or a hundred kilometers an hour. It happened so fast. But we threw ourselves off and ran to the hills. We took the same train back from Medias Aguas to the shelter. When we arrived, the Padre immediately took us to the hospital. When we arrived our shirts were drenched in blood.

As we continued the interview, the men told us about arriving to the shelter and their recovery. Ramon lifted his shirt and showed us the scars and wounds that were still healing on his back and shoulders. Ramon had been extremely worried about the fate of his uncle and cousin but found out what happened to them when he called home to tell his mother that he had been in an accident. Apparently, his cousin and another migrant, the ones who appeared in the newspaper, were able to successfully escape the kidnappers, but were apprehended by immigration officials. As the article said, his cousin had already been deported home. His uncle had also tried escaping when the truck slowed down between two speed bumps on the edge of town. But the kidnappers managed to catch him. They put a gun to his head and told him to call a family member who would be able to send money. Before he left, his uncle had sold some of his land and left $3,000 with his sister, Ramon's mother. They forced him to dial her phone number, and they demanded $450 dollars. She paid the ransom and they let him go. His uncle called his sister to thank her and tell her that he would continue on north. She guessed he was close to the U.S.–Mexico border by now. Ramon was relieved to hear the news, and to know that his cousin was safe and back in El Salvador. But still, as he explained to me, they still did not know the fate of the others who were kidnapped with them, "We don't know anything about the rest of them. The other four Salvadorans, and the seven Hondurans, we don't know anything [about what happened to them]."

I include much of this interview because it reveals many of the logics that underpin the *cachuco* industry. The kidnapping described by Ramon and Israel was a more systematic, planned affair than the chaotic raid on the train described by Sergio earlier in this chapter. The assailants had cell phones, sophisticated weapons, and access to large vehicles to carry out their operation. They strategically used other Central Americans to lure people into their trap. Local residents and even other migrants are often seen as useful in such operations, because the involvement of multiple seemingly unconnected actors adds to the chaos, confusion, and intentional deception important in such kidnapping operations. For example, did the woman selling food or her husband tip off the kidnappers? Were the soldiers who drove by in on it as well or was that just a coincidence? Other questions remained: What happened to the Suburban that was supposed to arrive and never did? Who was on the other end of those phone calls? Where was the truck headed?

We assumed the migrants were being transported to some type of "safe house" used by kidnappers to hold people while they attempt to extract ransoms from family members.[14] Padre José would later tell me of a safe house that he had discovered with the help of several migrants who had escaped. It was located in a neighborhood not far from Albergue Nazaret. When they entered the recently abandoned house, they found backpacks lying on the ground, empty alcohol bottles, a radio, and used condoms outside. He explained that these items were remnants of what he described as kidnappers' "orgies," sexually assaulting migrant women as part of the process. He saw a deck of cards, currency from Honduras and Guatemala, and the discarded ID cards of several migrants. Also telling were the pieces of paper with the names and phone numbers of family members in the United States, along with money order receipts, presumably evidence of paid ransoms. It is impossible to know, but I imagined a similar scenario likely unfolded after the kidnapping of Ramon's uncle and the others on the truck.

Here, a paradox emerges. Central American migrants, especially those riding the trains, are undoubtedly economically marginalized. So why would they be targeted for kidnapping and ransom? Surely criminals would make more money if they targeted the rich and affluent? The answer lies in the value, not only of the migrants themselves, but of their social relations. Kidnappers target migrants because they know they are likely embedded within extended familial and social networks across Central America and the United States. Those who are able to migrate often receive loans from family members, who "sponsor" their journeys either through helping to finance smuggling costs or sending money orders along the way. Kidnappers know that family members at home or in the United States are willing to pay high monetary prices in exchange for their mothers, daughters, sons, and brothers. Ramon's uncle's life was exchanged for $450 dollars. From other accounts, I gathered this was a relatively low ransom. I typically heard stories of ransoms ranging from U.S.$500 to $5,000. But even so, think of the profits that could be made from ten or twenty migrants' whose families pay their ransoms. Indeed, the strategy for organized criminals was to kidnap people en masse. That year, we started documenting reports of forty, sixty, and even eighty people being kidnapped from the trains.

But perhaps more important, kidnappers target migrants because they can do so with impunity. Central American migrants—*los cachucos, los indocumentados*—are structurally vulnerable while in transit in Mexico. They are largely invisible to the state, which fails to protect their most basic rights, and even when there are legal provisions for unauthorized people, migrants have such an embedded distrust of officials based on their previous experiences along the arterial border that they often choose not to report the violations they suffer. After Ramon's uncle was kidnapped, he preferred to put his head down and keep going.

SMUGGLING AND THE ECONOMY OF FEAR

In addition to the direct value of commodified and kidnapped bodies, the less tangible fear surrounding kidnapping became a powerful economic force in itself. This was particularly visible within satellite economies of the *cachuco* industry such as the smuggling economy. Scholars have analyzed how border enforcement and smuggling economies operate in a symbiotic relationship.[15] The more difficult a clandestine journey, the more necessary hiring a human smuggler becomes. While this is certainly the case for migrants crossing Mexico, as discussed in the previous chapter, migrants are not only evading the state, but a larger state-criminal nexus. The emergence of routine mass kidnappings along routes controlled by organized criminals adds another variable to the smuggling equation. As stories of migrants being kidnapped, sold into the sex industry or ending up on makeshift operating tables in hotel rooms to have their organs harvested circulated through shelters, the demands for smugglers rose. In 2008, the going rate to be smuggled from Central America to the United States was somewhere in the U.S.$6,000–$7,000 range. Most of the migrants I met in Mexico could not afford such a high fee and thus instead opted to travel on their own through Mexico. Many planned to hire smugglers once they reached the U.S.–Mexico border. Yet, as Los Zetas and affiliates began taking over the routes, many migrants who had originally hoped to travel on their own found mid-journey that they needed a smuggler to negotiate the human landscape across Mexico. Finding a smuggler, or what many more affectionately referred to as guides, willing to help you cross was considered a form of protection against the dual threat of organized criminals and corrupt authorities. Indeed, the need for smugglers as forms of safety against organized criminals and kidnappers signified an important shift in the dynamics of the arterial border. As migrants faced more uncertain and violent routes, they were compelled to take costly detours by bus and employ human smugglers. This development highlights the ways supply and demand ebb and flow through the capillaries of the arterial border.

As discussed in more detail in chapter 5, smuggling and smuggling relationships became associated, not necessarily with exploitation, but rather with safety. Despite dominant discourses that overwhelmingly tend to villainize smugglers and conflate smuggling with trafficking, people on the ground have a much more nuanced understanding of the practices that may be legally considered smuggling. Rather than relying on a migrant/smuggler or victim/perpetrator dichotomy, we can understand the social relations involved in mobility along a continuum. Many people identify as guides rather than smugglers, and even within the category of smuggler (*coyote* or *pollero*), there are *coyotes* who are connected to more organized networks, and others who work alone. Sometimes a smuggler-guide may be a friend or family member. During our interview at the safe house, Erik said to me: "You know that out of every five people who come here, at least one of them is a *coyote,* right? Or better to say a guide. They are guides more than smugglers." This idea was reinforced by Padre José during a joint meeting with shelter workers from both Casa Guadalupe and Albergue Nazaret. Padre José said, "Look, the smugglers that are on this route are still clean. They are not connected to organized criminals or the Zetas." In his calculation, a "clean smuggler" meant someone not connected to the more vicious and brutal drug cartels. At the same time, because organized criminals were demanding "taxes" for migrants to ride the trains, having a smuggler who was at least familiar with the major players and processes was important. Smugglers or guides help migrants negotiate the appropriate fees in crossing and thus, in an ironic twist, protect them from even more dangerous elements. As one of my interlocutors eloquently put it to me, "If you don't have a *pollero* with you on the train, you are fucked."

SHELTERS AS SPACES OF PROFIT

We picked up our plastic white chairs to move them away from the men's dorm room so that the migrants resting inside would not be able hear this part of my interview with Padre José. As we resettled them in the dusty lot on the other side of the fence he resumed his story, this time in a hushed voice. He was telling me about why his life had been spared after the criminals who dominate the area had vowed to kill him. A few months earlier he had received multiple threats that criminals were going to attack the shelter. After he and several migrants set up watch posts on the corners of the shelter, he spent several sleepless nights hidden in the back seat of his car. But the criminals never came. According to the gang's second in command, whom Padre José later met during a visit to the local hospital, they decided it was best to leave him alive, because if they killed him, the shelter would surely close. The shelter's presence was already highly contested in the community. The gang leader admitted that if the shelter closed, it would be much harder to track down Central Americans to traffic and recruit into their business of smuggling drugs, weapons, and bodies. As much as the migrants needed the shelter to stay alive, the gang needed it to maintain their operations. And so Padre José was spared.

This sobering realization of linkages between the groups that exploit and abuse migrants and those who serve and defend migrants is one of the central contradictions revealed in my research. Migrant shelters are intended to be spaces of respite, healing, and solidarity, and for the most part they fulfill this mission. However, they have increasingly become sites of new forms of violence and tension within and outside their walls. The complex role of shelters in local communities is discussed in more depth in chapter 6, but here I want to focus on the ways shelters have become highly important nodes in the economic industry of the migrant journey. In the same spaces where migrants receive the most basic of needs (i.e., food, shelter, and a place to sleep), they are also able to obtain money orders, hire smugglers, and sometimes find work.

Because I am not a Mexican citizen, I was not eligible to retrieve money orders in Mexico, but I occasionally accompanied shelter workers to local Western Union offices to collect the money orders for migrants staying at the shelter. One afternoon I accompanied Marco, who was the coordinator of Albergue Nazaret at that time. He left the truck with a handful of tiny slips of paper with each of the migrant's codes and returned to the truck with a handful of bills spread out like flowers between his fingers. Companies like Western Union make an enormous profit, not only from the remittances that immigrants send home from their destination countries, but also from various practices that take place in spaces of transit. Money orders are crucial to individual migration strategies, because people know they are likely to be robbed or worse, kidnapped, and will need money wired to them at different points along the way. Money-wiring centers thus facilitate the exchange of cash for human lives. Activists in

Mexico have gone so far as to condemn Western Union for complicity in the kidnappings and ransoming of migrants.

Shelters have also become spaces for outsiders to recruit potential people to smuggle, traffic, or recruit into illicit industries like drug smuggling and sex work. It was a daily challenge for shelter workers to identify possible *polleros* or criminals who entered the shelter to prey on migrants. Migrants were often approached near and within shelters by *polleros* looking for new *pollitos* (little chicks) to transport. At the same time, shelter workers must confront the uncomfortable truth that smugglers have become necessary to many migrants' crossing strategies, particularly in the context of the drug war. It becomes a difficult line to walk.

The abundance of opportunities to profit off of migrants occasionally tempts local actors. Padre José explained the slippery slope from charity to exploitation that emerged as increasing numbers of migrants began passing through Mexican communities.

> Before no one took migrants' money, because they thought, well, they are poor. They didn't take advantage of anyone or steal their clothes or their shoes. But later, they started making money by selling to them. Right, they would sell them, rather than giving them, things like water, bread, and tortillas. . . . and from selling [they] turned to extortion. Because [the migrants] were illegal and were treated like criminals under the Ley General de Población [General Population Law], they were able to get away with this. And the migrants accepted it, because they felt they were guilty. They said, we deserve this, because we are in a country that is not ours, and so we should give them our money.

The ability to profit from migrant's illegality has also seeped into the lives of shelter workers. Mauricio, the manager at Casa Guadalupe, had a second job playing the electric keyboard and guitar in a local band, which usually played at restaurants or for private parties, and occasionally in bars. One night Mauricio had a gig at a local bar near Oaxaca City, and the owner found out that he worked at Casa Guadalupe. The bar owner expressed an interest in having Central American women work as dancers in his strip club and asked Mauricio if he would be willing to help funnel women to work at the club, for a fee, of course. Mauricio rejected this offer, but explained how tempting it was given his financial circumstances and concerns about providing for his own family.

In some cases, people who are victims of violence become facilitators and perpetrators of what Simón Pedro Izcara Palacios calls "poststructural violence." Central American migrants who fear being killed are recruited to work for organized criminals and ultimately become perpetrators themselves.[16] I documented several cases where people volunteering at migrant shelters became actively complicit in the exploitation of migrants. This came full circle the last time I spoke with Sergio toward the end of my fieldwork, when he passed through Casa Guadalupe. I had seen him a few times in between, since he had been working at Albergue Nazaret for several months, where he was in charge of the kitchen. He was finally on the road again, hoping to reach Tacoma sometime in the next few weeks and reunite with his daughter Frida. He had learned that his ex, Frida's mother, was seeking full legal custody. There was a hearing set for the beginning of summer, and he needed to be there if he was to have a chance of getting even partial custody or visitation rights.

He had gained weight and was in overall good spirits, confident about traveling through Mexico now, armed with his temporary visa. He said the past six months had been challenging, but he did his best to maintain his dignity and, as he phrased it, *hacerlo correcto* (do the right thing). I was struck by this vague statement, and asked him to explain what he meant. He explained that things at Albergue Nazaret were complicated. Because he had taken over in the kitchen, which is basically the center of the shelter universe, he saw everything. He said that he helped keep an eye on what was going on at the shelter. He inspected people's belongings when they entered to make sure they did not have weapons or drugs and alerted the staff if a suspected *pollero* had entered. He said that at least once a month, they found people infiltrating the shelter trying to recruit migrant women to work in the bars nearby. This was what had happened with Erik. Padre José had arranged for Erik to work in a nearby parish but he often visited the shelter. On one occasion, they found him trying to talk two women into going with him for a work opportunity. Sergio said Padre José was furious and banned him from returning to the shelter. I confirmed this with Padre José a few days later. Sergio then told us that another apparent migrant we knew had also recently been banned from the shelter. He had shown up a few weeks earlier looking for work, and Sergio had told him he could help out in the kitchen. But then, according to Sergio, they found him trying to coerce some of the younger migrants to have sex with him. "You actually saw this?" I asked him skeptically. "Yes, in the middle of the night we found them," Sergio said. He went on to tell me that this man was not actually a migrant; in fact, he was a *pollero,* and that Padre José also banned him, and that we should not let either of them into Casa Guadalupe if they showed up.

It was quite a string of accusations, and to be honest, it was difficult to parse out fact from fiction. It was not uncommon in the shelters for migrants to whisper accusations against one another. We often spent hours trying to figure out the "truth," usually to no avail. The only truth, the only certainty was uncertainty. This was something Erik actually said to me in that first meeting at the safe house. "You can't trust anyone here, but you have to get along with everyone if you want to survive." These are the rules of survival in the *cachuco* industry.

In the previous chapter, I elucidated my concept of the arterial border as a dynamic political and material space where migrants confront the insecurities produced by state securitization. As this chapter highlights, the arterial border is also a space where local economies take root to profit from human mobility. The incentives to profit are so strong that even spaces of refuge like migrant shelters are not immune. The twin concepts of the arterial border and the *cachuco* industry, both of which proliferate through the marginalization of racialized and gendered migrant others, are thus not separate, but rather inextricably intertwined.

Like state violence, the *cachuco* industry thrives on impunity. Officials and criminals alike profit from what journalist John Gibler calls a "special breed of paramilitarized-narco-silence," "where murder is part of the overhead in an illicit multibillion-dollar industry," and "impunity becomes a fundamental investment."[17] By thinking about the productive aspects of the *cachuco* industry—that is, who profits from the silence and impunity that accompany migrant commodification, disappearance, and death, we may come closer to understanding the twisted logic of this human rights crisis. You cannot put a price on the life of a child or sibling or parent, but in Mexico this is exactly what has happened.

4 Embodied Mobilities

Mayra is in the kitchen, where she chops a mound of yellowing but still edible broccoli donated by a market vendor from a neighboring town. She is excited because today we are having chicken. It's not enough to serve people individual pieces, but enough for *caldo de pollo* (chicken soup), which she has been cooking for hours in an enormous aluminum vat over an open fire. "This will give people energy for the journey," she says, and a welcome change from the monotony of beans and tortillas. She stands firmly on her right leg, because the knee of her left leg rests on a white plastic chair advertising *Coca-Cola* in fading red letters. People don't ask Mayra what happened to her foot. In this place, when you see someone missing a foot or a leg or an arm, you can guess that it was La Bestia, the freight train. But in Mayra's case, La Bestia was just an accomplice.

That morning Mayra told me about her "accident," which turned out to be no accident at all. The single mother of three from Guatemala was riding on the top of a train car with about thirty other passengers, all men. One of the men—who was drunk—made an inappropriate comment to Mayra, and another jumped to her defense. The other passengers started yelling at the drunk man to get off their wagon and go find his own group. Upset, this man turned to where Mayra was sitting and said, "All this for a fucking old lady?" He kicked her in the jaw. She lost her balance and slipped down the side of the moving train. She managed to grab onto the ladder, but the train was moving too fast and sucked her underneath. Her left foot was immediately crushed and mangled and had to be amputated below her knee that day. Mayra reflected on her experience, "I was on the verge of losing my life, but *gracias a Dios,* that did not happen. I believe things happen for a reason, and for me, even with all I have suffered, my purpose now is to help others." While in the hospital, Mayra met Padre José, who brought her back to Albergue Nazaret. She has been working as the head cook of the shelter for several months and manages well with a pair of old crutches. She is waiting for a prosthetic foot and lower leg to be donated. She then plans to continue her journey north.

A young man whistles for me to come over to the "living room," which is basically an open-air room with a tattered old couch, some folding tables, and a small television. Several guys are piled onto the couch watching a *telenovela* on a fuzzy screen. The young man, Rubén, asks me where I am from and what I am doing there, and I tell him about my research. He playfully says that if I was his woman, he would never let me be out on my own *andando por la calle* (walking the streets). "You should marry me and help me get to the U.S.," he jokes. He then tells me he needs a favor that requires a "woman's touch." He tilts his head to reveal a head wound and a scabbed ear, which looks to be missing the very top. The head wound was from a machete and his ear was partially bitten off by some *delincuentes* (delinquents) he got in a fight with after crossing the southern border. He opens his hand to reveal several capsules of Aspirin. He asks me to help pick the scabs clean, open the aspirin capsules and sprinkle their contents onto the open wounds. This will help prevent infection, he explains. I am a little taken aback by the request, but happy to assist. As I proceed I notice the adolescent pimples on his cheeks. Despite the heat and humidity, he is wearing a hooded sweatshirt and when I am done he carefully pulls the hood up and over his head. Rubén tells me that the hood will help protect his wounds from the dust.

I ask him where he is going, and he says first to Matamoros, where he has some family, and from there he will continue on to Houston, Texas.

"What is in Houston?" I ask.

"My mother" he replies.

"How long has she been there?"

"Sixteen years."

"And how old are you?"

"I'm twenty"

"That's a long time," I say, imagining a four-year-old Rubén and his mother making that impossible decision.

"That is why I need a new *mamacita*," he says with a sly smile, diffusing the serious turn the conversation had taken.

I roll my eyes and we both laugh. He thanks me kindly, but then jumps up telling me that he has to go and get his things together. He knows that the train won't leave for a few more hours, but he wants to make sure he doesn't miss it.

I return to the kitchen where Mayra is watching over the lunch meals being served. She is worried because they are running very low on tortillas and won't get any more donations until tomorrow. She rations the tortillas to just three per person to make sure they have enough. But when a group of men arrive and tell her they have not eaten for two days Mayra gives them an extra stack to share. Everyone is responsible for washing and drying their own plastic bowls and cups and people file through the kitchen. As they deposit their utensils many say their goodbyes. Mayra seems particularly sad to see one of the few other women currently at the shelter say goodbye and leave with a group of men. She gives her a long embrace. In this hyper-masculine space, women often find comfort and solidarity in one another. As people leave, Mayra offers them packages of expired *Emperador* and *ChocoChips* cookies. For some migrants, these meager snacks will be the only guarantee of sustenance in the days to come. At least they were able to get some decent protein from today's *caldo de pollo*. "Vaya con Dios [Go with God]," Mayra repeats like a mantra as she hands out the cookies. As they leave migrants grab flattened cardboard boxes from a large stack in the living area. The cardboard will shield them from the beating sun and dust on the top of the train. It isn't much, but it is something.

A missing foot, a scabbed ear, an empty belly—these are a few examples of the ways the violence of migration becomes inscribed onto people's bodies. This chapter examines the embodied realities of transit migration. Migration is often treated as an abstract and disembodied action, but

Figure 9. A migrant dismembered by a freight train recuperates at Albergue Nazaret.

what are the corporeal effects of migration on people's bodies as they move through and across physical space? By the time Central Americans reach the U.S.–Mexico border, they have already experienced extreme physical and mental exhaustion. The experience may include days trekking through sweltering jungle and desert landscapes, running from authorities or criminals, staying awake on a moving train, being crammed into tight spaces (such as in the back of a trailer or boat) and surviving with very little food, water, and rest. Many people arrive to the shelters without having eaten or slept for several days. These everyday calamities compound more severe bodily experiences like fist fights, rape, infection, illness, and injury.

For some people, like Mayra, who lost her foot on the train, these embodied forms of violence are conspicuous (fig 9). Indeed, the image of the dismembered migrant has become almost iconic of the journey in Mexico. But for many migrants, their injuries, ailments and other bodily preoccupations are less apparent. Conditions like intestinal parasites or urinary tract infections are hidden, but cause considerable discomfort and distress. Beyond their physical state, the journey also takes a toll on people's mental well-being. The emotional tolls of having recently left a child behind, of suffering a traumatic incident, or the constant uncertainty of life in transit cannot be underestimated.

Through an examination of the visible and less visible traces of migration on people's bodies, this chapter contextualizes injury, suffering, and the embodied experience of mobility within larger social and historically produced contexts. In doing so, it seeks to move beyond individual medical diagnoses and explanations of suffering as the result of accidents, bad luck, or bad people doing bad things. Rather, as medical anthropologists have argued, illness and poor health among marginalized groups, and undocumented people more specifically, must be understood as the embodiment of structural, political and symbolic forms of violence.[1] Through scars, injury, and trauma, migrants embody the histories that propel and circumscribe their movements.[2] Neither assaults on migrants crossing danger zones nor their dismemberment when they ride atop freight trains are purely random events. They are not merely the result of chance encounters or accidents, but are produced by local and global political-economic forces that create social conditions in which such violence is rendered natural, expected, and even to be regarded as deserved.

BEYOND ACCIDENTS

Her smile is infectious. Just shy of five years old, Emeline's constant giggles and boundless energy bring balance to this place where broken bodies and broken dreams come to recover. She is wearing a miniature jean skirt, yellow tank top and a *piolín* (tweety bird) cap, which seems appropriate as the tippity-tap of her flip-flops flutters across the verdant courtyard. She runs between the rooms cheerfully greeting the other residents, many of them with doors and windows open. But mostly she stays close to her mom, nestles her body into her mother's lap. Her left side leans into her mother's chest, and her right hand grasps the cold hard metal frame of her mother's wheelchair. I note that she appears comfortable with the wheelchair, almost as if it is now an extension of her mother.

Six months earlier Emeline and her mother, Irma, were riding on the top of La Bestia when the train made a sudden jerking motion, throwing Irma off balance. Not unlike Mayra, she slipped down the side of the rail car and in a flash was swept beneath the train, crushing the better part of both of her legs. A farmer whose land lay next to the tracks transported her to the local hospital, where both her legs were amputated. Like many other migrants who are severely injured, often losing limbs as a result of falling from the train, Irma was brought to a shelter located in the southern Mexican border city of Tapachula.

Irma was one of the first female migrants I met along the journey. I had originally set up a meeting with the founder of the shelter, a remarkable woman named Doña Paula, but she was called away to assist a migrant who had fallen from the train the day before and was waiting to be amputated. She spent the day with him at the hospital, making sure he had an advocate and company. Her work, as with many shelter workers, is unexpected and constant. And so instead I spent the day with Irma and Emeline. It had been several months since Irma's accident, and she was well adjusted into the daily rhythm of shelter life. Within the green-and-white-painted walls of the shelter, migrants move across the courtyard in wheelchairs and rest in beds in open-air rooms. She joked with the other residents, and blushed happily when one of the volunteers returned from the corner store with a bottle of her favorite shampoo. At the shelter I spoke with people learning to adapt to their new embodied realities, looking forward to receiving prosthetic limbs, dreaming of home or of the United States.

Like Mayra, many of the migrants here were waiting for donations to pay for prosthetic limbs. The shelter does not receive financial support from public or church funds. Rather, it relies on donations from individuals and private organizations to assist in the payment of medical procedures, prosthetic limbs, and the shelter's daily maintenance.

Shelter workers also developed informal economic strategies like the selling of used clothing. To this end, Irma and I spent the afternoon sorting through garbage bags filled with donated clothing. Irma instructed me to throw the clothes into two piles, one to keep and one to discard. "What happens to the clothes in the discard pile?" I asked. "You see that pit out in the back? We burn them," she replied. I was surprised by how selective she was in the clothing to keep, throwing almost everything into the discard pile. She kept only the newest looking shirts and pants, nothing too worn or with too much writing on it.

Irma knew something about clothing. She had worked for years in a Sara Lee Intimate Apparel outsourced manufacturing plant in Honduras, one of over forty countries where the Sara Lee Corporation operates. Eventually, however, she found that this was no longer safe or lucrative. Organized criminals had begun to extort a weekly *piso* (tax) from workers, and the job did not pay enough for her to care for her three children. She therefore decided to migrate to the United States and seek employment there as a domestic worker. Her older two children were in school and stayed with her mother in Honduras. For now it was just Irma and her youngest, the delightful Emeline. The plan was to work for a few years and make enough money to return home to them.

As I spoke with Irma I noticed a poster on the wall behind her. It was hard to miss, though not particularly well-crafted or designed. It is actually just a sheet of grid paper with nine photographs of different sizes taped onto it. Because this shelter is located before most migrants meet La Bestia, the photos serve as a prelude for what is to come. There is one of hundreds of people aboard the train, the kind of thing you might see in any newspaper. Then there are two photographs of individuals on the train. One of the men wears a T-shirt over his head to protect him from the dust and sun and grips the side of the railcar. He looks directly into the camera and is smiling. The image conveys a sense of adventure and excitement.

But the significance of these images lies in the contrast with the other photographs on the poster, which are the ones that really compel you to look. Four of the remaining photographs are close-ups of migrant men lying in hospital beds. All of them have lost at least one leg. In one photograph, the bandages wrapping the stump of a severed limb are soaked in blood, suggesting that the injury was very recent. The man is connected to tubes all over his body and stares at the ceiling. The center photograph is perhaps the most compelling. It depicts a handsome young man, with his chest bare, lying on his back. He has one arm thrown behind him, casually propping up his head. The other hand is grasping what remains of his grossly mutilated upper leg. Taken together, these photographs juxtapose freedom of movement with confinement in bed, the idealized masculine bodies often associated with the adventure of migration and the debilitated, medicalized, tube-connected bodies of the injured. The poster is part warning, part lesson, and part tragedy, all wrapped into one.

News articles reference these migrant bodies as *mutilados* (maimed), *desmembrado* (dismembered), *lisiados* (crippled), *fragmentados* (fragmented). What does it mean to for a person to be "fragmented"? Their bodies are altered, reshaped, permanently different. Rather than focus on the medicalized tragedy of injury, I argue that these are tragedies of a larger order. These injuries and disabilities are socially produced and connected to global and local political and economic structures. Irma's migration was motivated by concern for personal safety and a desire to support her children, but instead of her being able to buy a bus ticket and travel safely with her daughter, Mexico's growing border and security regime all but forced her to board a dangerous freight train, which nearly took her life.

Irma set out to provide a better life for her family, only to return several months later with a significant disability. If she was already rendered redundant in the context of the local economy in Honduras, she would be doubly so as a wheelchair user, particularly in the job sectors that require workers to engage in physical labor, including putting in long hours on *maquiladora* production lines, one of the few opportunities for women in the formal sector in Central America.

Like Irma, the migrants in the photographs, many of them quite literally cut in half, physically embodied the brutal consequences of state enforcement policies that funnel migrants onto the tops of dangerous trains. More than that, collectively, they represent a global workforce whose lives teeter on the edge of disposability in an economic sense, but also in an immediate embodied sense. These migrants' "accidents" were anything but accidents; rather they must be understood as the result of specific state and larger structural processes of inequality and violence.

At the end of the day spent with the newly injured man, Doña Paula finally arrived back at the shelter. Everyone filtered out of their rooms to the modest chapel, where she held an evening mass. Bonded through violence and now disability, they joined together in the warm light of dusk for an evening of song and prayer.

LA CLINICA

While the image of the dismembered migrant has become associated with the migrant journey in Mexico, it is not necessarily representative of the embodied realities that most migrants experience. Rather, people were preoccupied with more mundane, but no less important, conditions impacting both their physical and mental well-being. I often learned about these issues during our initial intake interviews with newly arrived migrants at Casa Guadalupe.

On the bottom of our intake forms there was a section dedicated to recording people's health issues. People arrived with external wounds, blisters, and minor injuries that needed attention. Stomach and intestinal issues, including parasites and urinary tract infections, were common. One woman was desperate for contact lens solution to clean the hard lenses she wore, which had not been properly cleaned for weeks. Another woman needed emergency dental work for tooth pain. Other migrants alluded to less specific problems like trouble sleeping, uncontrollable shaking, and other symptoms associated with psychological distress, which many migrants referred to as *nervios* and *susto*.[3]

In addition to offering people a place to sleep, food, clothing, help retrieving money orders, and free phone calls, Casa Guadalupe was also able to offer migrants access to healthcare. It had a closet filled with expired medications donated by local pharmacies that could be given to migrants. But more important, it had established a partnership with a local hospital on the outskirts of Oaxaca City that agreed to treat migrants free of charge. This is not a state hospital, but a small, nonprofit hospital and drop-in clinic that treats the poorest of patients. It receives financial support from benefactors in the United States, helping to offset the costs of services given, often free of charge, to local people who cannot afford to pay. The hospital has a shelter to house the families of hospitalized patients, which is crucial, particularly as many of the patients travel from rural indigenous communities across the state where they do not have access to adequate healthcare. The clinic is a crucial place of support for migrants coming through Casa Guadalupe, because it willingly treats patients regardless of their immigration status or financial means. Emergency and non-emergency care is provided without questions being asked.

Accompanying migrants to the clinic was one of the more rewarding aspects of working at Casa Guadalupe. In a context where we often felt as if our hands were tied in our abilities to help people, the ability to offer access to needed medical services was concrete, immediate, and transformative. From a research perspective, I also found that moving beyond the confines of the shelter encouraged people to open up about their lives in new ways. Maybe it had something to do with the sterile setting of the clinic, the bare urgency of their situation, or perhaps it was just the sheer boredom of sitting in the waiting room for hours on end that created a space for people to talk openly about some of the more intimate details of their lives.

Reproductive Health

I first noticed the openness in talking about intimate details and embodied experiences a few months into my fieldwork, when three couples arrived to Casa Guadalupe together: Victor and Suli from Honduras, Alex and Vero from Guatemala, and Magda and Elvis, also from Guatemala. At the end of our initial interviews and group orientation session I checked in to see who wanted to go to the clinic. Everyone except for Elvis was eager to go. Alex had a mysterious rash on his arm, and Victor complained for a dull pain in his chest. As I would soon learn, all three of the women were concerned about issues related to their reproductive health. We were able to make a quick trip to the clinic in the afternoon, where Alex was prescribed an anti-fungal cream for his rash and Victor was given medicine to relieve what the doctor suspected to be heartburn. All of the women, however, were asked to return the following day for various examinations.

We decided to go just after lunch. Soon after we left the shelter, we wove our way through the cars, *colectivos,* and lines of buses as we crossed the jam-packed *periferico* that runs around the city center. While it was not an official market day, it was late October, and Oaxaca's sprawling wholesale market, the Central de Abastos, was teeming with activity as people made their final Day of the Dead preparations. I usually tried to bypass the market, but the women were fascinated by the crowds and spectacle, so we decided to walk through. I knew that the market was a hotspot for robberies, so I pulled my small purse to the front of my body and made sure the zipper was shut. Magda noticed and said, "I would never carry a bag like that in Guatemala." She grabbed the bra strap under her shirt, "I carry all my money and phone numbers in here."

As we entered the market, the smell of car exhaust was soon offset by the aroma of cocoa beans, dried *chiles,* and copal resin burning. Mounds of colorful *pan de muerto* and cleverly crafted sugar *calaveras* greeted us in the bustling labyrinth. We walked through a sea of bright yellow and orange marigolds, known locally as the *flores de los muertos* and stalks of sugarcane that people use to construct their altars. I told them we would construct an altar at the shelter, and the women seemed excited. Soon, however, we emerged from this short diversion on the other side, back into the world, ready to confront matters at hand.

As we walked the remaining blocks to the clinic and sat in the waiting room the women opened up to me about their various ailments. The fact that we were all women meant that they could share even the most intimate details. Suli, the most forthcoming of the bunch, told me she was concerned about her IUD. She wanted to ensure that it was properly inserted. It is common knowledge that women receive birth control injections or have IUDs inserted before they embark on their journeys to prevent pregnancy in the event they are raped. These contraceptive measures may also free women from the burden of their menstrual cycles while in transit. The physical demands of riding the train and lack of access to feminine hygiene products pose significant challenges to menstruating women.

While menstrual periods can be extremely annoying and unwelcome for a woman in transit, unexplained vaginal bleeding can be even more worrisome. This was in fact Vero's issue. She had had a Depo Provera birth control injection—dubbed the "anti-Mexico" shot by Central American migrants—to prepare for the likelihood of being sexually assaulted. For many women the injection stops menstruation, but Vero had been bleeding continuously for almost the entire four weeks she was on the road. As she explained it to me, she said that when she was especially nervous, stressed, or startled, the bleeding increased. She also described some internal pain that she associated with the bleeding.

The nurses called each of the women into the exam rooms. The doctor found a vaginal infection and parasites in Vero's stomach and asked her to come back for a vaginal ultrasound to determine if the bleeding was hormonal or caused by another internal condition. Like Vero, Suli was also ordered to receive an ultrasound at the clinic. The doctor determined Suli's IUD was fine, but also discovered a vaginal infection and both she and her partner Victor were prescribed antibiotics.

Where Suli and Vero were anxious about preventing pregnancy, Magda's worries spanned the other side of the spectrum. A 38-year-old mother of five sons, Magda arrived at the clinic desperate to know if she was still pregnant. She had not had a period in over five months, but was worried that she had lost the pregnancy during the journey. She had suffered two miscarriages in the past and knew the signs; the initial spotting and then the period-like bleeding for weeks, the cramps and labor-like contractions as the tissue passes.

Magda entered the exam room, where the doctor performed an initial pelvic exam. She did not detect a fetus. The doctor ordered a series of tests to confirm this. The following day, Magda's official pregnancy results came back: negative. The doctor told her that she did, however, have a severe infection and needed to purchase medicine for an injection into her lower abdomen. She was quiet, simply nodding her head as she received the news. She rationally explained to me that it was the stress of the journey that had caused her to miscarry. She was not immediately emotional about the result, but later that evening, when Vero called home to talk to her daughters and began to cry, Magda held onto her and they wept together.

As the cases of these three women demonstrate, sexual violence and reproductive health concerns are of primary importance to many Central American women. Vaginal and intestinal infections are often hidden, masking their prevalence in this population, although they may urgently need treatment. Researchers have found that many migrants are aware of the risk of sexual violence before they embark on their journeys, but do not have access to gynecological services en route.[4] In addition to infections and immediate injuries, concerns around pregnancy—both wanted and unwanted—were paramount for women in transit.

Sexual Violence against Male and LGBTQ migrants

While there has been significant public attention to the types of violence experienced by women along the journey, few have addressed gendered forms of violence experienced by male, lesbian, gay, bisexual, transgender, or queer (LGBTQ) migrants. As mentioned briefly in the introduction, sexual violence against male and LGBTQ migrants is also a reality of the journey, albeit one spoken of mostly in whispers and through euphemisms. For some men, sexual humiliation occurs during strip searches by state agents, as described in chapter 2. But more violent forms of sexual assault also take place. "You know men who have been raped, Wendy," Padre José once told me. "You know them and they have confided in me, but I won't tell you who they are." Mayra also reiterated to me that it was not only female migrants who were raped, but male migrants as well.

One person who did open up to me about his sexual assault was Jasiel. Jasiel openly identified as a gay male. His fingernails were painted cherry red, his eyebrows plucked thin, his skin shiny with lotion. A rosary of wooden beads hung around his neck. He walked with a slight limp; he had a bad knee. Jasiel was also victim of kidnapping, an escapee, a survivor.

At Casa Guadalupe, Jasiel kept to himself. When everyone else was sitting in the living room, lingering after meals, you could find him alone in the dorm room. While he was always polite and smiled when I passed him, I knew that tensions were high between him and others at the shelter. The two men he arrived with claimed that Jasiel was really a *pollero*. He had a visa to be in Mexico, and there was no reason he should be at the shelters except to recruit migrants to smuggle, they argued. One of the men went as far as to suggest Jasiel wanted to be kidnapped because he wanted to have sex with men.

Unlike some of the other shelters, at Casa Guadalupe, the shelter workers strongly encouraged the migrants to stay inside during the day and at night. Yet one evening Jasiel announced he was going out. He was dressed in cutoff jean shorts and a tight shirt that showed his midriff. Someone murmured, "What does he expect will happen to him if he goes out like that?" People who transgress social boundaries are commonly perceived to have invited the violence they experience.[5] One of the other volunteers, who also happened to be gay, gave me a sidelong glance and rolled his eyes.

It was several days before I would have the opportunity to speak with Jasiel himself. I remember the day well. It was Thanksgiving in the United States. "Today is the Día de Acción de Gracias," one of the other migrants told me, proudly demonstrating his knowledge of U.S. culture. It was early evening, past *comida*, so I was surprised to see Jasiel in the living room eating by himself. But he was not eating food from the shelter. He had a styrofoam take-out container of fried fish, mixed vegetables, and macaroni salad, no doubt from the *mariscos* (seafood) place down the street. I sat with him as he ate and asked if he would be willing to share his story. "Yes, but not in here," he told me. "Better we go to the dormitory."

I often conducted interviews on the bunk beds in the shelter dormitories. The rooms were musty, but they were quiet, cozy, and private. Jasiel began by telling me about his early life in Honduras and then moving to southern Mexico at the age of ten to work on his father's dairy farm. He told me about the challenges he faced growing up, in his own words, "how I am, abnormal, gay." Jasiel had a boyfriend back home, a much younger man. People judged them, but he said he did not care. Even though he was in love, he said, when a friend told him that he was going to the United States—to Tucson, Arizona—he wanted to go as well. Jasiel was riding a train through Oaxaca when it was stopped by armed men. Other migrants ran toward the hills to escape the kidnappers, but Jasiel was unable to do so. He rolled up his pants to show me the scar around his knee, explaining that he could no longer run. He was one of four people kidnapped and brought to a safe house where he was abused and raped for three days. He suspected that he had been targeted because of the way he looked. In his words:

> It is hard, hard to talk about what happened. . . . When I saw the women and how they raped them I screamed. And when I screamed, they started doing it to me. To me. Eight men. And all eight penetrated me. Can you imagine how I felt? I was in the hospital for a week. The priest kept me in the hospital, ten days later I left the hospital, and now I can sit down like I am sitting now, I healed physically, but here [pointing to his chest] something stayed, something stayed, a trauma, and I still cannot sleep well. I lie down and barely close my eyes and I see the men who grabbed me and raped me. And when one was done, another would say "I'll have a go," and another, and when he was done, "I'll have a go now," and another. . . . I wish they had

used a condom but they had nothing and so now I am scared that one of them gave me a disease. I've already done a ton of tests, and they came out negative, but who knows with time.

Jasiel eventually escaped his kidnappers after Mexico's Agencia Federal de Investigación (AFI) raided the safe house where he and the women were being held. His story serves to illustrate, not only the sheer horror that many individual Central American migrants must endure, but also its lasting impacts, both physical and psychological. Sexual violence, needless to say, has implications for sexually transmitted diseases, including HIV/AIDS.[6] Furthermore, it also impacts the mental health of migrants. Jasiel described his experience through a lens of trauma, something that will stay with him. When I suggested that perhaps he should talk to a psychologist at La Clinica, he responded, "No way! They'll think I'm crazy. What would they think of me, of who I am?"

MIGRANTS' MENTAL HEALTH

Aside from dealing with physical health concerns, La Clinica also assisted migrants suffering from mental health issues. Constant fear and insecurity was the modus vivendi for many migrants. People with whom I spoke were not only on edge about the possibility of being robbed or kidnapped but also unsure about when next they would be able to sleep or eat a meal. Intimidation by local police and military patrols made walking on the street or making a phone call risky. Migrants were often wary when meeting new people and found it difficult to trust others, since deception and trickery were common tactics used by organized criminals, as we saw earlier in the testimony of Ramon and Israel. Even within the walls of migrant shelters, a climate of fear and anxiety existed as migrants shared stories about the violence they have witnessed or experienced. In addition to this everyday fear and insecurity, some migrants exhibited symptoms characteristic of psychological stress and even post-traumatic stress such as nightmares, difficulty sleeping, depression, unresponsiveness, and high levels of anxiety. I met one woman who could not stop shaking she was so nervous and panicked about being at the shelter. She was convinced one of the other women staying in her dormitory was a *bruja*, a witch. Another woman cried uncontrollably. These are symptoms that are often associated with Latin American folk illnesses called *nervios* and *susto*. Anthropologists have found that *nervios* is more commonly associated with chronic depression while *susto* typically manifests after a specific traumatic event, like a robbery or rape.[7]

It was Wilson, one of the most friendly and warm migrants I met during my fieldwork (and someone I still occasionally keep in contact with through Facebook) who really opened my eyes to the emotional distress experienced by migrants. Wilson was someone I got to know over several weeks during his stay at Casa Guadalupe. I actually first met him and his traveling companion Josie at Albergue Nazaret. They were childhood friends from the same neighborhood in Villa Canales, just south of Guatemala City. They had been at the shelter for three full days and knew that this was the maximum amount of time migrants were allowed to stay. "But we don't want to go on the train," Wilson told me. "It's not safe for Josie." Wilson had a brother who lived in Texas and they were hoping to reach him so that he might be able to send some money to pay for bus tickets. When I ask where they were going, Wilson simply replied, "Wherever God sends us." A week after I returned from Albergue Nazaret, I opened the door at Casa Guadalupe, I was pleasantly surprised to see Wilson and Josie on the other side.

While many people at the shelter used free time to rest, Wilson liked to keep himself busy. He spent an entire afternoon filling a plastic bucket with water and throwing it onto the ground in an attempt to keep the dust down. He often liked to sing American pop songs with accented English lyrics. He spoke openly about his life in Guatemala, and the challenges he and his family have experienced, particularly with respect to paying *la renta* (the rent) to local gangs. I knew he had experienced extreme violence and insecurity growing up, but was not made fully aware of his inner turmoil until one evening at the shelter.

One day I was at the pharmacy purchasing medicine for another migrant when I received a phone call from Mauricio asking me to come back as soon as possible because there was something wrong with Wilson. When I arrived, Mauricio said Wilson was despondent. I found Wilson in the women's dormitory room, sitting on a chair and crying with his head in his hands. He was shaking. Josie was in the room with him and told me that about an hour earlier she had found Wilson lying on the ground in the back garden, completely unresponsive. Mauricio had to carry him into the house. I sat next to him and he said flatly, "Hello, Wendy." He was able to speak through his tears. I asked him what had happened, and he said that he could not feel his arms or his legs. He then said that he didn't know what to do, because he had no money. Earlier that day, his brother who lives in Houston had called the office and told us that he would be able to send some money to Wilson soon. When I told him this, he seemed to perk up and asked for more details about the call. But when I said that we needed to call him back, he put his head into his hands in despair, saying, "but I don't have any money to call him." Mauricio and I reassured him that we would help him make the phone call; Mauricio even gave him a phone card. This seemed to cheer him up a bit, but he requested that I take him to the clinic.

Apparently several nights prior some worrisome symptoms had started to arise. Wilson could not fall sleep, and when he did, he woke up hyperventilating. Josie was extremely worried about him, since he hadn't eaten anything for two days. When I asked Wilson if he had ever experienced anything like this before, he said he had when his mother passed away. She had died of complications related to diabetes when she was just thirty-eight. At the clinic, Wilson spoke to a psychologist. While Josie and I waited for him in the waiting room, Josie began to cry silently. She said she had to stay strong for Wilson, but in that moment she too needed to let out her emotions.

Through my work at Casa Guadalupe I was privy to some of these less visible physical and psychological health issues experienced by migrants in transit. Yet, the people who come through Casa Guadalupe and receive even the smallest level of care are a minority. Most migrants in transit do not have access to mental healthcare, and even when they do, like Wilson, they do not often get the long-term treatment that is necessary. The psychologist treating Wilson emphasized, for example, that he needed ongoing therapy. Wilson returned to the clinic to meet with the psychologist one more time. But the next day, he was gone.

Several weeks later Wilson called me on my cell phone. "Where are you?" I exclaimed as I heard his voice. "Wendy, we made a terrible mistake, a terrible mistake," he lamented. Wilson called to tell me that he and

Josie had eventually made it across the U.S. border and to his brother in Houston. But in the first week they were there, they were picked up on the street by U.S. Immigration and Customs Enforcement (ICE). "We should never have gone outside." His mistake had been leaving the house. Wilson was calling me from Guatemala. It had taken them weeks and weeks to reach Texas, but Wilson and Josie were deported on a plane just days after being apprehended. He wanted to know how much longer I would be at Casa Guadalupe; he was already planning his next attempt.

CARMEN AND EVER

Carmen had a prominent scar the shape of a crescent moon just above her right eye. As I would learn, it was her journey scar. We met Carmen and her partner, Ever, in chapter 1. They were the couple who were fleeing gang violence in El Salvador and expecting a baby. After a month living at Casa Guadalupe, they ended up settling in Oaxaca. I include more of their story here because it reveals the ways physical, psychological, and other forms of violence and vulnerability overlap in the experiences of undocumented migrants in Mexico.

Normally, men and women were segregated in different dormitories at Casa Guadalupe, but this afternoon Carmen and Ever were taking a siesta together. I knocked on the door and pushed it open to see if they were awake and ready for our interview. They were both sound asleep on the bottom of one of the bunks. I must have woken Ever up when I turned to leave, because he aggressively jolted off the bed with a look that was somewhere between fear and anger. It took a moment for him to register where he was, but then his face softened and he apologetically told me that he had just woken from a terrible dream. He explained that he often had nightmares, which were often different versions of incidents they had experienced during their two attempts to cross Mexico. In each iteration, there is some element of danger and Ever is unable to help Carmen.

The first time Ever and Carmen had attempted to migrate was the previous year. Ever had a brother who worked at a Black Angus Steakhouse in San Bernardino, California. This was their destination. Their journey through Mexico took about a month. In Chiapas, they were robbed at gunpoint soon after boarding the train, but Ever's brother was able to send them some money to finance the rest of the trip. When they reached the town of Altar in Sonora, Mexico, they hired a smuggler to help them cross the desert. However, just a day after crossing, they were apprehended by U.S. Border Patrol officers and separated. Ever was quickly shipped back to El Salvador, but Carmen was held in detention centers in Arizona and California for three months before she was deported in turn. Ever told me that Carmen was so traumatized by the experiences of that first journey that she had stayed in bed for months upon her return and barely spoke. He also spoke of the agonizing months that he spent in El Salvador not knowing what had happened to her, where she was and if she was okay.

During those months back in El Salvador, Ever became embroiled in local gang activities, and his life was threatened. They decided to try migrating again. Their resolve to leave was strengthened once they found out that Carmen was pregnant. This time the journey was more difficult. During their attempt to cross through La Arrocera, they were assaulted by four armed men. As in so many stories I had heard before, the men and women in their group were separated. Carmen and another young woman were forced to strip naked in front of everyone. She feared they would be raped; she had heard the stories. "Please kill me," she pleaded with her captors. "I'd rather you kill me than rape me." "I was not scared," she told me with a look of defiance on her face. Presumably to shut her up, one of the men hit her in the face, just above her right eye, with the butt of his pistol. When Ever witnessed her being hit, he decided he needed to do something. While the men were distracted with the women, Ever managed to escape. He described the powerlessness he felt, screaming at the top of his lungs for someone to help them. He was so desperate that he decided to run directly to the checkpoint they were trying to evade to solicit the help of the agents stationed there. He begged for their assistance, but the police showed no interest in helping him. Ever wondered if they might have even been in on the crime.

This was how Carmen had got her journey scar, which is now a constant reminder of the assault to both her and Ever. She never told me if she was raped or how she was released—that part of the story was filled in with silence.

After they had been at the shelter for a few weeks, Padre Luis was able to secure a job for them to live and work in a seminary school located just a few kilometers away, in a village just outside the city. Ever was formally hired as the school's cook, and Carmen assisted him in the kitchen. Almost immediately Ever created a garden and put up a chicken coop just outside their small two-room apartment, where he also raised several rabbits. The shelter staff stayed in very close contact with them, and we saw them regularly at the shelter or their apartment at the seminary. One day Araceli and I went to the seminary to drop off some items that had been donated for the baby. By then, Mari, Carmen's sister, had joined them to help Carmen during labor and the early months after the baby's arrival.

When they first arrived Carmen was just about five months pregnant, but had had no prenatal care up until that point. Both she and Ever were anxious to confirm that the pregnancy was still viable and there were no major issues. Over the next months, I often accompanied Carmen to her prenatal appointments. Her first appointment was at La Clinica, where Carmen and Ever heard the fetus's heartbeat for the first time. I will never forget the excitement as they exited the ultrasound room holding the small black and white grainy image. I have a photograph of the two of them, both dressed in clothing they had picked out of the shelter's communal closet, smiling broadly and holding the ultrasound photograph between them. I printed the photo for them, and we joked that it was their first family portrait.

On one of their next visits, Carmen learned that La Clinica only offers women the option of cesarean births, and she wanted to have a vaginal birth. C-section births are common throughout Mexico, and even more so in Oaxaca, where they are viewed as more efficient, predictable, and profitable. I have seen estimates that between 40 and 80 percent of all Oaxacan births end in a cesarean. There are only a few small private clinics that will allow women even attempt a vaginal birth. Several of the shelter workers at Casa Guadalupe joined together to reach out to one doctor who was an advocate for "natural" births, and they raised the funds to help pay for Carmen's medical expenses. As luck would have it, I was away traveling on the night that Carmen went into labor. My colleagues at Casa Guadalupe were there with her and sent me updates and photographs of the long night and the newborn baby, a girl they named Francesca. With some trepidation, Ever and Carmen were able to secure an official birth certificate for Francesca, and ultimately receive their own regularization papers to legally stay in Mexico.[8]

From the outside, all seemed to be going very well for Carmen and Ever. They had escaped death threats in El Salvador, made it through one of the most dangerous parts of the journey in Mexico and now had jobs, a place to live, and a healthy daughter. But, as I soon learned, beneath the surface, things were more complicated. The complexities of Carmen and Ever's relationship came to the surface one evening after a wedding celebration hosted by the board members at Casa Guadalupe for my husband Nick and me. Francesca, who was now about six weeks old, was dressed in a bright magenta ruffled outfit, and all the *socios* had a great time passing her around. At that time another young couple from El Salvador was staying at the shelter, and the five of them seemed to hit it off quite well, sitting together and dancing at the party. The following afternoon I was surprised to see Mari in the kitchen at Casa Guadalupe, since she had been staying with Ever and Carmen at the seminary. She was helping to steam vegetables, and I asked her how she was doing. "Triste" (sad), she replied. "Why?" I asked. "Because I am sad for the baby and for my sister," she replied.

According to Mari, after the party, when Ever, Carmen, and baby Francesca were on their way back home, Ever said that he wanted to stop by a cantina to get another beer. The sisters told him they did not want to go, especially with the baby, but he was insistent. Apparently, the sisters asked Ever for some money to pay for a moto-taxi back to the seminary and he became upset with them. One thing led to another and Ever ended up pushing Carmen forcibly, and she nearly fell. Thankfully, Mari was holding the baby. The two women were extremely upset, crying hysterically, and called members of the staff at Casa Guadalupe to come and pick them up.

The women and baby stayed at the Casa Guadalupe that night, but the next day Carmen called Ever to pick her up. Carmen was worried that she was not producing enough breast milk for Francesca, and she needed Ever to help get baby formula. While she had received excellent care during her labor, she did not have significant postpartum support and breast-feeding proved to be a challenge. Ever arrived to the shelter remorseful and promised never to repeat what had happened. They left the shelter together, but Mari decided to stay. Mari told me that while Carmen said this was the first time he had pushed her, she suspected otherwise. According to Mari, Ever had a history of alcoholism and abuse in his family. She claimed that at times he verbally abused Carmen and forced her to do things for him. For example, she claimed that four days after the baby was born Ever demanded that Carmen wash his shoes for him. Mari also suspected that Ever was cheating on Carmen, having allegedly seen suspicious text messages on his phone.

It is difficult to know the whole truth of the relationship between Carmen and Ever, and I hesitated even to include this part of their story in this chapter, because I am wary of reproducing an essentialist conceptualization of Latino men as macho or violent, but I do so for a number of reasons.[9] First, it importantly demonstrates the ways unauthorized migrants, and women in particular, are structurally vulnerable to abuse in contexts where they are disconnected from their familial and social networks and have few rights or access to systems of support. At the most immediate level, Carmen depended on Ever financially and needed him to help her purchase formula for the baby. Second, as anthropologists have argued, intimate partner violence must be understood in the context of larger economic, political, and social forces of violence and injustice.[10] That is, Ever's actions were not simply the result of his individual personality or culture, but were enacted within a longer trajectory of economic precarity, social violence, and inequality. Third, their story illuminates how intimate partner violence can linger just beneath the surface. Part of the horror of such violence is that it can (re)emerge at any time, perhaps triggered or perhaps without a clear reason. Finally, while the migrant shelter and clinic proved to be crucial during Carmen's prenatal care and the birth of her baby, as well as the immediate aftermath of her fight with Ever, these local ties ultimately proved temporary and circumstantial.

As such, the story of Carmen, Ever, and Mari illuminates some of the embodied realities of life in transit and the webs of violence and vulnerability that migrants must negotiate under social conditions of illegality. It demonstrates the threads of violence that connect people's lives in Central America to their more immediate experiences of violence—state, physical, gendered—as migrants in transit or as unauthorized immigrants in Mexico who experience embodied realities like pregnancy, motherhood, rape, injury, intimate partner violence, and trauma. Rather than treat each of these threads as singular and isolated, we must understand them as interconnected and produced by larger social, political and economic contexts in which people experience a paucity of care and support of their most basic human rights.

After the wedding incident we did not see much of Carmen, Ever, and Mari. Mari returned to El Salvador and her own two children, one of whom she had learned was ill. She hoped that Carmen would return with her and they could introduce Francesca to her grandmother and other family members, but Carmen decided to stay. The seminary gig did not last very much longer, but Carmen and Ever remained in Oaxaca and moved to another neighborhood where some other Salvadoran immigrants lived. They stayed in touch with me for a few months, mostly through phone calls and the occasional visit, but we eventually lost contact.

DESERVINGNESS AND HEALTHCARE

La Clínica was a crucial resource for many people who passed through Casa Guadalupe. Ultimately, however, the access migrants had to these health services depended on a specific local relationship between Casa Guadalupe and the clinic. These were not services that were widely available to other migrants in transit. How many migrants, like Rubén, were treating their own wounds and hoping they did not get infected instead of receiving stitches? How many countless women in transit are also pregnant and not receiving appropriate prenatal care? How many are suffering from painful infections that could easily be resolved with a dose of antibiotics?

Anthropologists have produced important work on the implications of illegality on migrant health, bodies, and lived experience.[11] James Quesada and his co-authors use the term "structural vulnerability" to describe how the racial, gendered, and class-based positionality of undocumented Latino immigrants in the United States negatively impacts their physical and emotional well-being.[12] Related to the larger concept of structural violence, such a framework is useful in making sense of the health concerns and issues experienced by unauthorized Central American migrants in Mexico, where legal status precludes them from seeking care or justice when their rights are violated. Even where healthcare is available, many migrants do not seek it because they fear deportation or discrimination, choosing instead to treat their ailments on their own or not at all.

For these reasons, providing healthcare to unauthorized migrants in transit raises legal, practical, and moral questions of deservingness. "Embodied experiences of 'illegality'-in both the experiential sense and the epidemiological sense of the term—are profoundly influenced by local moral assessments of who is or is not deserving of society's attention or investment," Sarah Willen observes.[13] For unauthorized migrants in Mexico, provisions for care and access to legal protections are grossly inadequate. At the time of my fieldwork, there were no legal guarantees of healthcare for unauthorized migrants. However, some local clinics and hospitals, like the clinic in Oaxaca, did provide care without question. These arrangements were often negotiated through the efforts of shelter workers. The legal landscape around this would change officially in 2011 with Mexico's new Migration Law, which guarantees access to education and healthcare for unauthorized migrants in Mexico. The law marked an official shift in discourses of deservingness, but although it is a positive step, it has not amounted to much in the way of concrete or systematic access to healthcare for unauthorized migrants. Moreover, the law has since been largely overshadowed by Mexico's more punitive approach to Central Americans in the wake of the 2014 unaccompanied minor crisis and the implementation of Programa Frontera Sur, which has pushed migrants further into the shadows in Mexico, making them less likely to engage with official institutions to seek medical or legal attention.

One notable development in the moral economy around healthcare for unauthorized migrants in Mexico has been the establishment of Médicos sin Fronteras (Doctors without Borders) clinics in several locations along the migrant trail. I first learned of the work being done by MSF during a return trip to Albergue Nazaret in the summer of 2013. Near the shelter office there was a bulletin board with various informational posters, brochures, and newspaper articles, as well as drawings and notes of gratitude by migrants who have passed through the shelter. There was a poster warning about the dangers and incidence of dengue fever, which had been a problem for migrants staying at Albergue Nazaret. When I visited, clinicians wearing white shirts came into the shelter courtyard and announced their drop-in hours and consultations for people in need of medical treatment or mental health services.[14] Where access to medical treatment once depended on the availability of Padre José or one of the other shelter workers to transport people to a hospital willing to treat an unauthorized migrant, these crucial services were now incorporated into daily life at the shelter.

Yet organizations like MSF expose the contradictions of medical humanitarianism in contexts of illegality, transit, and crisis. Peter Redfield refers to a "minimalist biopolitics," where health is governed "without any certainty of control as responsibility for rule is ever deferred by humanitarian organizations such as MSF to absent political authority."[15] Humanitarian efforts exist when the state fails to protect certain populations. The irony is that the more humanitarians there are, and humanitarian regimes become institutionalized, the less pressure there is for the state to step in.[16] Anthropologists have been led to take a critical look at humanitarian aid, and Didier Fassin has called into question the "moral untouchability of humanitarianism."[17] Much of this work traces the relations of power and governmentality as they play out within humanitarian regimes, the economies of compassion that emerge between the aid apparatus, donors, and clients, and the overall unintended consequences of top-down models of aid.[18] Indeed, relations of aid and care, including those within Mexican migrant shelters, are often founded on paternalistic relationships that reproduce new forms of social inequality. While these are crucial lines of inquiry, particularly as shelters become more institutionalized, it is also crucial to maintain a focus on the responsibility of the state to protect the most basic rights of people within its territory. In Mexico there is a glaring disjuncture between the discourse of humanitarianism and the passage of the 2011 Migration Law and the implementation of the Programa Frontera Sur securitization program, which has pushed unauthorized migrants into more clandestine routes, in many cases bypassing migrant shelters. Indeed, Albergue Nazaret, where MSF has set up its clinic, now receives only a fraction of the number of people that passed through there in years past because many migrants are no longer riding the trains. How can medical humanitarians and the state respond to the immediate embodied needs of a transient population whose routes are in constant flux? To begin, it seems that the push for accessible and safe healthcare for migrants in transit must be made at the local level through institutions invested in the well-being of *everyone* in the community. Beyond this, however, we must trace the pathways of inequality that create the conditions of structural vulnerability for populations like migrants in transit. The so-called accidents suffered by Mayra and Irma on the train, like the other everyday forms of violence, illness, and injury experienced by Central American migrants, must be understood as socially and politically produced.

5 Intimate Crossings

The railroad tracks, which had been fairly deserted, begin to fill with people staying at Albergue Nazaret and the cheap motels downtown. Street vendors are busy selling tacos and tortas, watching as the spectacle of Central Americans preparing for the train journey unfolds. I am with Jesus and two other men from the shelter who are eager to scope things out before they embark on the next leg of the journey. Most migrants are clustered together in small groups, sitting in the precious shade of the few trees and abandoned rail cars. As we walk along, we pass a lone man sleeping on his backpack on the ground; his white socks read *USA* in red, white, and blue.

There is a police pickup truck at the far end of the tracks. It makes a U-turn and slowly drives down the frontage road with several uniformed men dangling large automatic rifles haphazardly. It is undoubtedly an act of intimidation, but no one seems to care. We are in a de facto sanctuary zone; the clandestine flows visible for all to see. The scene embodies the way unauthorized migrants are "present yet absent" in the spaces they occupy, what Susan Coutin calls the "erasures of presence."[1] In these liminal spaces, the supposed protectors are often the most feared, and the most feared can become crucial to everyday strategies of survival.

It is a stifling hot day, and one of the men in my group wants to buy a cold drink. We walk to the center of town to a bodega on the ground floor of a hotel. I wait out front with Jesus as two men come down the hotel stairs and out the front door. Jesus leans his head into mine and whispers that the men are Zetas going to scope out the tracks. The Zetas had already become notorious for their brutal tactics and recent foray into the business of migrant kidnapping. Two weeks earlier I recorded the testimonies of three women who were tracked by Los Zetas in this very area, before narrowly escaping. I wonder if these are the same men. According to Jesus, they live at the hotel and are well-known locally. Jesus understands the social dynamics at the tracks in ways I do not—the major players, what is going on just beneath the surface. While just a short jaunt into town, I begin to appreciate his presence in terms, not just of my research, but also my safety.

We walk back to the tracks, and the men in my group spot an elderly man they call Tío (Uncle) slumped against an old rail car. He appears to be sleeping, but when the guys call to him, he sits up straight, waving them over. As they chat with Tío, I notice two adolescent boys sitting on a plaid blanket adjacent to the rail car. Their youthful, almost innocent presence seems out of place among predominately adult male migrants who sit in groups talking, joking, and playing cards. In contrast, these boys sit quietly alone, careful not to make eye contact with anyone. Their clothes and looks suggest that they might be indigenous Maya, most likely from Guatemala. I wonder if the two men Jesus identified as Zetas have taken note of them— like women, adolescents are also considered valuable.

I am surprised when an older hefty man walks toward the tracks and stops at the boys' feet. His shirt is fully unbuttoned revealing his round stomach, tattoos on his chest, and gold chain necklace. They look up and their eyes widen as they register the bag of freshly roasted chicken, tortillas and two-liter bottle of Coca-Cola he is carrying. The man tells the boys to get up off the blanket, and he spreads it out before them. Then he sits down beside them and opens the bags of warm food and pours the coke into two small plastic cups. The boys come alive as they swiftly grab their tortillas, stuff them with chicken and into their mouths, as if this is the first meal they have eaten in days. The man seems pleased but does not eat with them. He begins to make small talk with the people in my group.

Even though I am sitting closest to him, he turns to Jesus and asks him: "Quién es ella?" (Who is she?). Jesus replies, "I think she is some kind of psychologist or something." Still not looking at me, he asks, "What is she doing here?" "She is just talking to us," he replies defensively. It is an unsettling dynamic, the two men talking across me as if I am not even there.

The man catches my gaze and asks if I would like a taco. "No, gracias," I say politely. "Are you sure? Here have one," he says again, and I cannot tell if this is a friendly gesture or a veiled threat, letting me know that he is watching me. "No, gracias," I reiterate. One of the other guys asks him what his plans are, what his story is. He tells us he is from Honduras and on his way north. Once again Jesus leans in to me and whispers "No es cierto. Es Mexicano" (That is not true. He is Mexican). This is code for saying he is in fact a *pollero,* a hired smuggler and not to be trusted. We know that many smugglers pose as migrants in order to infiltrate the shelters and recruit new clients. Things quickly fall into place: this is a smuggler and the boys are his clients. I wonder how much he was paid to transport the two boys. I know a Guatemalan woman in Los Angeles who paid $5,000 for each of her two children to be smuggled to the United States. Did their parents pay similar fees? My mind turns to these hidden webs, the families spread out across the Americas that underpin people's journeys. For some, transit marks the initial separation from loved ones, and for others, it brings the hope of reunification. But I know that right now they have more immediate and pressing concerns.

The boys finish off the last of their tortillas. The smuggler tells them to get some rest before the train is ready to go. Everyone knows the next stretch through Veracruz is one of the most dangerous. This is the calm before the storm. I turn my attention back to my group and see they are now passing around a joint. It turns out that Tío is a local dealer. Jesus senses my discomfort and says we need to head back to the shelter. Later that evening I hear the sounds of the train leaving in the distance. I imagine the boys and their smuggler precariously perched on the top of the train, with bellies full as they ride toward the uncertainties of future.

.   .   .   .   .

I often think about this encounter, this transgression of sorts, along the tracks that afternoon. While marred in suspicion on all sides, it was a brief glimpse into this largely invisible world, the shared intimate space between a smuggler and his clients. As I watched their interactions, the look on boys' faces when they registered the bag of chicken, the way the smuggler laid out the food for them like a little picnic, I could not help but think about his dual role as both perpetrator and protector. The journey, comprised of weeks or months of alternating movement and stasis, marks a unique social world between departure and arrival where migrants and their smugglers, guides or companions are bonded together in irreversible and poignant ways. In his assignment to transport these two boys, the smuggler risked his own life alongside them as they rode on the top of the freight train. Day after day he was responsible for meeting the boys' most basic needs of sleep and sustenance. Perhaps more important, his close watch also likely provided some type of protection from abuse or disappearance, particularly in light of recent kidnappings and rumors of women and children being specifically targeted. Indeed, I suspected his questioning my presence was somehow linked to his protection of the boys. Can human smuggling, an act that is almost universally constructed as detached exploitative criminality, be reconsidered through a lens of intimacy or even care?

The social imaginary around human smuggling tends to be static and one-dimensional. Smugglers are presented as elusive criminals who exploit their clients. They are the boogeymen of the migration industry, an omnipresent danger, but disembodied and difficult to see. Yet the types of social relationships that develop in transit are more complex. As Padre José reiterated, there are "clean smugglers," those who are not embedded with more organized criminal groups. But more than this, along the journey, family members, friends, or lovers can double as smugglers or guides. And complete strangers can quickly become allies and caretakers.[2]

This chapter examines the strategic social relationships and forms of intimacy and care that develop along the Central American migrant route in Mexico, seeking to shed light, not only on state border enforcement, but also on migrants' social worlds and relationships. As their journeys become more uncertain and violent, the intentional and sometimes serendipitous social relations migrants forge become key to mobility and survival. In doing so, they defy simple binaries of exploitation/altruism, victim/perpetrator, smuggler/migrant. At the same time, however, these bonds can be temporary and tenuous, and in some cases depend upon and reproduce new forms of inequality.

The malleability of these relationships and configurations exemplifies some of the complexities within the intimate economies of mobility along transit routes.[3] As feminist scholars have argued, state and structural processes are inextricably linked to intimate emotional life.[4] State legal systems reshape the intimate lives of transnational migrants and their families.[5] And while there is an emphasis on the ways social relations have been fractured and undone by exclusionary state immigration policies, this research also shows how ordinary people—parents, grandparents, and children—strive to maintain relations of care and kinship across borders. There is no denying that people and families around the world are being torn apart, and that migrants' journeys are often violent. The question is, under such conditions, how and in what new and unexpected ways are people being brought together?

Moving beyond the family unit as the primary site of analysis, this chapter conceives of intimate relations more broadly to examine the types of arrangements, strategies, and forms of intimacy that migrants engage in, sometimes with strangers, as they grapple with precarity and uncertainty en route.[6] I argue that the forms of relationality and intimacy that develop along migrant routes can be read as strategic, processual, and produced within specific social, economic, and political contexts. The stories in this chapter move primarily between and around Albergue Nazaret and Casa Guadalupe. By examining the logic of intimate economies within these spatio-temporal worlds of transit, we see how they are embedded within intersecting fields of power, from interpersonal gendered dynamics to transnational flows of labor. The need for particular types of relationships of mobility have emerged in response to perceived and real threats of gendered violence and vulnerability.

NEED A MAN?

It was the eve of the two-year anniversary of November 20, one of Oaxaca's deadliest days of police repression during the 2006 social movement.[7]

Padre José had just arrived at Casa Guadalupe to participate in a silent march and mass planned for the next day. We were in the midst of a small evening gathering. The shelter's *socios* (board members) and a group of migrants staying at the shelter gathered in the living room to enjoy *mollotes*, thick slices of bread slathered with beans and topped with *queso fresco* (Mexican farmer's cheese) and spiced *café de la olla*. People shared their stories of previous attempts and returns. One migrant began to talk about his experience crossing the U.S.–Mexico border near Tucson and the fact that smugglers often lie to their clients about how many days it will take to cross the desert. This was our first joint meeting since the November 5 kidnapping of twelve women. Sergio, the migrant who had witnessed the kidnapping and was staying in the safe house was present. Padre José told us that he was now recommending that all women and children—and all men traveling with women and children—skip the train and instead take the alternate route through the Sierra Mixe to Casa Guadalupe.

Sergio, took the opportunity to share some advice with one of the newly arrived male migrants in the room who was traveling with a female companion. He looked him directly in the eye. "Look, I am telling you this not just for your sake, but for her sake as well. You are not just responsible for yourself, but for her too." The other people in the room nodded their heads in agreement, and the man indicated he understood. Another migrant chimed in, "Women need a man who will at the very least defend her."

In his gripping book *La Bestia*, translated as *The Beast: Riding the Rails and Dodging Narcos on the Migrant Trail*, the journalist Óscar Martínez uses the neologism *cuerpomatic* ("bodymatic") to describe how women's bodies and sex are used like credit cards to buy safety or favors from gangs, officials, smugglers, and even other migrants along the journey.[8] Sexual acts become forms of payment, and women's bodies sites of transactions in ordinary encounters. While it is true that many unauthorized migrant women often feel they have no choice but to give in to such demands or risk deportation, kidnapping, or even death, the gendered dynamics between male and female migrants/smugglers/guides are more complex. That is, the construction of women's bodies as *cuerpomatic* fails to take into account the agency of female migrants and the complex arrangements and forms of reciprocity that also develop along migrant routes. Just as in the opening with the two young boys and their smuggler, female migrants are caught up in multiple economies of intimacy along the journey. In some cases, these economies are quite visible, such as the prolific sex work industry along the Mexico-Guatemala border that profits from the labor of Central American women. But less visible are the intimate relations forged en route between female migrants and other migrants, smugglers, guides, and shelter workers. Their stories are not just about victimization and suffering, which is by far the dominant narrative perpetuated in the media and even within shelters. Rather, as the stories in this chapter attest, even women who have suffered extreme forms of violence, are resilient, strategic actors in their own migration trajectories. I argue then, that rather than thinking about gendered dynamics as purely exploitative, we may conceptualize them as also strategic and relational. Female and male migrants perform multiple "intimate labors" as they move through the landscapes of transit.[9]

For some, like Mayra, the cook at Albergue Nazaret who lost her foot, it entails inserting themselves into the practical and affective daily work of migrant shelters. But for others, intimate forms of labor inform more personal types of relationships. For example, in the sections that follow I examine what I call protective pairings between migrants in transit. I borrow the term protective pairings from literature that describes the reciprocal yet often unequal relationships between prison inmates.[10] In such scenarios, male and female migrants simulate kin relations, generally spousal relations, as a migration tactic. Male migrants exchange security and protection for female carework such as procuring food, washing clothes, tending wounds, and in some cases, sexual acts. Both partners perform intimate labors in processes of exchange and reciprocity that go beyond the realm of straightforward financial transactions. In this way, such intimate labor, even that involving sex, differs significantly from traditional constructions of sex work, smuggling, or exploitation.

A focus on the intimate economies of mobility complements new directions in kinship studies that have moved away from traditional understandings of kinship based on biology/culture.[11] Instead, through analysis of protective pairings and other strategic arrangements, we see how forms of relatedness, kinship, and intimacy are emerging and flexible, existing in particular social and political contexts.[12] Moreover, in several examples I examine, protective pairings and simulated kin relations are explicitly

Figure 10. Two couples chat near the tracks in Veracruz as a train approaches.
Photo by author.

gendered arrangements that rely on heteronormative ideas of masculinity
/femininity and often reproduce such notions through gendered labor
roles. Yet it is through these types of gendered relations and the intimate
economies of mobility that women and men are able to negotiate their
movements and their lives.

JESSENIA AND ABEL

"I think it's a boy," Jessenia told me as we crossed the pedestrian bridge
over a busy intersection on our way to the clinic. "Girls are beautiful and
all, but a girl would never have survived on that journey. Boys are much
stronger. At least that is what I am hoping for. I don't want to have a
daughter knowing that what happened to me could ever happen to her."

Six months prior, Jessenia had been kidnapped, raped, and held hostage for close to a month in the back room of a small bodega in the town of Huehuetan, Chiapas.

I met Jessenia on a bright Oaxacan summer morning, a few hours after she arrived to Casa Guadalupe with a man she introduced as her husband, Abel. I immediately noticed how her oversized T-shirt pulled tight around her belly. She looked to be about six-months pregnant. I assumed Abel was the father of the baby. They were affectionate and giggled as they sat together on the couch. He called her *mamita* and she rested her hand on his knee. On their intake forms, they listed each other as spouses. I also noted that they listed different sets of children in different locations, hers in Honduras and his in Maryland, where he had lived and worked for fourteen years. But this wasn't all that unusual, because migrants arriving at the shelter often had complicated family arrangements spread across borders.

Things became clearer several days later when Jessenia told me her story. We had just finished washing the plates from lunch and retreated back to the women's dormitory. We sat across from one another on the bottom bunks and I got out my voice recorder, placing it on a plastic chair between us. As in most interviews, we started by talking about life back home. She was a single-mother of three boys, aged nine, eleven, and fourteen. Her ex-husband had been abusive, and she had left him and moved in with her mother when her youngest son was an infant. Money was tight, but for years the mother-daughter team managed, both working odd jobs to put food on the table. But recently her eldest son had started talking about going to medical school. "He wants to be a doctor. But you know, that is a really expensive career." Jessenia started to worry about paying for education, not just for her eldest but also for the younger two. Her mother was only sixty-two and in good health, but she had seen friends struggle to care for their aging parents. As the only daughter, she worried about providing for her mom in the years to come. She figured that this was her window of opportunity; she could go to the United States and leave her boys with her mother while she was still able to watch over them. After a few years of working, she would be able to return to Honduras, maybe purchase a home and support everyone. Jessenia was under no illusion that this would be easy, and unlike other migrants who had family members to help pay for their journeys north, she knew she would have to work her way across Mexico.

In the early morning hours, before her sons were awake, she set off from her home in Honduras, alone and determined. She crossed Guatemala and the Guatemala-Mexico border with little trouble. She had heard that many Central American women found work in the cantinas and bars in the region—Central American women were highly desirable in the local sex industry—but she was adamant about only engaging what she called *trabajo inocente* (innocent work). So when she heard about a job packing mangoes, one of the region's most important agricultural exports, she jumped on it. The job was in Huehuetan, known among migrants as the site of one of the first military checkpoints in Mexico's interior. It was tiring work, but she was content knowing that she would soon be able to continue her journey north.

At this point in the interview I noticed Jessenia's demeanor shift. Her voice became more of a whisper, but at the same time she spoke more quickly, almost as though she was afraid someone was listening in on our conversation. I asked her about what had happened in Huehuetan. Jessenia typically worked an evening shift and a local bicycle-taxi driver would take her back to the apartment she rented with a few other Central American women. But one night in early December, Jessenia had agreed to take on an extra late shift and did not get out of work until 2 a.m. Her usual bici-taxi driver was nowhere to be found. The only person still around was her boss, a man everyone called Gordo. She described Gordo as a "deportee" from the United States and rumors swirled about his ties to gangs and drug traffickers, though Jessenia admitted that she had never found him to be particularly threatening. When Gordo exited the facility and told her he would take her home, she agreed. This was a moment she would become fixated on, a decision she would soon regret.

Not even a full block after they started walking, Gordo began to make threats. She realized he was drunk and possibly high on something. "You would not know it looking at him, but it was like he transformed into a monster." He grabbed her hand and pulled her down the street, telling her that she had better obey him or he would beat her. He brought her to the storage room behind a bodega owned by his brother. She described the room as empty except for a few soda crates and dirty mats on the floor.

Gordo sent her to the adjacent bathroom to clean herself. Jessenia described the terror she felt crying in the bathroom, already certain of what would happen next. She told me the next part of the story in euphemisms, sparing herself the pain of repeating the details of a night that would become weeks of captivity. Jessenia was held in that room for nearly a month where her boss repeatedly drugged her with unidentified pills, raped her, and eventually impregnated her. As she described her experience, she kept going back to those soda crates and mats, the material objects that kept her company for those unimaginable weeks.

Jessenia eventually escaped with the help of one of her neighbors, who was able to track her down at the bodega. She brought Jessenia back to her apartment where she bathed her, fed her, and washed her clothes. The two women were convinced that if Gordo found them he would kill them both. "He was searching for me, *me buscaba, me buscaba, me buscaba,*" she repeated. Jessenia and the neighbor lived in terror for weeks. I asked her why she didn't just return to Honduras at that point. She strongly considered it, she told me. But then she found out she was pregnant.

This was when Abel, one of Jessenia's co-workers at the mango-packing plant, who had heard what had happened to her, sought her out through her neighbor. "He told me not to worry, that he was here now. I told him that I wanted to abort the baby. He asked me how many children I had. I told him three. He asked how many I had aborted and I told him none. How many had I given up? None I told him. And he told me not to worry, because he could be the father and that he was going to help me in any way that he could." Abel proposed that they travel together. He was preparing to leave Huehuetan and looking for a companion. Jessenia admitted that she was surprised and a bit uncomfortable with Abel's offers. She worried that she would be a burden and that he might tire of her and abandon her. But she needed to get out of her current situation, out of Huehuetan, and away from Gordo.

On a more immediate level, Jessenia now felt that she needed a man, particularly to finish crossing through La Arrocera and the multiple checkpoints. Abel and Jessenia had both heard the horror stories of La Arrocera and the likelihood of assault and rape for migrants traveling by foot. Abel decided to purchase a cheap bicycle, and instead of taking *combis,* the pair would ride through the backroads. The journey was rough.

Jessenia described the fortnight she spent riding on the handlebars of the bicycle during the day and sleeping on cardboard mats or the floors of strangers' homes at night. She told me about men who robbed them but then let them continue.

After being robbed, the pair decided it might be best to stay in Mexico for a little while to work. They met another migrant who told Abel about a job near Tonalá, a bit farther north on the Pacific coast of Chiapas. They spent the next few months living in a small apartment, in her words, like husband and wife. "At first, he would not touch me, because of the baby. But now, we are more like a couple. I feel as if he is my husband, because of the help he gives me. I mean, look, he does more for me than my actual husband did!" Jessenia tells me about the rhythms of their daily life, how she prepared the food and cleaned his clothing when he was working. And while there was a semblance of normality, they both ultimately decided it was time to continue on the journey. Jessenia was nervous about going to migrant shelters, because she had heard rumors that men preyed on women at shelters, but Abel promised her he would take care of her. And when she was offered ten pesos to have sex with another migrant at Albergue Nazaret, it was Abel who stepped in to defend her.

When the ultrasound technician entered the small room at the clinic, Jessenia told her that she was worried about the baby because of the train journey. "What train?" the technician said as she squirted cold lubricant onto her belly. "The train from Arriaga to Ixtepec," Jessenia stated. The technician gave her a curious look, "Is your partner from Arriaga? Is that why you rode the train?" The technician had no idea that Jessenia was a migrant. At that time, the plight of Central Americans in Mexico was still relatively unknown. "No, he is here with me," Jessenia responded. "He also wants a boy. He already has a name picked out."

While Jessenia outwardly projected a fairly stable image of her relationship with Abel, in private she revealed another side of the story. On several occasions she confided in me that she was worried Abel would tire of her and leave her during the journey. One afternoon I found her upset because she noticed him flirting with another female migrant. Another night he was out late and she told me, "Well, he either got picked up by *la migra* [i.e., the Instituto Nacional de Migración (INM)] or he is with a *muchacha*." "Qué muchacha?" I asked her perplexed. "You know, in a *can-*

tina," she replied raising her eyebrow. "He has a lot of manly needs." Jessenia's tone and attitude quickly dispelled the admittedly romanticized narrative I had created in my own head. I realized that Jessenia was not worried because of her deep emotional connection or romantic love she has for Abel, but rather, because of the crucial role he played in her own migration trajectory. She told me that despite his protests to the contrary, she knows the relationship won't last once they get to the United States. "*Así es* [that's how it is], but he is my help now and with him I have a better chance of arriving."

When we walked back to the shelter from the clinic I asked Jessenia if she had told her mother and sons back home about the baby. She had not. "When I left, my mother told me to be careful. Don't get involved with a man she said. I don't want any more children around here." Jessenia was too ashamed, fearful of what her mother would say and, even more so, of the anguish the news of their mother having been raped would bring to her sons. How would she explain it to them? What would life be like with this new baby? Jessenia expressed a deep ambivalence. "The burden is heavy. I'm afraid that my sons will be indifferent to the baby, that they will not love it. I am not sure I will love it. How could I?"

And yet that day in the clinic, when she finally got her ultrasound, the energy around her almost seemed to lighten. She was captivated as the technician counted off ten fingers, ten toes, four heart chambers. She looked back to me with her eyes wide to make sure I was following along. The technician told her that the baby was not in the right position to determine the sex. "Ni modo" [It doesn't matter]," she said with the tiniest hint of a smile on her face.

Jessenia's decision to leave Honduras was motivated by her affective ties and aspirations to care for her sons and mother. "The only thing I can do now is work. That is my obligation. I have to arrive, I have to work," she repeated to me in many different ways. It became clear that if she did not get to the United States and make enough money to send home, all of this would have been for nothing. The already high stakes had been raised. Yet her lived and embodied experiences of mobility across Mexico reveal another layer in her story of intimacy, kinship, and care. The social bonds she created while in transit—the neighbor who rescued her, her strategic partnership with Abel, the staff at Casa Guadalupe, even the ultrasound technician at the clinic—were all crucial to Jessenia's well-being, mobility, and survival. But although meaningful, these relationships were ultimately temporary. Indeed, several days after the ultrasound, Abel left Jessenia at Casa Guadalupe. He decided to continue on with another group of migrants. Jessenia was upset, but also determined to keep going.

No Soy Pollero

It is late morning and I'm in town with a friend when I receive a text message. It is from Flor: "Can you come to the shelter now?" I usually don't receive messages from Flor, so I have a hunch something is up. When I arrive, Flor opens the door quickly and pulls me into the living room. She is uncharacteristically agitated. She tells me that three people, two men and a woman, just arrived and she wants me to do their intake interviews. Then she whispers, "One of them, the one named Alberto, is a *pollero*." Apparently, Alberto had come through Casa Guadalupe not six months earlier, though he was going by a different name. He was particularly memorable because on that trip he was traveling with a young girl, his daughter, which at that time—before the 2014 influx of unaccompanied minors—was a fairly unusual combination. The father and daughter stayed and left the shelter without incident, but later when Flor and Mauricio called Albergue Nazaret, they were warned that Alberto was a well-known *pollero*. So when he showed up at the front gate this morning, now traveling with his "wife" and her brother, Mauricio confronted him on-the-spot. Alberto vehemently denied the accusation claiming the staff at Albergue Nazaret had a personal vendetta against him. Because he was with a woman, Mauricio reluctantly let them inside, but both he and Flor were too upset up to do the intake interviews. I tell them I would take care of it and see what I can find out.

I enter the men's dormitory and see two men sitting across from each other on the bottom bunk beds. The older of the two men, who looks to be Afro-Honduran, is the first to greet me. He introduces himself as Alberto and when he smiles I notice he is missing three of his upper teeth. The other man, Dionisio, says hello from the bed. I do not see the woman at first, but she soon enters the room carrying a tube of toothpaste and a toothbrush. She introduces herself as Marta and sits on the bed next to Alberto.

I worry the group may be hesitant to speak to me after the tense encounter with Mauricio and Flor this morning, so I make a couple of jokes to break the ice. They quickly reassure me that they are happy to complete their interviews. We go through the intake forms rather mechanically. Alberto gives me his details. He is forty-two and from Honduras. He has nine children, spread out between Honduras, California, New York, and Georgia. He is a construction worker and has migrated a dozen times between Honduras and the United States. His lists his wife as Marta. I collect Marta's information next. She is 30 years old. She is from El Salvador and has one daughter. This is her third attempt crossing Mexico. She lists her husband as Alberto. Finally, I collect Dionisio's details—he is twenty-seven, from Honduras, and Marta is his older sister. His wife is in Los Angeles. This is his first attempt at crossing Mexico.

The intake interviews spill into a more natural conversation, and I end up spending much of the day with the three of them. I learn that they are waiting for a money order from Dionisio's wife. When I ask them where they are going, Dionisio says Los Angeles, and Marta says either LA, with her brother, or Georgia, with Alberto. Both Marta and Dionisio defer to Alberto when talking about their migration plans and futures. He is the most experienced, knows where all the shelters are located, and has contacts on the northern border to help them cross into the United States.

Alberto and Marta are physically affectionate, like Jessenia and Abel, and casually refer to each other as husband and wife. I decide to ask them about gender dynamics along the journey. "Women cannot migrate alone," says Alberto in response to my question. Here is the next part of our exchange:

WENDY: A woman cannot migrate on her own?

ALBERTO: On the train, no. All the other men will want to take advantage of her.

WENDY: So women do not travel alone on the train?

ALBERTO: In reality, never. The majority say that they are with their husband so that the rest do not bother them.

WENDY: And this is just until they arrive?

ALBERTO: Yes.

WENDY: And so women need men, more or less for protection, and men need women for . . .

ALBERTO: Look, what I'm telling you is that it helps them both out. For men who are traveling alone, they don't help them as much in the houses or shelters. Sometimes they don't give them anything to eat or a place to sleep, but if a man is with a woman asking for something to eat, they regularly give. So that man is responsible for the woman just as the woman is responsible for the man who protects her. And it really helps the man out because it makes it easier in the homes and to arrive.

The irony, of course, was that Alberto was describing something approximating his own arrangement with Marta. Later that afternoon, during a trip to the store, Marta revealed that she and Dionisio had just met Alberto about three weeks before at the shelter in Tapachula. This was not uncommon during my fieldwork. Couples that initially presented themselves as husband and wife would later confide that they had only known each other for a matter of weeks. When I press Marta on this revelation she laughs and tells me that she never wants to get married again. But she likes Alberto and he is experienced and knowledgeable. Despite the suspicions raised by Flor and Mauricio, Marta assures me that Alberto is not a paid smuggler, but more of a *guia* (guide). Indeed, migrants often distinguished between guides and smugglers, the former having a more innocuous association.

As Alberto pointed out, these protective pairings are not one-sided. Rather, they are strategic partnerships involving reciprocity and exchange. At their core, the relationships between Jessenia and Abel and between Alberto and Marta were not based on idealized notions of love or long-term commitment. Nor were they traditionally understood smuggling relationships where cash is exchanged for guidance and/or transport. Rather, these relations were grounded in different types of intimate exchange based on highly gendered understandings of domesticity, protection, safety, and survival along the migrant route. The men offered a modicum of protection in navigating dangerous geographies, and the women performed traditionally female tasks like cooking and cleaning, as well as providing the men with a sense of legitimacy and companionship as they traveled to migrant shelters. This becomes especially important in a climate where Central American men are feared as delinquents, gang members, and sexual predators, and Central American women are associated with immorality and prostitution. The simulation of marriage through the performance of heteronormative coupledom, as opposed to brother and sister, for example, becomes a highly strategic legitimizing practice.[13] Such simulated kin relations can thus be read as crucial strategies as unauthorized migrants seek shelter and attempt to remain undetected by authorities.

CLARA AND VALENTINA

Sometimes the complexities of intimate economies of mobility become apparent through more formal smuggling arrangements. While we knew that smugglers and guides like Alberto likely passed through the shelter posed as family members, it was usually only after migrants had been abandoned by their smuggler that we would gain deeper insight into these relationships. Here, the story of Clara reveals the ways in which smuggling relationships are both intimate and yet ultimately tenuous. I first met Clara in the front patio of Casa Guadalupe. She had arrived with another woman, who had long, ribbon-threaded braids and was wearing a black-and-white woven headscarf typical of the Zapotec region of the Oaxaca Valley, and with a little girl, who, I soon learned, was her seven-year-old daughter, Valentina. Clara's husband had migrated to North Carolina several years before. Clara explained that she had had no intention of migrating to the United States until she received a telephone call from her husband telling her that he had hired a *coyote* for her and their daughter. He had already paid half the total fee, so she had no choice but to go.

Three days later, the *coyote* came to her town to pick her and Valentina up. He was already accompanied by two women in their early twenties. The five of them traveled for three weeks together in a private automobile through Guatemala and southern Mexico. Clara's first impression was that the *coyote* had a nice face and challenged her own stereotypes of how *coyotes* behaved. She recounted their daily routine driving to houses on the outskirts of towns where they would be given decent places to sleep and food to eat. The women developed relationships with one another, and they helped watch over and play with Valentina. Relations between and among smugglers and clients often involve daily practices of care, including the facilitation of transportation, lodging, food, and medical attention when needed.

Clara said that the *coyote* did not abuse them at all, nor did they have any trouble with the police or gangs. When they approached police or military checkpoints, the *coyote* would drop them off and men on *motos* (scooters) would pick them up and drive them around the checkpoint. The routine became predictable, and Clara and Valentina had learned to trust the other women and the *coyote*.

Once in Oaxaca, the *coyote* informed the women that he knew someone in the town of Mitla, a town less than an hour bus trip from Casa Guadalupe, and that they would stop there. Instead of dropping them off at a private residence, he took the women and Valentina to a *cantina* (bar). For the first time on their journey, they saw him drink alcohol and smoke cigarettes. The *coyote* told the women that he needed to step outside for a few minutes, and before they knew it, he was gone. They waited at the cantina for several hours, but he never returned, taking all their belongings with him. They had been abandoned.

Once they realized this, the women made the difficult decision to split up. The other two women were adamant about continuing their journey and decided to try and hitchhike their way at least to Mexico City. Clara felt this was too risky, especially with Valentina. With no other choice, she began to knock on stranger's doors looking for help. After being turned away several times she encountered a local woman—the woman with the headscarf and ribbons in her braids—who told her she could help. The woman had heard about Casa Guadalupe through her church, and after giving them something to eat, accompanied them on the 45-minute bus ride to Oaxaca City. When I interviewed Clara, it was clear she felt betrayed and even personally hurt by her *coyote*. He had become someone she trusted, and depended on. This betrayal was like salt in the wound of the financial loss her family would incur. She also confided in me the ways the abandonment affected Valentina, who had also learned to trust the *coyote*. She explained that Valentina was not sleeping well at night because she was fearful that her mother would abandon her too, just like the *coyote*, and her father before him.

The ultimately tenuous nature of the social bond between smugglers and clients does not negate the lived experiences of mobility, intimacy, and affect that may develop. Human smuggling is a form of labor that involves day-to-day intimacy as smuggler and migrants share the same physical spaces for weeks. They are also subject to the same threats and obstacles posed by state and criminal infrastructures. Yet, as the case of Clara and Valentina exemplifies, and what distinguishes such cases from protective pairings, is that these intimate labors are underscored by the exchange of capital for services in highly unequal power relations. While migrants may willingly enter into such arrangements and in some cases legitimate bonds form, even working with reputable smugglers or guides is laced with uncertainty. In Mexico, the human smuggling industry has grown in response to increased state enforcement and new fears posed by organized criminals who control the journey. We have seen a renewed dependence of human smugglers and guides to negotiate this double-pronged threat. However, the potential safeguards presented by smugglers and guides do not negate underlying possibilities of deception, exploitation, or in this case, abandonment. As discussed in the next section, these dynamics can permeate even the strongest of social relations.

MONEY IS THICKER THAN BLOOD

I am just stopping by Casa Guadalupe after a long day to drop off a box of donated items. Flor and Araceli are chatting near the front door. Flor asks if by chance I brought any backpacks. A family has just arrived, and the mother needs a backpack. Araceli gives me a skeptical look. "You should go and talk to them. It is a little unusual."

When I enter the room, I see a three-year-old child on the bed sound asleep. He is totally passed out, despite the squeals of his eleven-month-old sister as she pulls herself up and down on the side of the mattress. I notice the baby's earrings, two tiny gold studs. Karen, the mother of the children, who looks to be in her early twenties, tells me these were a parting gift from Padre José at Albergue Nazaret. The shiny earrings stand in sharp contrast to the baby's soiled shirt and frayed diaper. I wonder if we have any pants in the donation bin that would fit her. Both kids' clothes and bodies are filthy. We give them toiletries for the shower and show them the bag of donated kids clothes.

In addition to Karen and her two kids, there is also another woman in her late twenties, two men in their late twenties or early thirties and an older man who looks to be in his sixties. I assume Raul, one of the younger men, is the father of the children, but I learn that he is actually their uncle, and that Juan, the older man, is the father. The other two young adults, Vicki and David, are also siblings and Karen and Raul's cousins. The family left Guatemala a week ago.

We chat while the three-year old sleeps. They give me updates on the staff at Albergue Nazaret; it had been several weeks since my last visit. They tell me about *la migra*, the INM, harassing them when they were staying at a hotel in Huixtla (a town in Chiapas). The owners of the hotel had reported them to the INM as *indocumentados*. However, rather than apprehending them, the authorities had demanded that each person pay them two hundred pesos.

When I leave the dormitory Araceli pulls me to the side, "Do you think Juan is a *pollero?*" she asks. The thought certainly crossed my mind. There seemed to be tension between Juan and Karen's brother and cousins. And then there was the age difference—at least thirty years difference between Karen and Juan. Like Alberto, we often suspected certain people were smugglers, but it was difficult to be certain. This was part of the everyday uncertainty of shelter life.

I return to the shelter early the next morning to take Vicki to the office to make a phone call. Entering the front gate I see Juan come out of the dorm room looking disheveled, as if he had just woken up. He greets me and tells me he is looking for his son. The three-year-old is now riding a tricycle in the back yard. I notice that he is still wearing the same dirty clothes as yesterday.

I enter the living room and Raul is on the couch. I smile but he does not smile back. I sense something is wrong and ask him how he is doing. "I'm here," he replies curtly. Vicki and David are in the corner arranging their bags. They also seem upset. Since I left them last night something has shifted. Raul blurts out, "Juan is a *pollero* and he is leaving us to return to Guatemala." Araceli must have overheard him because she immediately comes into the room. We sit down in the living room and ask them to explain. Raul tells us that Juan is stealing their money and breaking the agreement they made. They had already paid Juan fifteen thousand *quet-*

zals to transport them to Los Angeles, where he promised them jobs. They were to pay the other half upon their arrival. But apparently last night Juan had received word from his associates in Guatemala that there was a group of fifteen *pollitos* waiting to be smuggled, so he was leaving them here.

Juan comes into the room in the middle of Raul's explanation. He begins to deny the accusations. "Yeah, it would be great if I really was a *pollero*, at least then I would have money to feed my children. But look at us, look at how hungry we are. We don't have anything. This is why we are returning to Guatemala." Vicki chimes in and tells us he is lying. She tells him to return the money they gave him. He says he does not have anything. Juan leaves the room and heads toward the men's dormitory. Minutes later Juan returns with Karen, who is still wearing her pajamas. Karen is angry. She begins shouting at her brother, telling him that they are not *polleros*. Raul responds by telling her that Juan is just using her and using the children. They argue for several minutes. Raul then disengages with her and turns to Araceli and me, "Where can we make those phone calls? We want to file a complaint. We need to tell people what is going on." Araceli asks me to step outside with her. We are both at a loss, caught in the midst of this family drama, we do not know who to believe. As we talk, Karen and Juan emerge from the dormitory still dressed in their pajamas haphazardly carrying the two children and with multiple bags hanging off their arms. They do not say anything and proceed to the front gate. At the very last minute, Araceli says to Karen, "Good luck." Karen looks back, smiles, and says, "Thank you," before closing the door behind her.

Raul and Vicki treat their hasty exit as proof of their guilt. Raul expresses his frustration at the time and money wasted. "If it weren't for Juan, we would be so much further than Oaxaca. We could have been taking the train this whole time. The only reason we are going to migrant shelters is because of the children. The American dream is not even my dream. I am only here for Vicki." He explains that his sister Vicki was adamant about migrating to the United States to support her daughters. They then tell me that Juan and Karen regularly smuggle people across Mexico with their children. Vicki explains, "She is with him for the money. Imagine, right now they are going to get fifteen *pollitos*. Imagine how much money that is. Juan is able to get a lot farther with the children. Eight days after having a cesarean birth, Karen was riding on the train with her newborn and Juan. Can you imagine?" Not only is traveling with a woman useful at shelters, as Alberto observed, but children can also be an asset in transit. The children, which I now suspect Juan and Karen left dirty and unkempt for strategic reasons, were part of their business strategy in crossing Mexico, used to elicit sympathy and concern from locals and shelter workers who offered to help them.

I have spent considerable time trying to make sense of that morning. The explosive tensions that erupted between siblings, the seemingly exploitative relationship between parents and children, the accusations of exploitation and abuse. The heartbreaking reality illuminated one of the more difficult discoveries of my research: the ways even the most intimate of social and kin relations may be implicated within intimate economies of the journey. I asked Vicki how her own cousin and Raul's own sister could abandon them like that. "Money is thicker than blood," she said.

LEAVING YOUR HEART BEHIND

I spent the afternoon with the three cousins. They were anxious to make phone calls home. At first Raul wanted to file an official complaint denouncing Juan, then decided against it. "He is still the father of my nephew and my niece," he said. Vicki called home to talk to her daughters. She did not mention the situation with Karen and Juan. Instead they talked about mundane things. "What did you eat for breakfast? How did you cook your eggs?" I could hear one of her daughters ask her the same in return, "I also had eggs for breakfast, *mamita*. They put *chile* on everything here!" It was as if these quotidian details were the sustenance needed for people to go on. She told them repeatedly, "Listen to your grandmother. Do your homework. I love you, do you hear me? I love you." Vicki told me how nice it was to hear her daughters' voices. But she said that she had to be careful not to cry. "If I cry, my soul will split apart."

Phone calls, like that between Vicki and her daughters, are a form of virtual care that has become prominent in the strategies of migrant mothers and fathers within what scholars have termed the transnational "circulation of care." Some scholars postulate a "care deficit," inasmuch as women in the global South leave their own children behind to care for the children and parents of the affluent in the global North, but others refute this by pointing to the networks of care that unite transnational families from the global South, even for those who do not cross borders.[14] Kristin Yarris has examined the ways caring practices shift to grandmothers who stay behind with their grandchildren in Nicaragua, for example.[15] In addition to intimate labors performed through protective pairings, and even smuggling, I argue, we might also turn our attention to the forms of care provided by parents while they are in transit. Sometimes this involves caring for children who are accompanying their parents, as in the examples of Irma and Emeline or Clara and Valentina. But caring relationships are also maintained through phone calls and, more recently, social media platforms like Facebook, WhatsApp, and e-mail. Because we offered free phone calls to migrants at Casa Guadalupe, I was often privy to the conversations people had with their families back home. They offered a glimpse into people's lives, the backstage, so to speak, of their migration stories. Indeed, it was most often family that motivated people's migration—to provide for, to escape from, to reunite with someone—*a* mother, *a* son, *a* husband.

The intimate relations that circumscribe migration decisions contribute to the affective dimensions of life in transit. In periods of stress, frustration, and fear migrants often expressed their feelings about the emotional tolls of leaving and yearnings for family. At the same time, it was almost as if migrants' families existed in a parallel universe. That life, *real* life, was somehow distinct, compartmentalized, detached from the immediate realities people were experiencing on the journey. One mother explained it to me like this, "When you are here, it is only your body. You leave your heart behind." In some cases, like that of Jessenia, it was difficult to reconcile the embodied reality of life in transit with the affective ties of life back home. Yet through these phone calls, these brief moments of connection, the intimacies of mobility that both drive and sustain people's journeys, collapse into each other in ways that are filled with both heartbreak and hope.

.   .   .   .   .

I will never know the fate of those two young boys on the railroad tracks, of Jessenia and Abel, Alberto and Marta, and the family from Guatemala.

Did the man who brought them the roast chicken accompany the boys all the way to the United States? Did Karen and Juan really go back to the Mexico-Guatemala border and pick up a new set of *pollitos* to smuggle? Was Jessenia's baby born a U.S. citizen? Speculating on the likelihood of migrants' arrival, or of detention, deportation, violence, or disappearance, can be endless. All Central American migrants face great risks when they cross Mexico, and yet record numbers of people continue to make the trek. In doing so, migrants and their bodies become swept up in global political and economic currents that profit from their mobility. Human smuggling industries are produced at the nexus of global economies of migration and transnational regimes of security and border enforcement. Yet as local conditions shift, so do the everyday logics and intimate economies migrants engage in as strategies of mobility and survival.

As this chapter has shown, Central American migrants' journeys illuminate such intimate economies, as well as the intersections between migrants' intimate and economic lives, often presumed to be separate realms.[16] The lines that separate smuggler, guide, companion, friend, lover, and family members can become blurred during a single journey. Highlighting migrants' agency and strategies for survival also challenges the often gendered constructions of migrants and human smugglers as either victims or criminals. Migrants, including female migrants, are not simply passive victims; they are resilient actors. Focusing on the interplay between state and global processes, on the one hand, and migrating individuals' strategies in shelters and clinics, and on railroad tracks, on the other, serves to deepen our understanding of mobility as a social process, and even a form of resistance to cascading forms of violence.

6 (In)Security and Safety

The shelter's gate was padlocked shut with a heavy chain, and there was no sign of movement or recent activity inside—it looked all but abandoned. A handwritten sign at the church across the street simply said: "Migrant, continue on your way." Inside the church I found a man sweeping the floor. When I told him I was looking for the priest that helped migrants, he replied: "He is not here . . . and we don't serve migrants anymore."

It was the summer of 2007, and I had recently read Sonia Nazario's popular book, *Enrique's Journey*, which describes the harrowing journey of a Honduran boy crossing Mexico in hopes of reuniting with his mother in the United States. In the book, Nazario, a journalist who traveled alongside migrants on the trains, describes several towns in the state of Veracruz that had become known to migrants as places of kindness and generosity. Local residents gathered together to toss bags of food and water bottles to the hungry passengers.[1] Inspired by her descriptions, I ventured to Veracruz to find some of these communities and, more broadly, to understand how local residents were responding to the influx of Central American migrants passing through.

In Orizaba, Veracruz, a city lying in the shadow of the majestic snow-capped Pico de Orizaba volcano, I headed to the tourist office to see if they might be able to help me locate the migrant shelter. The young woman sitting behind the desk was friendly and eager to help when I greeted her, but when I explained to her that I was looking for the shelter, her faced changed instantly. "The shelter is closed," she told me. "It has been closed for almost two years," and then she added, after hesitating, "since the rape of the girl." According to news reports I later read, in 2004 it was alleged that a thirteen-year old girl had been assaulted by three Salvadoran men staying at the shelter. The girl's father heard her screams and discovered her with her alleged attackers. He immediately called on his neighbors to help him catch and lynch the three men. An angry mob of neighbors formed and followed the migrants back to the shelter. The priest defended the migrants, keeping them safe inside, marking the beginning of a week-long standoff and protests. The men claimed they had just crossed the tracks to buy marijuana and had nothing to do with the girl, but all three were eventually arrested. The alleged main culprit was sentenced to thirty years in a Mexican prison, and the shelter was forced to close its doors.[2]

"Look, the priest who used to run the shelter is still here and works at the local parish. You could talk to him." She wrote down the name of the neighborhood where the church and the closed shelter were located and said any taxi driver would know where they were. I thanked her for her help, and as I was leaving, she said, "Be careful. Personally, I would not want to go there."

I hailed a cab from a busy downtown street and gave the driver the name of the church. Sure enough, he knew the location. Moreover, he was familiar with the story of the shelter closing and the alleged assault. As we drove he shared some of his observations about how the city had changed over the years with regard to Central American migration. Migrants were more vis-ible now, he said, especially near the train tracks. At first he expressed sym-pathy for migrants and what they faced on the journey. But as he ruminated about the impact they had had on his city, he shared how upset he had become about the problems they created, notably, their committing rape and other crimes. He explained to me that while local people used to assist migrants, they stopped out of fear of repercussions from the police, even though it is technically legal to offer them humanitarian aid. His reaction, a mixture of sympathy, disapproval, and fear, was one that I encountered repeatedly among other local people along the journey. As he drove me to the other side of the city, we crossed the railroad tracks, which seemed to be in one of Orizaba's more run-down areas. "This is where the migrants stay now," he told me. "You can talk to them here." "But how will I know who is a migrant?" I asked somewhat naively, and he chuckled. "It is obvious. The way they dress and the way they talk. They talk differently."[3]

We drove up into a hillside residential neighborhood and stopped in front of the closed shelter and church, where I encountered the man who told me that the priest was not there and no longer helped migrants. I asked the driver, who had waited for me, to drop me off near the railroad tracks. He took me back down the road where several groups of people were clustered near the tracks with backpacks and bags, resting in the shade of an abandoned *palapa* (thatched-roof shack) and some palm trees. I thanked him and got out. Even though we were still in a fairly urban area, and there were modest houses and corner stores nearby, sheep were munching the grass along the tracks. Trash was littered between the railroad ties, and two men were selling things like used jackets, cheap black cotton gloves, plastic bags filled with white bread rolls, and bottles of water and soda from a small wooden stall. I struck up a conversation with the men, who explained to me that many Central American migrants were unprepared for the frigid temperatures they would encounter, especially at night, riding on top of the train through the mountains and tunnels that lay between them and their next stop in Mexico City. These two Mexicans, one of them a former immigrant who had lived in the United States himself, made a living selling them needed items, as people do all along the route across Mexico (fig.11).

I mentioned that I had gone up to look at the shelter and church. The men knew the story quite well. They offered a few more details. Apparently, after the closing of the shelter the priest had still helped migrants at the church, but recently some migrants had stolen things from the priest's rosary box. That was the "last straw" that led to the posting of the sign telling migrants to keep moving—there was no help for them there.

I spent much of the rest of the afternoon chatting with several groups of migrants near the stall and along the railroad tracks. Among one large group of around ten people, I noted several couples. I did not know it at the time, but I later discovered that such pairings were likely examples of the instrumental intimate relationships I examined in the previous chapter. Most people in this group were from Honduras, but there was also one

Figure 11. A vendor sells bread to migrants outside the main entrance to Albergue Nazaret.

man from Guatemala and another from El Salvador. The group told me that they had met in Tenosique and had been traveling together ever since. They were on their way to La Lechería on the outskirts of Mexico City. They said that the police had not bothered them as long as they stayed on the tracks. They did not dare venture into the center of town.

As we chatted a man pushing a cart with thick stacks of colorful paper passed us several times. Looking more closely, I realized that they were stacks of Mexican pesos and Central American banknotes. He was a money changer, eking out a living by converting migrants' cash for them, so that they did not have to risk the trip to a bank or currency exchange shop. Some of the migrants joked with the man that if he let them borrow some money on credit they would pay him back. While the atmosphere was almost jovial, it led into a discussion about some of the true costs of migration, the thousands of dollars it takes to pay a *coyote* and the danger of falling off the train and being killed or dismembered.

The next day, I traveled to another of the smaller towns mentioned in *Enrique's Journey*, Fortín de las Flores, a lushly landscaped town with a resort popular with residents from Mexico City. Here, the train runs through the center of town and homes line the tracks. I chatted with a few residents who mentioned that they had noted more migrants coming through, and more women in particular, but did not have much contact with them. I then came upon a house where I found a woman called Edna sitting alone in her verdant front patio, on which there were several plastic tables. She told me that in the evenings she sold food from her home. She was methodically shredding chicken, pulling the pieces of boiled warm flesh from the bones and into a large plastic bowl, in preparation for the tacos she was making that evening. She invited me to come and sit with her, and I told her about my project. It turned out that Edna was one of the generous women that I had read about—or at least she had been.

Edna explained that formerly many of the women in her community, including several of her neighbors who live along the tracks, had prepared food to give to migrants, but no longer did. The parish had organized food drives and brought in large bags of bread, crates of fruits and vegetables, and rice and beans for the locals to cook and put into small plastic bags to throw up to the migrants. Edna said that migrants, whom she called *pobrecitos* (poor things), still occasionally came to her home to ask for help, and while she might give them a glass of *agua fresca* (fresh fruit juice), she no longer helped them as she had done before. "Ya no damos [We don't give anymore]," she repeated several times. She suspected that there were now a significant number of *maras*—gangsters—living in the community, and it was simply too difficult to distinguish between them and migrants—in her mind, they were part of the same process. Another woman whom I interviewed told me that migrants now congregated closer to the city of Córdoba. I asked her if she could direct me there, but she refused, saying: "They are delinquents, they are gang members. I won't tell you where they are. It's too dangerous."

· · · · ·

While I did not discover them on this trip, there is a collective of local residents, primarily women, called Las Patronas, who do still organize to provide food and water to migrants on the train. I will return to their inspiring work in the next chapter. But as I learned on this initial trip to Veracruz, while there were still traces of local residents aiding migrants in transit, there was also evidence of the insecurity and fear that permeated the area. This chapter addresses some of the more complex and intricate dynamics surrounding transit, aid and security as local communities grapple with an increasing presence of outsiders and multiple actors make claims in the name of security.[4]

Thus far the book has focused primarily on security as it is constructed and implemented as a top-down project by the state. I have examined how state securitization impacts migrants, but "security" has many forms, each of which is constantly being negotiated and challenged by actors at the local level.[5] I draw on the work of Daniel Goldstein and others who examine the contradictions that emerge as neoliberal "phantom states" in Latin America are both present and absent in local spaces.[6] Not unlike the insecurity described by Central American migrants about their home communities, Mexicans also grapple with the insecurities produced by drug war violence and a neoliberal security state.[7] In many transit towns in Mexico, the state is highly visible through policing and militarization in the name of national security, but largely absent when it comes to providing basic protection and services like healthcare, education, and access to justice. To fill the voids left by phantom states, local communities may take it upon themselves to enact forms of community policing and vigilantism, which might be conceptualized as the neoliberalization of security itself through privatization.[8]

The privatization of security is particularly pervasive in addressing social violence attributed to delinquents and gangs, what Daniel Goldstein calls the "spectral figure of the *ratero*—a quasimythical being who haunts the margins of the city."[9] For many Mexicans, the *ratero* is perfectly embodied by the transient Central American migrants who move through the shadows of their cities, never wholly known. Much as in Central America, the language of *delincuencia* often attributes violence to moral and individual failings rather than structural causes.[10] The lines between migrant, smuggler, gang member, and narco quickly become blurred as rumors of robberies, rape, and kidnappings permeate everyday conversations.

So how do local actors and groups along the migrant journey negotiate the issue of community security in contexts of social, political and economic insecurity? On one hand we have migrant shelters, which are born out of visions of compassion, humanitarianism, and rights for migrants who suffer extreme violence during their transit journeys. Shelters are seen as places of security for migrants, but also for local communities. Shelter staff argue that by keeping migrants contained, they keep communities safer. And yet for state authorities and many local residents, migrants are simultaneously constructed as threats to everyday community safety and security. They are characterized as illegal transitory intruders who do not have a legitimate claim to rights, resources, or pity within the communities they pass through. Far from being deserving victims, Central American migrants have been blamed for the increases in violence and insecurity local residents experience on a daily basis. The claims that shelter workers might make for buttressing security within shelters are thus quite different from the claims made by local residents, or even migrants themselves. Moreover, the state is not a monolithic entity; police, military, immigration officials and local politicians may have competing interests and visions of security. Thus, migrant shelters have become hotspots where the anxieties and politics around security come to the fore as multiple actors enact their own visions of moral duty, community protection and justice. As I discuss next, these anxieties, which manifest as discrimination and sometimes violence, are often expressed through highly gendered and racialized narratives of migrant "others."[11]

hay de todo: EVERYDAY DISCRIMINATION

Throughout my fieldwork, as has been noted, I documented considerable ambivalence displayed by Mexican residents with regard to Central American migrants—many people with whom I spoke were at once sympathetic to the plight of migrants, and dependent on them as consumers, but simultaneously fearful of their presence. Migrant men, particularly from El Salvador and Honduras are often associated with criminality, delinquency, and sexual predation. Meanwhile, Central American women are often associated with prostitution, since they make up a significant percentage of the workers in Mexico's prolific sex work industry, particularly in southern Mexico.[12] As Patty Kelly notes in her ethnography on sex workers in Chiapas, Central American women are not only more vulnerable to exploitation and anti-immigrant harassment, but are constructed as immoral and sexually deviant, sometimes by their Mexican co-workers.[13]

During interviews, migrants regularly commented on the discrimination and everyday anti-immigrant sentiment they encountered in Mexico. Edwin, a Honduran migrant who ended up settling near Huixtla, Chiapas, but who had lived for over a decade in the United States, told me: "The situation for Central Americans here in Mexico has become more difficult. There are fewer work opportunities, and they always denigrate us. We are labeled here . . . the majority suffer greatly on Mexican soil . . . there is more racism, just like in the times of the KKK." While Edwin's analogy might be a bit hyperbolic, it underscores the idea that racism and discrimination are bound up with other markers of difference like nationality.

Cindy, a woman from El Salvador whom I introduced in chapter 2, reflected on the discrimination she experienced trying to secure work in Mexico. When she arrived to Tapachula, Mexico, she said, because she was Salvadoran and did not have papers, "Me trataron de la patada" (They treated me like dirt). Her first job was washing cars, but she claimed the car wash owner eventually fired her because as the only woman working among men, she became a "distraction." She eventually found work as a seamstress with a woman in Tapachula who helped her get FM3 documents to live in Mexico. She explained the gendered dynamics at play with regard to Central American women:

> While it is true that some Central American women come to steal husbands away from Mexican women, we all have to pay for those. They think of us all as prostitutes, and yes there are prostitutes, and so I imagine that is why they don't want us. Where I worked, my co-worker hated me until the day I left. She was the daughter-in-law of the boss, and when I was making my food, she would come in and put soap in it.

From Cindy's perspective, gendered stereotypes about Salvadoran women as prostitutes were central to the discrimination she experienced. Sandra, a woman from Honduras mentioned in the Introduction to this book, who had been living in Oaxaca City trying to earn money to continue her journey, recounted her experience looking for work at the large outdoor market in Oaxaca, the Central de Abastos, which I walked through countless times on my way to the clinic. She traveled from stall to stall asking if anyone needed an extra hand. Eventually, she found a female stall owner who offered to hire her for the day. She sensed that Sandra was not local and asked her if she was from Chiapas. Sandra said no, and told her she was from Honduras. The stall owner then demanded to see a form of identification, but Sandra told her she did not have an ID. The woman then proceeded to accuse Sandra of being a liar and of being a prostitute. As we talked she told me that in Oaxaca women from Central America are often associated with prostitution because the strip clubs on the outskirts of the city are known for hiring them. She herself had been solicited several times to engage in sexual acts with men. I asked her if she had suffered any form of physical sexual abuse during her time in Mexico. She responded, "No, but the abuse and discrimination I have suffered is just as bad."

In addition to gendered anxieties around migrant women, I found that migrant men—both Central Americans and deported Mexicans, encountered discrimination in southern Mexico. Central American men, particularly young men from El Salvador, complained about being unfairly associated with street gangs like the Mara Salvatrucha, the very same gangs that they were often fleeing. Mexican deportees, especially those who had lived in the United States for many years, were also stigmatized. For example, at Casa Guadalupe I met Alfredo, a man in his late thirties, who was brought to the United States by his parents when he was just two years old and spent most of his life living in East Los Angeles. While proud of his Mexican roots, Alfredo barely spoke Spanish, and he described feeling like a "fish out of water" since being deported. He had gone to the shelter to find assistance in securing employment. Alfredo was convinced that his "*cholo*-style" appearance—he wore a white tank top and loose-fitting khaki pants, had a shaved head and visible tattoos—contributed to his inability to find employment in Oaxaca, because locals did not trust him.[14] He asked to borrow a long-sleeve shirt to cover some the prominent tattoos on his arms. In fact, Mauricio, the manager of Casa Guadalupe, initially refused to let him inside because he stereotyped him as a gang member.

Subtle forms of discrimination also circulate between migrants and locals and among migrants themselves. Central American migrants are not a homogeneous group who share an inherent sense of solidarity or unity. On the contrary, everyday tensions and forms of differentiation may come to the surface within the enclosed spaces of migrant shelters. For example, I remember one afternoon talking to several people from Guatemala who said they did not trust the other migrants in their room because they were from El Salvador, and people from El Salvador are drug addicts and *delincuentes* (delinquents/criminals). I registered complaints from migrants who felt they were being unfairly treated by the staff—not getting the freshest food or not having access to the best donated clothes—because they were from certain countries. While not the norm, at times the tensions between migrants were palpable. Here is part of an interview I conducted with a male migrant named Esteban from El Salvador:

WENDY: Is there a sense of friendship between Salvadorans, Hondurans, and Guatemalans?

ESTEBAN: Oh no, there are problems. The Guatemalans don't like us, and we don't like them. Look, those from Nicaragua, Salvador, and Honduras we stick together. But when we are in Guatemala, they rob us. They rob us. We do not get along with Guatemaltecos or Costa Ricans.

WENDY: Including migrants?

ESTEBAN: Migrants and non-migrants. It's like this, look, we [pointing to a female migrant] are united, for example if I have ten pesos and I buy food, and she is close to me, I will share with her. The Guatemalans, no. They are just out for themselves. Just for themselves. They are really selfish and don't know how to share. And Salvador, Nicaragua, and Honduras, yes, we three stick together.

WENDY: Interesting

ESTEBAN: The Guatemalans don't get along with us. Sometimes there is one that will, every once in a while. But no, they don't like us, and we don't like them either.

WENDY: And why is this? What is the history there?

ESTEBAN: I don't know. For my whole life, they haven't gotten along with us. Maybe it is an old thing, but El Salvador and Honduras had a military war and they still like us, but with Guatemalans, we have not had a war with them but they still don't like us. And we don't like them. But Nicaragua, Salvador, and Honduras, yes, we get along.

This interview excerpt demonstrates not only the stratification based on national origin that may exist among migrants, but also the ways these divisions are potentially embedded or at least rationalized by historical contexts. Discrimination against and sometimes between Central American migrants is a reality of the journey, but as one migrant put it, "En Mexico, hay de todo" (In Mexico, there's everything). Like anywhere and everywhere, *hay de todo*. There are those who help migrants and those who prey upon them.

But before dismissing discrimination as a natural condition of humankind or as evidence of Mexicans as just as discriminatory and anti-immigrant as U.S. citizens, it is important to understand the anxieties around immigrants both in a political economic context and in the context of everyday insecurity for Mexican residents. Scholars have documented the chronic insecurity, fear, and violence along the U.S.–Mexico border and in states with a deep history of involvement in the drug economy.[15] Along the arterial border, where the war against drugs and migrants is being fought simultaneously, transit zones are zones of insecurity and fear for migrants, but also for local residents. As examined in the next section, migrants become scapegoats in ways that perpetuate stereotypes that maintain social hierarchies, legitimize community policing, and consolidate political power and profit.

CONTESTED SHELTER: MIGRATION POLITICS AND SEXUAL VIOLENCE

I promised Doña Consuela that I would attend the inauguration. I met her several weeks earlier during one of the regional meetings for shelter workers organized by Movilidad Humana. She told me that she was helping to open a new shelter in her community located close to the state border between Oaxaca and Veracruz. She took out a piece of paper and jotted down a few notes for me to remember. There was no official flyer or brochure, just a date and time and her phone number on a piece of scrap paper. But when I arrived to the shelter the next month, accompanied by Padre Luis, Padre José, Araceli, and my husband, Nick, I was immediately impressed by the scene that unfolded before us. There were several large

Figure 12. Mothers watch their daughters perform at the celebratory opening of a new migrant shelter in Oaxaca. Photo by author.

white tents set up on the grassy area just in front of the shelter. The tops of the tents were decorated with colorful plastic buckets and *papel picado* (traditional paper cut-out) banners. We sat in the neatly lined up folding chairs and watched as a parade of local politicians and religious leaders came up to the podium to lead the crowd in prayers and speeches that touched on themes of inclusiveness and welcoming strangers. There were performances by girls dressed in traditional *traje* (regional dress) and many of the female residents also wore their elaborately embroidered Tehuana skirts and blouses, with their hair braided with long silky ribbons (fig. 12). When the speeches were over and the shelter was officially opened, groups of local residents moved through the crowd handing out plates of steaming homemade tamales from large aluminum pots and cups of *tejate*, a traditional, non-alcoholic drink made with maize and cacao. It was a rather jubilant affair and a feeling of solidarity permeated the air as the community both symbolically and formally welcomed migrants.

As we chatted with local residents and toured the rooms of the new shelter, Padre Luis whispered to me, "See, they are doing it right here. They are involving the community from the very beginning. You must have the support of the community. This is something we can learn from and work on so that as more migrants pass through, we do not have problems like the other shelters."

By this, Padre Luis was referring to tensions that had emerged around other migrant shelters, including Albergue Nazaret. Not unlike when I first arrived in Veracruz and heard the stories of the rape and the closing of the shelter, when I first arrived at Albergue Nazaret, I heard a remarkably similar story. In the early summer of 2008, a few months before my fieldwork began, there had been an alleged assault on a young girl in the community by an unauthorized Nicaraguan male. While the staff at Albergue Nazaret found no evidence that the man had ever passed through the shelter, and in fact argued that he was not a migrant, but rather a known smuggler in the community, local politicians used the incident as a way to incite fear and anger in the local community around the presence of the shelter. Padre José spoke of a phone call he had received, telling him that he needed to return to the shelter immediately, after an angry mob approached the gates threatening to burn the shelter down. According to news reports, close to fifty residents, armed with sticks and gasoline canisters, gathered together with municipal police agents wielding pistols and clubs at the front of the shelter. The mob shouted threats against Padre José and chants of "¡Que se vayan los migrantes! (The migrants have to go!)"

The shelter was not burned down, and Albergue Nazaret continued to operate, but the incident left a bad taste in the mouths of many residents. Padre José was adamant that corrupt politicians, who seemed to be linked to organized criminals, were behind it. After the incident, he enlisted local university students to survey neighborhood residents on their feelings about the shelter. It turned out that 90 percent of people were in favor of helping migrants, and 58 percent of residents reported feeling no threat from the presence of the shelter, or to their local opportunities, in light of the flow of migrants. He said that only small percentage of the people believed the shelter should be closed.

Because most of the people I came across were affiliated with the shelter, I did not get a good sense of wider public sentiment, though

I occasionally noted hesitation and skepticism in my encounters with local residents. For example, I spoke to a schoolteacher who said he "did not know who to believe" after seeing clips of interviews of both the victim's mother and Padre José on television. I interviewed several members of a family that lived about fifteen minutes away from Albergue Nazaret who conveyed their skepticism about the shelter and, by extension, Padre José. They did not like going near the shelter, and prohibited their children from going to the area near the shelter alone. Another resident I interviewed lamented the fact that her daughter had to pass close to the shelter and the railroad tracks every day on her way to school. She hoped the city would build a bridge across the tracks so that she did not have to worry about her children crossing tracks lined with migrants. Another family described their horror at several migrants having entered their elderly mother's home looking for food and provisions when she was alone there. They later built a new security fence around their home.

What I found interesting about these narratives was the way migrants were constructed primarily as threats to local women. Sexual violence— whether real or perceived—is central to anti-immigrant sentiments and anxieties, which are premised specifically on fears of migrant men as sexual predators whose presence directly threatens young local women. Throughout history, the threat of rape by dangerous men—whether they are immigrants or African Americans in the Jim Crow U.S. South—has been used to justify more militarized tactics—either by the state or by vigilante groups, or in the case of Albergue Nazaret, a mix of local state authorities and residents.

Indeed, rape discourses have a deeper history around the politics of immigration and border security that draw parallels to such dynamics along transit spaces in Mexico. In the United States in the 2000s, the border vigilante group known as the Minutemen strategically used the threat of rape and the alleged existence of "rape trees"—trees and bushes where the undergarments of migrant women are supposedly hung as trophies— to justify their actions. The idea of rape trees constructs migrant women as victims and migrant men as hypersexual criminals and smugglers who rape their own women and who can only be stopped through increased enforcement. Not only does such discourse make invisible the role of U.S. Border Patrol Agents as perpetrators of sexual violence, but it also masks the ways militarization creates the conditions under which women travel remote clandestine routes with smugglers in the first place.[16] As Amy Lind and Jill Williams argue, such discourse allows "the re-inscription of the US nation as a land of female chastity and safety in the face of foreign (in this case, Mexican) barbarism, while also invisibilizing the state's role in facilitating and carrying out violence against women."[17]

What is interesting in this case, however, is that the so-called rape trees—found at multiple points along the migrant route, and not just along the U.S.–Mexico border—are also used by humanitarian aid groups and migrants' rights activists to make visible the plight of Central American migrants and women in particular. As mentioned in chapter 2, the region known as La Arrocera is also rumored to be filled with rape trees, illustrating the brutalities suffered by Central American women in transit. The brutalizers, however, are not migrant men, but criminals and state officials, a crucial distinction. Rape trees have become an important symbol for politicians and activists across the political spectrum in their respective efforts to legitimize and criticize state securitization projects, while making their own claims for safety.

While I am not aware of any formal vigilante or self-defense groups, known in Mexico as *autodefensas,* specifically to protect residents from migrants and other outsiders, the angry mob that threatened to burn Albergue Nazaret down, like the angry crowd of neighbors that confronted the priest in Veracruz, demonstrate how residents participate in local protection strategies in contexts of perceived threats. In a third case documented by the Washington Office on Latin America (WOLA), a migrant shelter was shut down in a popular transit community on the outskirts of Mexico City, where it faced opposition, threats, and aggression by local residents who blamed the shelter for an increase in crime. The WOLA report includes a photograph of a banner that was strung across a central street stating: "The neighbors of the Colonia Lechería are united. If we catch you robbing or abusing the people, we will lynch you."[18] Lynching and other forms of community policing and vigilantism are on the rise in Mexico and other parts of Latin America.[19] The targets are typically people seen as outsiders—gang members, delinquents, and migrants. Daniel Goldstein, who contends that outsiders are often seen as potential robbers, molesters, or rapists in Bolivia, calls lynchings examples of "neoliberal violence." He states, "Having learned to depend entirely on their own devices for the realization of what they perceive to be their basic rights as citizens (including the right to 'citizen security'), these Bolivians look to their own resources—including violence, torture, and the administration of death—as their only recourse."[20] Indeed, the threat to lynch Central American migrants is eerily similar to the justifications used to lynch African American men by white supremacist groups in the United States and outsiders in other Latin American contexts.[21] While I have no evidence of local residents actually carrying out such vigilante violence, if Central American men are constructed and feared as sexual predators threatening local women, it is easier to make the case to close down shelters and justify more punitive security measures.

My point is not to defend the actions of Central American migrants or to deny the very real possibility that some of them may have been involved in sexual assault—indeed, I have documented numerous allegations of migrant men assaulting other migrants or coercing them into sex work— but the spinning of discourses that equate foreignness with sexual violence obscures the fact that gendered violence is not only produced and reproduced on a much larger scale, but also exacerbated within conditions of state militarization and impunity.

CRIMINALIZING HUMANITARIAN AID

As migrants and migrant shelters can be constructed as threats to community safety, migrants' rights defenders also become implicated in the local politics of security. Shelter workers are charged by authorities and residents with being enablers of crime, or criminals themselves. Under Mexican law, it is legal to provide humanitarian aid to unauthorized migrants as long as there is no cash remuneration. However, defining humanitarian aid has proven blurry and contested in several cases. Perhaps the most famous case was in 2005, when a local middle-aged woman affectionately known as Doña Concha was arrested in the state of Queretaro by the former Agencia Federal de Investigación (Federal Investigations Agency; AFI) after feeding six hungry migrants in her home. Doña Concha was charged with human trafficking and sentenced to six years in prison. She served thirty months in prison before being released after a human rights organization took up her case. Once she was released, Doña Concha continued to offer aid to migrants passing through her town. In a news interview, Doña Concha reported being saddened by the fact that the other residents in her town do not help migrants themselves; they do, however, still send them her way.[22]

The year after Doña Concha was imprisoned, Padre José was violently arrested and imprisoned near Albergue Nazaret after attempting to help a group of migrants locate their loved ones who had been kidnapped. According to Padre José, the local municipal police commander was behind the kidnapping. Before I met him I had seen the dramatic photographs of Padre José standing behind the bars of a jail cell surrounded by a group of migrant men. I would later see the video captured in secret by a local resident documenting the events leading up to his arrest. In the video you can see a group of male migrants exiting a house when a convoy of municipal police trucks arrives. The policemen, wearing white shirts and black pants and many of them holding pistols (something the Municipal Police commander would later deny, despite the evidence) swarm the migrants and throw them into the back of one of the vehicles. Padre José exits the house accompanied by several migrants who are trying to protect him. Next, a group of six agents violently pick him up and throw him into the back of a second truck. When I interviewed him about the incident, he spoke of the agents' brutality: "They insulted me, told me to shut up. They told me that my place was in the church and not here. The more I spoke, the more they beat me." The irony of such abusive treatment being meted out to a priest by officers driving trucks marked *Seguridad Pública* ("Public Security") could not be starker.

This would not be the last time Padre José was accused of illegally aiding migrants. Toward the end of my fieldwork, Padre José and Araceli were both formally accused of human trafficking in a charge submitted by the Oaxaca office of the Instituto Nacional de Migración (National Migration Institute; INM) to the state attorney general. Several migrants picked up by INM officers who had recently passed through both Albergue Nazaret and Casa Guadalupe had claimed under interrogation that they were not migrants, but in fact victims of human trafficking. It becomes very difficult to determine where such accusations originate—from the migrants themselves, from authorities, or even from local residents.

While the relationship between shelters and the state is often antago-
nistic, many shelters and international bodies continue to call on the state
to take a more active role in fulfilling promises of protection and security
for migrants in transit and shelter workers. Organizations like Amnesty
International have issued urgent action statements on behalf of shelters
and the individuals who have been threatened or targeted. In August
2012, the Inter-American Commission on Human Rights urged the
Mexican government to guarantee security in relation to one specific
migrant shelter. It released the following statement: "the work done by
defenders of the rights of migrants is of fundamental interest in the entire
region, because they protect the rights of persons from several countries
in the continent. The Commission reiterates that the acts of violence and
other attacks perpetrated against human rights defenders not only affect
the guarantees of any human being, but they also undermine the fundamental role that human rights defenders play in society and leave all those
for whom they fight defenseless." An interesting development is that
human rights defenders are here considered "a group in special situation
of risk."[23] Human rights thus need to be protected, not only for the most
marginalized and vulnerable populations of unauthorized migrants, but
also for the defenders of human rights themselves. Yet despite such
requests, Mexico has largely failed to protect the rights of shelter workers,
who have thus taken it upon themselves to implement their own forms of
securitization.

THE SECURITIZED SHELTER

The same summer that I traveled to Veracruz, I also traveled to the city of
Juchitán in the Isthmus of Tehuantepec. Culturally speaking, Juchitán is
often recognized for the strong presence of women in public spaces like the
central market and openly tolerant attitudes toward third gender peoples
called Muxes.[24] I was attending a traditional Zapotec wedding with the family of my friend Carlos's wife, who invited me to stay in their home for the
weekend. Because I was a guest, one of the daughters insisted that I sleep in
her bed while she slept in the hammock in the courtyard. The family took me
to the famous central market where the open arcade is filled with vendors

selling gold jewelry, brightly painted bowls, and iguanas, a regional delicacy. The morning of the wedding I awoke at dawn to the harrowing sound of a pig screeching as it was slaughtered just outside my window. The wedding was a glorious and colorful affair and gave me an opportunity to meet some of the local families in the area. Since I knew that the train passed through the region, I was curious to hear people's thoughts and impressions on Central American migration. People shared stories of seeing groups of migrants walking through their neighborhoods and bathing in the nearby Río de Los Perros, but mostly people seemed ambivalent about their increasing presence. Several people directed me to a nearby town where it has been rumored that a priest recently opened a shelter for migrants.

Accompanied by my friend Carlos, the next day I set off on an old painted school bus to the next town. We exited and quickly hailed a taxi. "You want to go where?" the driver asked. We told him that we heard there was a new shelter and wanted to visit it. "There is no shelter here, but there is a place near the tracks where migrants go." He made a U-turn and took us down the frontage road near the railroad tracks. Dust swirled around the cab as we passed rows of abandoned rail cars, graffiti, and trash on the ground. It was not far from the center of town, a distance that we could have easily walked, though we may have passed right by it. As the taxi driver described, there was not a formal shelter per se, no signage or doors, just an open dirt lot with a few makeshift structures.

I paid the driver and walked across the dirt lot. The first thing I saw was the open-air chapel, painted in bright Mexican pink. There was a hammock strung across the center and a person bundled inside like a cocoon. On the other side of the lot was a white plastic table with a few folding chairs and plastic stools around it. The table was set up underneath a tarp with frayed edges, tied together around four large tree branches, which functioned as stakes. A group of men noticed us and started gathering around the table. When we asked if the Padre was there, the guys said no, he was out of town. There were two young volunteers standing behind a concrete counter with plastic crates of vegetables and behind it a large *comal* (griddle). This was the kitchen. We chatted with them for awhile. They were students from Guadalajara and had traveled to the shelter as part of their university social service requirements. They told me that the priest whose name was Padre José let them stay in the house he rented.

We turned our attention back to the guys sitting around the plastic table. My friend Carlos was a smoker and took out his pack of Marlboro reds and matches, which he graciously offered to everyone. Several of the migrants accepted. Two of them lit theirs immediately, and one of them put his cigarette in his shirt pocket. Three of the men identified as Garifuna, the largest of Honduras's mixed-race African-Carib descendent communities.

As we sat around the table, on a whim I pulled out my Rand McNally map of Mexico. One of the young men—I distinctly remember him because he was wearing a purple Sacramento Kings basketball jersey— asked if they could look at the map. The group was excited and gathered around the map (fig. 13). This was well before people had smart phones or even before internet cafes had really become widespread. Since many of these guys had not seen a map of Mexico, this was the first time they were able to visually see the journey. I placed my finger on the map, "This is where we are now." "No way!" "Don't fuck with us!" said the guy wearing the Kings jersey. We all laughed. The moment captured a feeling that I would have over the course of my fieldwork, the simultaneous feeling of being both screwed over and overwhelmed with the magnitude of the journey, but also the feeling of solidarity that all these other people were also going through the same thing. It was what Victor Turner might call *communitas*—the sense of solidarity that people experience through the shared experience of liminality, in what might be characterized as a rite of passage for these young men.[25]

Once we had a good laugh around how short a distance they had actually traveled, the men took turns tracing their routes with their fingers. As they followed the highways and railways, they talked about where they came from, where they had encountered trouble and where they hoped to go next. The map was like a treasure chest, somehow connecting them to what were only abstractions of the possibilities ahead. This was my first trip to Albergue Nazaret.

Flash forward six years to 2013. It had been several years since the longest portion of my fieldwork had ended. I was in Oaxaca for a few weeks and Araceli and I decided to make a trip down to Albergue Nazaret. We arrived late at night by bus and were dropped off in the middle of town. Once again, we hailed a taxi and told the driver we'd like to go to the

Figure 13. Migrants discuss their travel strategies around a map during my first visit to Albergue Nazaret. Photo by author.

shelter. This time there were no questions asked. He knew exactly where it was and was not surprised to see outsiders going there. I was surprised when we pulled up to a building with no windows, just high walls capped with a swirl of barbed wire. Not only had the front entrance changed, but the structure had come to resemble a fortress. We sent Geovany, who was now the main coordinator of the shelter, a text so he knew we had arrived. We rang the bell and someone opened a tiny window in the security gate to confirm who we were. Geovany came over and we both give him a hug. We told him to go back to sleep, to get some rest before sunrise.

There were over a hundred people at the shelter that night, but all was still quiet. I paced across the upper patio near Padre José's room. He was out of town, as were his personal bodyguards, who now also lived at the shelter for his protection. The bodyguards were provided by the state after he filed a complaint against the Zetas in 2010. I could not help but think about the ways the security of the shelter and Padre José himself was ensured by the very forces that he openly denounced.

As the dark sky started to lighten, I heard the first sounds of morning. The metal of a bathroom door closing. A face being washed at the sink. I looked down, and there was movement. The early risers who needed to start boiling the water for coffee and the preparations for breakfast. Geovany emerged from his room still sleepy. As the shelter's coordinator, he oversaw all the shelter's the daily activities. Marco, the previous manager of the shelter, had left years ago. Indeed, different casts of characters had come and gone over the years, but Geovany, the young and sharp-minded migrant from Guatemala I met in late 2008, was still there. Half a decade ago we had been sitting together in an internet café desperately trying to retrieve important photographs that we had accidentally erased from the shelter's digital camera. At that time, he had only been there for three weeks. He had aspirations to go to college, maybe in the United States. But he stayed, moving from being Padre Jose's right-hand man to shelter coordinator and eventually one of the most prominent activists in the movement. The journey, this place that he had to bear to get to his destination was now his permanent reality. It became his home.

I looked down over the shelter through the wires of the fence. People were walking around now, and a migrant from Cuba was collecting and stacking the flat mattress pads into a pile. The workers at Casa Guadalupe had been gossiping about the influx of Cuban migrants passing through. There was a rumor that one of the volunteers was engaged to one of the men. I wondered if that was him.

I moved to the top of the stairs. At the bottom was a baby wearing nothing but a diaper. It looked as though she had just discovered the joys of climbing. She excitedly moved her way up. She would make it up a few steps, so proud of herself, while her parents laughed, picked her up, and put her back on the ground level. Then she would begin her ascent again. And on and on. Up and down. The kitchen was still the central meeting point. There were two families working in the kitchen preparing the morning meal. Steaming blue and green plastic bowls of black beans sprinkled with cheese lined the counter. Where was Mayra? Where was Wilson? Where were Sergio and the others I had met in this same kitchen years earlier?

In front of the *palapas* (palm-thatched open-sided structures) there was a bit of shade. A migrant in a wheelchair was resting on a couch with two women. He looked to be flirting with one of them. He was one of the people living at the shelter while awaiting his visa. This was the temporary home of a whole group of people. Since the law changed in 2011, the Mexican government had begun issuing humanitarian visas to migrants who had suffered extreme forms of violence on a more regular basis. In response, some shelters had become longer-term living spaces for migrants waiting. They became regular fixtures. You could tell who they were, because they often had jobs, like the Cuban guy who collected the mattresses from the ground in the morning. An older man tended the shelter's garden. A small plot of trees and plants surrounded by a small wire fence. That was where I had first interviewed Padre José.

There were other noticeable changes. There was a plaque displayed on the wall noting that the building had been built through a gift from the Vatican. There were new posters telling migrants that no weapons were allowed inside the shelter. The MSF clinic had been set up adjacent to the shelter, and migrants could easily walk over during afternoon drop-in hours. There was now a computer room, which was filled with people checking their Facebook pages. There was artwork around the room. I spotted a half-played game of checkers, blue water and white coke plastic bottle caps on painted squares. When people arrived, they were given tiny slips of paper to exchange for their meals. Things seemed orderly. There were more rules and procedures. The shelter was becoming more legible as an institution. Was this what progress looked like?

Some of the shelter workers were excited to show me the office and the footage from the security cameras that had recently been installed. "Security cameras?" I thought to myself. "And barbed wire fence?" The shelter looked more like a penitentiary than anything else. It had been seven years since my first trip, when I sat around the plastic table looking at maps with the group of Honduran migrants and my friend Carlos smoking cigarettes. Besides the chapel, which was still painted pink, the shelter was unrecognizable. The once open lot on the side of the railroad tracks had been completely fortified.

While there is something to be said about the contradictions of the securitized shelter, I am continually reminded of its necessity, of the very real fear and violence experienced by migrants and those who protect them. Since completing my fieldwork, I continue to receive a steady stream of news from the shelters through e-mail and social media, which has become a key way for defenders of migrants' rights' to disseminate information about missing persons and issue calls for action and solidarity. It has also become a means to document the violence that continues to threaten migrants' safety.

In 2011, a nineteen-year-old indigenous Mam man from Guatemala named Julio Fernando Cardona Agustín, set off to Mexico as part of the "Paso a Paso Hacia La Paz" (Step by Step toward Peace) caravan in search of his brother who had gone missing along the journey. Geovany had sent out a message with photos of Julio Fernando's body, a chilling sight, with eyes swollen shut, blood behind his head, and stitches zigzagging across his thin, bare chest. Julio was found near the railroad tracks in the La Lechería area on the outskirts of Mexico City, where the lynching banner mentioned earlier was hung. There were also photos of him alive, one a headshot, routinely taken at migrant shelters, and another on a bus holding a blue-and-white-striped Guatemalan flag. You could see that same youthful and kind face under the blood and swollen lips and cheeks.

There were several stories circulating about what happened to this young man. The local police claim he fell off the train, but his body had none of the signs of having fallen, and he was not in a zone where migrants typically board trains. Eyewitness accounts from other migrants claim that he was sleeping just outside the local migrant shelter when he was picked up by a police patrol. Some suggested that he was sold by the police to local thugs for four hundred pesos. During the night migrants heard him being beaten in the distance and from the autopsy, it appears that he died of blunt force trauma to the head. In the morning, his body was found near the railroad tracks. Two days after his body was found, sixty migrants staying at the migrant shelter where he was found marched in the streets demanding justice for their fallen brother. A few days after I received the initial email and photographs, I received an official press announcement signed by a number of organizations, shelters and individuals in Mexico demanding an end to the injustices migrants suffered at the hands of state and local actors. In their announcement, they specifically proclaimed the Mexican state's role in violence against migrants and shelter workers. In a climate where migrants are often blamed for violent conditions, they make the explicit point that migrants are not responsible for violence; rather, state and local authorities are culpable for failing to guarantee the security of local communities.

A few months later, I received another email from Geovany. This time, his message included five photos of the body of another male migrant found in the early morning close to Albergue Nazaret. From the photos it appears that the migrant was beaten to death with a large concrete brick, which was still saturated in blood. In his message, Geovany wrote:

> These lamentable acts prove to us that this continues to be a zone of insecurity for migrating people. And we are just one day away from receiving the caravan of mothers looking for their missing children. What are we going to say to these mothers? That their children continue to be murdered?

The discovery of dead migrants near migrant shelters is an unfortunate reminder that spaces of safety and refuge are also spaces of insecurity and violence along migrant routes. Migrant shelters, railroad tracks, and bus stations continue to be zones where people in transit are preyed upon. At the same time, these spaces have become ground zero for public political protest and activism, the theme I take up in more depth in the next chapter.

CLAIMING SAFETY

This chapter has chronicled the everyday and highly localized ways concerns for safety and security play out in transit communities. Migrants do not travel in a vacuum, but rather become deeply intertwined in the relations, economies, and social climates of the communities they pass through. The majority of these transit communities are also spaces of insecurity, located in poor rural areas or on the impoverished margins of cities. Within these communities, migrant shelters have emerged as epicenters where the politics of immigration are contested as local residents, shelter workers, and state actors make competing claims about safety, security, and human rights. Unlike refugee camps or detention centers, where foreign others are physically contained within the walls of their institutions, the barriers between migrant shelters and local communities are fluid. Central American migrants are highly visible, and local residents continually grapple with their everyday presence, often in contradictory ways. The cycle of violence-immigration-security that emerges in spaces of transit is both concretely and discursively reproduced within larger conditions of insecurity and violence. National security does not equal human security, which does not equal community safety. On the contrary, securitization begets insecurity, which is constantly being challenged by a range of actors at the local level who have their own visions of security and safety.[26] In Mexico, the lines between security as a state project blur into ideas around citizen security as a project of community action. This blurring is especially heightened in the context of Mexico's drug war, where migrants and residents alike live with chronic fear, insecurity, and violence perpetrated by both the state and by organized criminal groups. The push for public safety by governments are often attempts to "flex their muscles" over targets they can easily overpower in order to assert their sovereignty.[27] But for local communities, demands for community safety also represent attempts to regain control of situations that seem uncontrollable. In this way, we might even conceptualize them as forms of resistance in the chaos and uncertainty of everyday life.

My goal is not to undermine the vital work of migrant shelters or to minimize the concerns felt by transit communities, but rather to understand how the larger landscape of violence shapes migration and complicates the meanings of security and safety in local spaces. Structural conditions such as militarization, corruption, and the lack of state-supported resources and policies create strains and pressures on migrant shelters and local communities. In turn, these forces create the conditions for existing and new types of inequality and marginality to be (re)produced in local spaces and social relations, creating new insecurities, not only for migrants in transit, but also for the communities they pass through and the people who dedicate their lives to serving migrants. This offers an important perspective on the anthropology of migration, which almost exclusively focuses on the experiences of migrants themselves and less so on the reverberating effects migration may have on other populations. In these ways, violence—and security—travel both vertically and horizontally across social groups.

7 Constellations of Care and Justice

Every day throngs of Mexican and international tourists venture into the lush jungle in the northeastern corner of Chiapas state to visit the spectacular Mayan ruins of Palenque. The town of Palenque bustles with internet cafes and restaurants catering to the constant flow of youthful backpackers and tour buses that fill up the hotels and resorts that line the road to the ruins. It is known for its bohemian scene where you'll find travelers selling handmade jewelry and whispers of "magic mushrooms." Yet just a few kilometers away there is another type of high-intensity movement of foreigners passing through the area. Palenque is not only home to one of the most impressive archaeological sites in Mexico, but located on a major Central American migrant route north.

After Hurricane Stan washed out the train line between Tapachula and Arriaga in 2005, the difficulty and danger of using that route increased. People sought alternative routes, including paths that took them through the Petén jungle. It was considered easier to cross the border here, especially since the trains on it were running. Of course, as the route became more popular with migrants, it was not long before the migration economy took hold in the region. In 2009, I started to hear increasingly from migrants that the area around Tenosique, located near the border with

Guatemala in the state of Tabasco, was now one of the most dangerous locations.

In early 2009, I took a trip to the region accompanied by my husband, Nick, who had joined me for several months in the field. Araceli had recently met a woman named Doña Alicia who was helping to set up a new shelter and gave me her phone number. After traveling on an overnight bus from Albergue Nazaret in the Isthmus of Tehuantepec, Nick and I reached Palenque in the morning. We checked into a hotel and then ventured to a pay phone to call Doña Alicia to see if she might have some time to meet with us that week.

"Where are you right now?" she asked.

"In the center of town."

"Where?"

"Near the Panadería Estrella."

"Okay, I'll be there in fifteen minutes," she said before abruptly hanging up.

Sure enough, fifteen minutes later, a pickup truck pulled up in front of the Estrella bakery. In the driver's seat was a hefty middle-aged man with a mustache. Next to him was a middle-aged woman with short hair wearing a colorful *huipil* and red skirt. In the back was a girl who looked to be about twelve. She was the couple's youngest daughter. Doña Alicia invited me to sit in the cab closely nestled between her and her husband and Nick jumped into the back with their daughter. This was the first time I met Doña Alicia, but she was warm and friendly, and our conversation flowed naturally.

We drove away from the city center toward the *colonia* where the shelter was located. Doña Alicia gave me the details on the history of the shelter and her involvement. While her husband greeted me when I entered the vehicle, he was noticeably silent during our conversation on the drive. Doña Alicia must have also noted the uncomfortable silence because as soon as we got out of the truck, she explained that her husband did not approve of her involvement with the shelter. "He doesn't know why I do this. He doesn't trust the migrants. He thinks they are criminals. But he knows that he can't stop me."

The shelter was just a few kilometers from Palenque. On both sides of the railroad tracks that run straight through the *colonia* in which it is located, there are small homes and storefronts. As we walked toward the shelter, locals stood in their doorways looking out onto the train yard and old abandoned railcars. Small groups of migrants sat on the ground in the shade of the train cars, resting between them. Doña Alicia mentioned to me that many residents were still wary of the migrants, and migrants tended to keep to themselves, out of sight if possible.

As we walked down the tracks, Doña Alicia told me of her involvement with the shelter and with helping migrants. In response to the more visible presence of migrants passing through the town, a group of women from her church decided to start bringing food down to the tracks. They started off on an informal basis, slowly increasing their interactions with these outsiders. This relatively simple practice started to have a big impact on her. "I would lie awake at night thinking about them. About the people I met down there. I couldn't sleep knowing that they were out there hungry." She explained that the migrants used to hide at the end of the tracks, where they hoped to remain undetected by police and residents. "It was tiring, always walking up and down, especially in the summer. It is cool now, but you wouldn't believe the humidity in the summer." Dona Alicia told me about one day that they were walking the tracks and they heard about two migrants who were injured. They spent the day searching for them, and it occurred to them that instead of searching out the migrants, they should have a central space where migrants could more easily find refuge.

Our first stop was an empty lot, overgrown with weeds, a few streets behind the tracks. She explained that this was the land where they planned to build the permanent shelter. For now they were operating out of a temporary space and small shack located directly on the railroad tracks, which was just a short distance away. Behind a chain-link fence, there was a dirt lot, on the far side of which was a small, dilapidated white wooden structure with a black laminate roof. You could literally see through the walls in several places. Twelve migrants—eight men and four women—were sitting on small logs and concrete stones in the front yard. One woman stood out to me because of how visibly scared she looked sitting, almost cowering in the corner next to a male migrant. Later in the day, when we sat to chat with the migrants, she was the only person who did not say anything.

The inside of the shelter was basic: in the main room, there was a metal stove, a few tables with non-matching dishes, some wooden chairs, and an altar with the Virgin of Guadalupe. The back wall of the shelter was plastered with newspaper that served as wallpaper. A cardboard box contained some medical supplies and a calendar that listed the names of the various church groups that would be donating meals on each day of that month. We walked to the back of the house, where there was a *bomba* (water storage tank) and two pit toilets, covered with pieces of ripped cardboard as lids. Even though it was mid-morning, we passed by another small room where migrants slept on the ground. Doña Alicia explained that while they didn't have the capacity to house migrants overnight yet, they allowed them to get a few hours of sleep in the shelter during the day. Doña Alicia introduced us to Don Mario, a small, older man in his sixties, who was from the neighborhood and watched over the shelter. Don Mario was paid a small stipend to oversee the house and take care of what needed to be done.

While most people immediately around the land seemed to be accepting of the general idea of the shelter, the neighbors most commonly expressed indifference or annoyance with migrants. She gave me a few examples of people telling the migrants to move away from their homes. There had also been an incident where a local resident had swindled a migrant who needed assistance cashing a money order. To prevent such incidents, Don Mario had begun to cash all money orders for migrants.

Doña Alicia and her daughter led me through the narrow rows between old abandoned train cars where small groups of migrants huddled together (fig. 14). Far from treating these men and women as dangerous criminals or undesirables, Alicia marched up to each group to ask them how they were doing and if they were hungry. Many of the migrants seemed taken aback by her forward attitude and how she extended her hand to personally greet each person. In those moments, the very simple act of handshake was a radical act of compassion and connection.

Most of the migrants we spoke to indicated they were in fact hungry, and Doña Alicia told them about the shelter. When we returned later that day, several of the people we met were dutifully lined up out the door to the tiny kitchen in the wooden shack. We stayed and chatted with them. One of the migrants who had been at the shelter for several days explained to us that there was a great level of tension at the moment. Several days earlier there had been a violent kidnapping involving Los Zetas a bit further down

Figure 14. Doña Alicia walks the tracks to invite migrants to a meal at the shelter in Palenque. Photo by author.

the tracks. He told us he was sure that there were Zetas around the tracks now hidden in plain sight among the migrants. "Not just Mexicans," he said, "but Zetas from Central America" as well. He said that it was hard to trust anyone, because they never knew who might be involved. Several of the men we interviewed had already decided not to continue on, but rather to return to their homes in Honduras and Guatemala.

Later in the afternoon, three migrants dressed in worn and soiled clothing arrived to the shelter. They were visibly famished. Doña Alicia stopped what she was doing and graciously invited them inside and told them to sit down while she scooped out heaping bowls of hot beans for them (fig 15). The men were grateful. There was no table in the room where they sat, but they held their bowls in their laps and ate in silence with a large picture of the Virgin of Guadalupe overlooking them in the background. One man's face was red and bloated—he had a terrible rash all over his cheeks and neck. I accompanied Doña Alicia to buy him some antihistamines at the

Figure 15. A typical meal of black beans and *queso fresco* served at Albergue Nazaret. Photo by author.

neighborhood pharmacy. I offered to buy the meds for him that day, but I knew that if I hadn't been there, Doña Alicia would have paid out of her own pocket. She told me she regularly dipped into her own funds to help out at the shelter. As we walked back along the tracks to deliver the medication, she told me about how things were changing in the town with regard to migration and violence. They constantly received reports of violence in nearby areas, like the kidnapping story told to us earlier that day. On several occasions, the shelter has been forced to close its doors to migrants as a safety precaution, though Doña Alicia greatly lamented this. I told her what I had seen in Veracruz and some of the other violence-related tensions that I had documented in my research. She gave me a sideways glance:

"You are only studying the violence?" she asked.

"Well, yes," I responded.

"But, Wendy, you cannot understand violence without also understanding hope. They are two sides of the same thing. You have to see what we are doing here. . . . We work on the tracks with tears in our eyes, but also with hope in our hearts."

In that moment and with those words, Doña Alicia challenged me to reconceptualize not only the ways I was thinking about violence, but also the ways I was thinking about migrant care, intimacy, and activism. Violence not only produced suffering but also sparked new forms of solidarity and gendered care relationships at the local level. Throughout my fieldwork I was inspired by local women like Doña Alicia who dedicated their days to caring for migrants in need. The most public figures in Mexico's migrants' rights movement, those who are the founders and coordinators of migrant shelters, are primarily men, often priests. Their work is often described through discourses of leadership and courage in their work defending migrants' rights—and rightly so. The work and dedication of people like Padre José has been absolutely critical to the movement. But theirs is not the only work that goes on. On the contrary, much of the everyday labor performed in shelters and during activist events is done by women, often middle-aged mothers and grandmothers. This work—which includes cooking, cleaning, childcare, domestic tasks, and caring for the sick—is often associated with "women's work" that typically takes place in the private realms of households. Yet what does it mean that these women are caring for complete strangers, and strangers often constructed as dangerous "others" in spaces that are both highly contested and often outside their own domestic spheres?

To begin to answer this question, I look to feminist scholarship that includes work on transnational circulations of care, intimate labor, and "motherist" activism in Latin America.[1] While the focus on transnational care typically looks at parent and grandparent relations and care practices in sending and receiving communities, I ask if women like Doña Alicia who spend their days caring for migrants in spaces of transit are not also nodes within larger constellations of care. Through their participation in formal and informal acts of care and activism, they become crucial to the lived experiences of migrants and thus to the wider processes associated with transnational migration. In this chapter I link the everyday intimate labors of local women quietly assisting migrants in transit to a more formal and public movement of Central American mothers who make an annual trek across Mexico to search for their children who have gone missing on their journeys north and raise awareness of the plight of Central Americans in Mexico.

In doing so, I consider the plurality of care and activist practices as they relate to gendered ideals of motherhood within spaces of transit. While many make claims about their participation through a lens of motherhood, I argue that women's care cannot be reduced to their motherly instincts, their natural role as nurturers, or even a simple sense of morality. Gender and motherhood become the foundation for work that is implicitly and explicitly political and often transgresses social boundaries within local communities. By connecting the labor of mothers and families in Central America and Mexico, we see how they are interconnected, not only within transnational economies of migration and violence, but also within transnational constellations of care and social justice. While some of these women are quite literally crossing borders and others stay "in place," they are all contemporary expressions of transnational feminisms and the "global intimate."

All in all, this chapter offers "counterstories" of women actively working to resist larger structures of inequality.[2] Women are not simply victims of violence, as is often emphasized about Central American migrant women, nor are they simply victims of the global economy whose families are torn apart. Rather, we must see women as participants in their own struggles for family survival, but also in larger struggles for migrant and human rights and justice. Although women remain embedded in gendered hierarchies and inequalities, they act within these webs of social relations as forces of resistance.

CARAVAN OF HOPE: THE MOTHERS OF THE MISSING

There was an excitement in the air as we gathered in the plaza awaiting the arrival of the caravan. High school students in plaid uniforms gathered around their teacher and his guitar, periodically checking to see if the bus was coming down the road. Two young men held a large hand-painted banner reading "Welcome Our Salvadoran Brothers and Sisters" (fig. 16).

Near them, an elderly couple held up a banner that simply asked, "Donde Están?" (Where Are They?). Next to them stood Sonia and Paty, two women from the local community near Albergue Nazaret who

Figure 16. Local residents gather to welcome a caravan of mothers and other relatives of missing migrants in Oaxaca. Photo by author.

regularly helped out at the shelter. During my first visits to Albergue Nazaret I stayed in both of their homes, where they fed me *tlayudas* (a Oaxacan specialty street snack) and quesadillas in the late-night hours after I returned from the shelter. I was excited to see them and Paty made sure I knew about the *comida* at her house that afternoon after the march. I assured her I would be there.

As I chatted with Sonia and Paty, a chartered bus pulled up to the curb where Padre José stood, dressed all in white, as usual, with a handcrafted wooden cross around his neck. The door of the bus opened, and a tiny gray-haired woman stepped off, to the sound of gentle applause from the crowd. As each person descended from the bus, Padre José gave them a long, warm embrace. Nearby, the high school teacher strummed his guitar, while the students sang a song to welcome the visitors. Local journalists carrying voice recorders and cameramen were there to document this historic encounter—this was the first caravan of Central American mothers and family members of missing migrants traveling the migrant route in Mexico.

Inspired by this inaugural caravan in 2009, activists continue to make an annual pilgrimage through Mexico to raise awareness of the brutalities of the migrant journey by physically retracing the steps of their missing loved ones. The caravan stops at key sites along the journey, where families and activists come together to speak out publicly about violence and impunity in Mexico. During these caravans, mothers and family members also literally search for clues and seek information that will perhaps tell them what happened to their children. The caravans are coordinated by grassroots organizations based in Central America and Mexico. This particular caravan had been organized in conjunction with the Comité de Familiares de Migrantes Fallecidos y Desaparecidos de El Salvador (COFAMIDE; the Salvadoran Committee of Relatives of Killed or Disappeared Migrants).

As the women and family members gathered together in the plaza, they grasped large poster boards with pictures of their missing loved ones. Underneath the photographs the full names of each person were printed in large black font on bright white printer paper. Above the photographs were the words *Desaparecido/a* (Missing) or *Fallecido/a* (Deceased) and below the names were the dates on which their families had last had contact with the disappeared (fig. 17). The posters were larger versions of the missing persons signs I had seen on my first trip to Mexico's southern border. But while those images could be easily ignored or viewed with a measure of detachment, at that moment it was hard to look away. The people in these photographs and those who loved them were not anonymous.

After a few opening remarks by Padre José, the large crowd began to march through the city streets, carrying banners and the posters of the missing. As we walked, I noticed a green military truck with soldiers pass in our wake, once again a reminder of the state's shadowy presence. One of the mothers had printed out a stack of photocopies with a picture of her missing son, details about his disappearance, and her contact information on it, which she handed out to the visibly uncomfortable shopkeepers and residents watching the scene from their doorways. She handed me a flyer,

Figure 17. A caravan of mothers and other relatives of missing migrants arrives at Albergue Nazaret. Photo by author.

saying, "I am looking for my son. Have you seen him?" During a caravan in November 2011, one mother was actually able to locate her son who had been imprisoned in Chiapas for the past seven years. Over the years, several stories of location and reunion have come out of the caravan, keeping hope alive for many.

As we walked through the streets I met and accompanied several family members. I met Beny, whose brother had gone missing ten years ago during his trek across Mexico. He suspected that his brother had disappeared while crossing the U.S.–Mexico border, but he could not be sure. Beny works in a laundromat and once had aspirations of migrating to the United States himself. But after his brother's disappearance and the death of his father, he was the only one left to care for his mother, who he simply described as *triste*—sad. When he was not working, Beny spent his free time with his mother or looking for clues of what happened to his brother. It was only in the past year that he had learned about the work being done by COFAMIDE. This was his first time participating in such a public demonstration.

I also met Teodora, whose daughter had gone missing two years earlier. Teodora was in her fifties. Five years ago her daughter had left El Salvador to work in Los Angeles, leaving Teodora to care for her two young grandchildren. In the early years, her daughter had called home every few weeks to check in on the family and her kids. She started living with a man in Los Angeles, and while Teodora had never met him, she trusted her daughter's judgment and assumed that he was taking care of her. But not long after they moved in together, her daughter's phone calls stopped. She had had no indication that her daughter was in any danger or what might have happened. All she had was silence. Teodora wanted there to be some type of investigation into the man her daughter lived with to see what happened, but struggled to make any progress with the U.S. justice system from El Salvador. Teodora spoke, not only about her anguish as a mother not knowing what had happened to her child (something stressed by many of the mothers participating in the caravan), but also about the hurt inflicted on her grandchildren, grappling with their mother's disappearance. What Pauline Boss calls "ambiguous loss"—the anguish and uncertainty experienced when a loved one goes missing—is not just felt by mothers; it spans the generations.[3]

As we neared Albergue Nazaret, we crossed the tracks, and I could see on the horizon a group of migrants staying at the shelter who had come out for the final stretch of the march to walk in solidarity with the families. In front of me was a migrant with one leg moving slowly as he carefully pressed his crutches into the dusty trail beside the very same railroad tracks where he had lost his leg. A migrant woman from El Salvador whom I had met earlier stood at the front gate as the caravan entered. I recognized her by the high heels she was wearing, but her face was different—her eyes were red and puffy and her cheeks were flushed and shiny. Tears streamed down her face as she clapped welcoming the mothers to the shelter. She too was a mother from El Salvador; she too was separated from her children.

Once at the shelter, the family members took seats upon a temporary stage that had been erected in the chapel. The women lined their posters side by side in front of them, looking out into the audience. And then they told us their stories. One by one the women took the microphone and told their stories of motherhood, loss, and pain. Some made concrete demands like the need for the Mexican state to create a DNA database to document the remains of unidentified bodies and family members of the missing. Others spoke more abstractly about their suffering. As one mother spoke her voice became louder and her tone more intense. She told the story of her son who had gone missing during his crossing. She lamented the uncertainty she felt when his phone calls stopped coming. She then began to speak, to no one and to everyone, of the importance of keeping in contact with your family members. The migrants hanging out in the back of the shelter silently watched her, perhaps thinking of their own parents and families. The pay phone was just steps away. Finally, one of the last of the mothers took the microphone, but she was so overcome with emotion she could not speak. As she struggled to push the words out of her mouth the other mothers on stage openly wept. We all wept.

As these mothers retraced the movements of their missing children, they expressed in spatial terms the rippling effects of clandestine migration on individuals, families, and community. Their testimonies hinted at the collective suffering in households throughout Central America and the chronic uncertainty that accompanies disappearance. They wanted to witness this journey and to know the landscapes where their children, and thousands of others like them, have disappeared—some years and others decades ago.

Yet they also highlighted a certain defiance and political prowess in drawing connections between individual loss and the structural inequalities within which they lived. As Judith Butler has argued, "assembly is also a way of making a demand with the body, a corporeal claim to public space and a public demand to political powers."[4] Caravans for justice, where activists journey across relevant spaces in search of justice, protection, and solidarity, have emerged in contexts worldwide.[5] Latin American women have a strong historical tradition of drawing on their roles as mothers and caregivers to make strategic alliances in various political movements. Examples of such women's activism include most famously the Asociación Madres de Plaza de Mayo who protested against their disappeared children in Argentina's dirty war (1976–1983), the Committee of Mothers and Relatives of the Political Prisoners, Disappeared, and

Assassinated of El Salvador "Monseñor Romero" (CO-MADRES) who protested their missing family members in El Salvador's civil war and the mothers of female factory workers killed in Ciudad Juarez.[6] As Laura Briggs documents in her analysis of feminist organizations that challenge transnational adoptions, organizations of families of missing children in Latin America have emerged as some of the most important groups in demanding legal accountability for war crimes.[7] More recently, there has been a growing surge of motherist movements in Mexico as the families of people killed or disappeared in Mexico's decade-long war on drugs demand justice for their loved ones. These organizations demonstrate the ways in which motherhood becomes a powerful vehicle to make political claims that challenge the state and its role in the reproduction of violence and disappearance.[8]

A central thread of the discourse within the movement is the call for an end to impunity—that is to say, an end to the ability of both state and non-state actors to systematically disappear and murder migrants without accountability. Linda Green argues that impunity is more than a legal process; it is also "a social process that is enabled in part by a characteristic mixture of silence and memory among its victims and historical amnesia and widespread indifference on the part of the dominant society."[9] Building on this definition, we can begin to locate sites of resistance to violence and to impunity in the work of social memory and public collective struggle. In making their own histories known, these women refuse to let their children be forgotten. Furthermore, while the women who are on the front lines of these movements for migrants' rights are suffering, they are neither suffering alone nor in private. Rather, they are making their suffering highly visible, through the media, in public marches, events, and their annual caravan, not only to compel people to see what they have gone through, as women and family members who have lost a loved one, but to raise awareness about the structural and state conditions that contribute to violence against migrants and the suffering of mothers and families across national frontiers. Caravans for justice are bringing international visibility to human rights violations in Mexico and publicly challenging the state to act and end the many forms of systemic impunity. They also show that violence is not only a destructive social force, but can also be the basis for collective struggle and transnational solidarity.

As I looked around at the audience toward the end of the mothers' speeches, I noticed that Paty and Sonia were no longer there. On that day they were not just spectators or casual participants; they had work to do. Geovany, the coordinator at Albergue Nazaret, asked if I wanted a ride to Paty's house for the *comida*. When we arrived, Paty, Sonia, and several other women I recognized from the shelter were busy in the kitchen. Sonia had just taken a large pan of chicken cooked in mustard sauce off the stove, Paty was heating tortillas on a hot griddle, and someone else was scooping portions of spaghetti onto plates. The scene reminded me of the busy chaos of a kitchen on Thanksgiving or Christmas Eve.

I tried to help, but Sonia pushed me to go outside and sit with the other guests at the long tables that had been set up. The women came out carrying plates loaded with food and served them to the guests. There were pitchers of *agua fresca* (fresh fruit drink) on the table, no doubt also homemade. I was seated between an activist from Mexico City and the Salvadoran consul in Tapachula. These were people who were often asked to give their expert opinions for news stories and in many ways represented the public face of the movement. And while it was truly an honor to be sitting there among them, I also thought about Paty and Sonia and the others in the kitchen, whose labor was less visible, but no less important to the movement. Paty's modest backyard patio was a tiny microcosm that linked together multiple nodes in this transnational constellation of care.

THE GRANDMOTHERS OF THE ISTHMUS

The last time I saw Sonia and Paty and the other women from Albergue Nazaret was during my final month of fieldwork. I had recently learned I was pregnant and shared the news with Padre José, who was thrilled. It was an unusually quiet day at the shelter. The train had recently departed and only a few migrants were still there. As we sat at the table in the kitchen he spoke to me about the important role and amazing gift of motherhood that he had witnessed throughout his long career. That day he was going to minister to men in the local prison and offered to drop me off in the next town over at the home of the family where I was staying. I took him up on the offer, and he said that first we just had to pick up a few people who would be accompanying him to the prison. We drove through the modest streets of town, away from the tracks and into the residential neighborhoods that surrounded the shelter. One by one, Padre José traveled to the homes of the women who had so kindly invited me into their homes during that year and they hopped into his small SUV. The last stop was Marta's house, where everyone got out of the car. Marta was ready with two long bags of Styrofoam cups for coffee and a sack filled with snacks. Padre José took these from her. Then he went inside the house and quietly blessed a newborn baby sleeping in a hammock. The women remained in the courtyard, excited to see one another and catch up on the week's happenings and gossip. This was their community. Since I knew that this would be the last time I would see them for a while, I asked if I could take a photograph. "What a great idea!" someone exclaimed.

Everyone lined up in front of the clotheslines strung across the courtyard. Padre José was in the middle, with his arms gently embracing the smiling women around him in their floral skirts and sandals. We joked while I was taking the photograph: "Padre José and the grandmothers of the Isthmus!" You would never guess it from the photograph and they would probably laugh if I ever told them this, but to me, these women were part of the central core of the migrants' rights movement. To this day the picture remains one of my favorites and it brings a smile to my face to remember the extraordinary ordinary women who made it their life's work to serve migrants. This, I think, is what Doña Alicia wanted me to see.

Maria

Every week, Maria, a tiny woman with stick straight gray hair usually dressed in a long, flowing skirt, arrived to Casa Guadalupe with her Bible in hand. She almost always wore white, with a prominent silver cross hung around her neck, and it was rare to see her without a smile on her face. Maria was one of about a dozen local residents who served as *socios*, board members of Casa Guadalupe during my time there. Like many of the others, she intimately understood the challenges faced by migrants and immigrants. Having lived in the United States for many years, Maria knew what it was like to live in the shadows of society as an immigrant. Indeed, she credited her own experience in describing her motivation to work at Casa Guadalupe. As a grandmother in her late sixties, she had returned to her native Oaxaca, where she lived in an apartment on the outskirts of the city above an internet café run by one of her sons. She used to offer migrants staying in the shelter work cleaning her house and doing odd jobs, but she had stopped offering after a migrant stole two cell phones from her home. Even so, she still devoted time to come to the shelter each week to lead a prayer group. She always invited the staff and migrants to participate. One afternoon she asked me to join her and a group of about six migrants from El Salvador and Honduras in the living room. She opened her palms and asked everyone to join hands. We stood in a small and intimate circle, everyone holding hands and eyes closed. Maria led the group in a prayer:

> Señor danos un corazón acogedor. Ayudanos a ser compañeros de los que sufren, de los que caminan; que nos ayudanos todos. / Lord, give us a welcoming heart. Help us to be companions of those who suffer, of those who walk, so that we can help everyone.
>
> Que nuestras vidas se gastes por nuestros seres queridos, trabajando y sirviendo a los más necesitados. / That our lives will be spent on our loved ones, working and serving those in need.
>
> Que los que sufrimos y los que caminamos en la tierra encontremos albergue en otros. / That those of us who suffer and those of us who walk on the land will find shelter in others.
>
> Señor, vuelve a nacer, día a día, en los corazones de nosotros, haznos mas humanos. / Lord, continue to be born, day after day, in our hearts, to make us more human.

I am not a particularly spiritual person and not well versed in the prayers that were being recited, but I found the experience to be quite profound, as did the migrants in our circle. Moments of prayer, mass, and religiosity often seemed to take on an extra meaning for migrants in transit. Migrant shelters are spaces where people are not only physically nourished but mentally and spiritually as well. But beyond the content of the prayer, it was the actual act of praying together that moved me. Here we were, people from four different countries, mostly strangers to one another, but for a few moments, intimately connected in this space through these words. It struck me that the very simple gesture of holding hands alongside migrants, like Doña Alicia's handshakes with migrants on the railroad tracks, these moments of physical connection, were powerful acts of solidarity and humanity. This was particularly true in a social context where migrants are deemed as people to fear. Maria's weekly routine, while certainly motivated by her religious faith and conviction, transgressed social boundaries in ways that I found to be extraordinary and radical. I came to see the weekly visits by Maria as one example of the everyday and often invisible forms of care and solidarity at migrant shelters.

Mayra

In addition to the work of local women, I also documented solidarity that formed between local women and migrant women, who also contributed to the everyday care at shelters. In chapter 4, I introduced Mayra, the Guatemalan mother of three who lost her foot in a train accident and was working in the kitchen at Albergue Nazaret. Several months after I met her, she traveled to Casa Guadalupe with another group of migrants. Away from her usual hustle and bustle at Albergue Nazaret, I had the opportunity to learn more about her personal trajectory from migrant to shelter worker. This is an excerpt from my interview with her:

> Sometimes you feel bad, remembering all the bad things that happen[ed] to you on the road, all the things that continue to happen, and for women it is more difficult, and even more if she has children, she just wants her family to do well financially, to see her family happy. This is part of the problem, when you can't make them happy, when you realize you are not the solution. Women suffer more than anyone, seeing the needs of her children, her siblings, her own mother. And then, on the journey, women continue to suffer things. Thank God I did not suffer this, but I have met many women who have been raped. And not just women, but men too. At the shelter, I've spoken to men who have been raped, and they arrive really traumatized, and they can't get it out of their head, they can't forget what has happened. But thank God, I have had the strength to share what I can with them, to be able to listen and talk to them and to help them. Now I never complain, I never ask, "Why me?" I think of what God suffered to save us. Now my purpose is to help others.

This excerpt captures many of the central threads of life on the journey— the desire to provide for one's family, the gendered dimensions of risk, suffering, and sexual violence that migrants experience, and the ways people reconcile pain. For Mayra, the tragic loss of her foot—her confrontation with her own mortality and limits—became a pivotal turning point in her life. Rather than framing her injury and the deferment of her American Dream as failure, Mayra found new meaning and purpose in the midst of her journey through caring for others. Mayra's care took the form of cooking, but also listening and talking to migrants who have suffered extreme violence. Throughout the journey there are seldom safe places for people to express themselves emotionally and grapple with both the extraordinary traumas they have suffered and the more ordinary, but not necessarily less painful, trauma of family separation. Beyond serving the most basic needs of food, sleep, and medical attention, migrant shelter workers like Mayra play a crucial role in supporting the mental health of migrants in transit. What I found particularly interesting in Mayra's statement was the way she used motherhood as paramount in describing the specific form of suffering that women endure. Such gendered discourses were often used to explain the work of women along the journey.

THE HEART OF A MOTHER: GENDERED LABOR AND THE MEANINGS OF MOTHERHOOD

As I have shown in this chapter, much of the everyday labor at shelters and activist events is performed by women. When I spoke to migrants and shelter workers about the presence of women volunteers at shelters, they often attributed it to women's and especially mothers' natural tendency to care for others, reifying rather essentialist notions of gendered labor. For example, Sergio, the migrant who witnessed the November 5 kidnapping, who was introduced in chapter 3, interpreted women's participation by saying that it was "because they have children, and they know that migrants follow the same path as their own children. That is why mothers are more inclined to help than men. They are motivated by their maternal instinct." Padre Luis used a very similar rationale while discussing the involvement of women:

> I was so impressed seeing the work of those women and how capable they are. They are more sensitive [than men] to the needs of migrants and are willing to take risks no matter the circumstances. And why? It is because

they have the heart of a mother. Not just of a woman, but of a mother, and so they understand the suffering of a child, and this is the reason that the majority of women are more sensitive to the realities of migration.

While valued, "women's work" in the shelters is still very much connected to ideals of traditional femininity and motherhood. Indeed, much of the work being described—cooking, cleaning, tending to wounds, coordinating phone calls, and so on, is the type of female labor that is taken for granted in households and societies around the world. Feminine care is often associated with the private, while masculine work is associated with the public sphere. Such explanations potentially depoliticize the work of these women—and perhaps sometimes intentionally—by attributing it to a vague biocultural imperative of women as natural nurturers.

On the one hand, it could be argued that such discourses reinscribe women within gendered hierarchies where their labor is seen as less valuable than the labor of men. In this way, their actions do not threaten the status quo too directly, and their resistances are mostly under the radar. On the other hand, through these everyday forms of intimate labor, women are consciously moving their labor outside their own immediate households and challenging larger systems of social inequality and discrimination.

In doing so, these forms of women's work created tensions and conflicts that sometimes surfaced within their own families and communities. For example, Doña Alicia's husband was clearly wary about her involvement with the shelter and worried for her safety. On a daily basis, her time and energy was spent caring for strangers—whom her husband characterizes as criminals—rather than her own family. Similarly, Araceli experienced her family's disapproval of her work at the shelter. As a single mother of two children, Araceli spent her days at Casa Guadalupe educating migrants on the risks of the journey, helping them make phone calls to their families, and accompanying them to the local clinic. She comes from a close-knit family and still lives on the family property. As I briefly mentioned in chapter 6, toward the end of my fieldwork, Araceli had become embroiled in a local scandal when she was accused of being a human trafficker by the Oaxacan office of the Instituto Nacional de Migración. As she described the situation to me, I was surprised to see that her biggest concern was not the actual legal implications of this accusation for her professional life, but the reaction of her family, and especially her father. She was horrified when her name was mentioned in a local newspaper in relation to the case, because she feared the stigma it might bring to her family. "They don't understand what I do," she explained, "I intentionally don't tell them much, because I don't think they would approve." For both Araceli and Doña Alicia, their family members believed they should conform to more traditional ideals of femininity and motherhood, which place them with in their homes and not in intimate interactions with potentially dangerous strangers.

The examples of Araceli and Doña Alicia show how women both challenge and conform to patriarchal power relations within the gendered structures of migrant shelters. I found that women themselves explained their motivations to help these outsiders more by their sense of social duty and shared experiences of gender inequality, economic precarity, and everyday violence rather than by some inherent sense of solidarity based on biology or instinct, even if such explanations were also used.

This dynamic is captured in a public statement released by a well-known organization of women called Las Patronas, to mark their twenty-year anniversary. Las Patronas is a collective of a dozen women who for twenty years have prepared plastic baggies filled with seasoned rice and beans and water bottles to throw to migrants riding on the tops of the train. Las Patronas, which takes its name from the town in Veracruz where they are based, has a dual meaning. Many migrants have called Las Patronas the female patron saints of migrants along the journey. These were the women I had searched for in Veracruz years earlier when I first started this project. I actually met Lizbeth, one of the primary organizers of Las Patronas during the caravan at Albergue Nazaret. When we spoke, she said to me, "We have to work everyday because migrants are hungry everyday." Here, the statement by Las Patronas reveals the ways in which women strategically claim their "natural" roles as caretakers as a platform for radical activism and political engagement.

> Much is said of the help that we give to migrants, but the truth is that they have also helped us along the way. Thanks to the work we do, we have assumed a position as humans and as women that we didn't know or ever thought would be able to make such a difference

Many told us that we could not help others, that we would go to jail, that we would face justice, the aid we were giving was illegal. The only thing illegal is leaving another human being to die of starvation. They told us that we were women facing problems that were out of our reach. And yes, our work started from our position as women from traditional families, of customs that did not permit feminine actions inside the home or your community, we passed the days caring for, giving love to our families, and it was just that that gave us the character to care for many others. Thinking that each of the men and women on the train were part of our family, and therefore it is only natural to take care of them.

Like this, we gained one of the most precious pieces of knowledge over the past twenty years: that to be a woman in our country is not a limited position as we were led to believe; on the contrary, in our society to be a woman should be a place of power and possibilities . . . endless possibilities, insofar as we are allowed to extend our love as humans, sisters, wives, mothers . . . the way God loved the world. We recognize ourselves as women capable of generating changes, our participation in community decisions and societal problems is not only necessary, but is a matter that opens doors to spaces, struggles, dreams, and expressions of humanity that appears nowhere more than in those who dare to look beyond their daily lives and decide to love.

God created man and woman, and he did not teach us to stand still in the face of adversity and misfortune in the world, but to fight it, no matter our differences. God gave us liberty and it is a powerful liberty.

Do not stop walking and dreaming, let's make that dream a reality. Growing and discovering. We are not a moral issue, we are a social issue. All of us are needed. We'll keep walking. We will not stop.[10]

By claiming their work as not moral, but social, Las Patronas articulate an idea of womanhood that is ambitious, outward facing and intensely political. At the same time, the statement reinforces the idea that their care for migrants is a natural extension of their care for their own families. For Las Patronas, the domestic and the public are not mutually exclusive.[11] It is through their gendered labor that these women transform public spaces and thus challenge traditional gendered dichotomies. Mario Bruzzone argues that that the women of Las Patronas disarticulate the domestic from the private through their performance of domesticity—through cooking for and feeding migrants—in public spaces, thus "exploding" the domestic-public binary.[12]

Lynn Stephen argues that the distinction between feminine/feminist and the corresponding private/public obscures the heterogeneity of experience of women involved in social movements.[13] Drawing from these anthropological insights, we must look to the ways women describe their own experiences and the diversity of histories, motivations, strategies, commitments, and possibilities that inform their participation. Rather than describing the work of shelter workers as a homogeneous movement, we may understand the social landscape around migrants' rights in Mexico as an infinitely rich and diverse collective action around a broadly articulated respect for humanity.

The migrants' rights movement both reproduces and challenges patriarchal hierarchies at a local level—through intimate care at shelters or throwing food to migrants along the train tracks, women are performing traditional feminine tasks, the second or even third shifts of their daily labor. But it is through these intimate labors and firsthand experiences working with migrants that women have increasingly become involved in civic engagement and public activism. For example, at regional meetings, conferences, and public events organized around migrant shelters and migrants' rights, women often outnumber men. In the intimate spaces of dormitories and shelter couches and the public spaces of train yards, these women at once conform to and resist their traditional gendered roles as caregivers as they seek to bring a small bit of humanity to the everyday uncertainty and fear that permeates the journey for migrants in transit— even when it may be looked down upon or met with ambivalence by their families and communities.

By linking together the visible labor of women in public-facing articulations like Las Patronas and the caravans of Central American families with the less visible gendered labor of local women, like Doña Alicia, in migrant shelters, we gain a deeper understanding of the ways women articulate their resistance to transnational processes that both depend on and reproduce violence and inequality. In a place where impunity reigns, this type of collective action poignantly demonstrates the power of solidarity in resistance.

Conclusion

THE UNFORGOTTEN

"Do you speak English?" asked the coordinator of the shelter.

"Yes," I replied.

"Very good. Come with me. I want you to talk to one of the migrants here. *El negrito.*"

It was already midday, muggy under the bright sun of Chiapas. At this shelter, located near the Mexico-Guatemala border and run by the Scalabrini missionaries, migrants were not allowed inside during daytime hours. Instead, they loitered in front of the shelter on the sidewalks and open lot across the street. I would later learn from a female migrant that a well-known smuggler lived in the house across from the shelter.

I recognized Theo, *El negrito,* immediately. His dark brown skin and tall, thin body frame made him stand out among the other men. When I greeted him in English a wave of relief crossed his face. "I have been here for several weeks and I don't know how to speak Spanish!" he said to me laughing. How did he get here, I thought to myself, to this tiny shelter located in a residential neighborhood on the outskirts of a Mexican border town? The coordinator left me with Theo to chat. We moved to a shady spot across the street underneath a tree. Intrigued by the presence of these two outsiders speaking English, a small group of men joined us, and Theo agreed to tell me a bit about his story.

Theo was from Sudan and was a college graduate with a degree in Physical Sports Therapy. He spoke multiple languages, including English and French. While educated, there was very little opportunity for him in his home country. He explained that many of his peers were departing on boats headed north toward Europe. "Everyone was going to Europe, so I thought I would try my luck by going to the United States. I figured there would be more opportunity in the United States."

I met Theo in 2006, a year when thousands of migrants were heading to the Spanish Canary Islands from ports in the West African country of Senegal. But instead of boarding one of these boats, Theo stowed away on a massive container ship headed to South America. After crossing the Atlantic, he traveled by foot and bus, with the help of anyone who could speak English, to find his way north through Central America and to Guatemala, where he stayed for several weeks. Like his Central American counterparts, he crossed the Suchiate River by raft and followed the lead of another migrant, who directed him to the migrant shelter.

As he spoke, Theo carefully wove together thin shreds of palm leaves and wood. He explained that to help pass the time, he made small handicrafts common in his home country. He proudly held up a small instrument that vaguely resembled a Brazilian *berimbau*. The other migrants, clearly impressed by his handiwork, showed me examples of other things he had made. They playfully joked with him in Spanish, and Theo, who had learned a few expressions, returned their teasing, much to everyone's delight.

Theo's presence at the shelter was definitely an anomaly, although over the years increasing numbers of people from Africa and Asia have traveled by ship to ports in Brazil, then head either south to Argentina or north in hopes of reaching the United States.[1] While this is an interesting development and one worthy of more study, I recount my encounter with Theo for a more basic reason.

The goal of this book has been to trace the particularities and complexities of clandestine transit journeys across Mexico. I have sought to illuminate how structural and state policies around migration and security affect the intimacies of people's lives, social relations, and bodies, as well as the ways individuals, local communities, and activists respond to insecurity, violence, and injustice. An ethnographic perspective is able to render visible what is often invisible in mainstream accounts of migration and violence.

Yet many of the broader processes that I describe in the book transcend the particularities of Central American migration across Mexico. People around the world—educated and uneducated, men and women, children and adults, migrants and asylum seekers—risk their lives as they flee conditions of war, poverty, and persecution. In doing so, they must negotiate the increasingly perilous and ever-changing conditions of global clandestine transit journeys. While the dynamics of hiring a smuggler, finding transportation, and seeking aid to cross the deserts of Niger or the waters of the Mediterranean are unique and distinct from those processes in Mexico, they speak to the social, political, and economic consequences of a more heavily militarized and bordered world. Through ethnography, we may gain a deeper understanding of the ways global inequalities are reproduced and resisted in the spaces between home and destination in contexts worldwide. And by tracing the contours of power and violence, we may work toward public scholarship that is useful in larger struggles for rights and justice at home and abroad.

This type of global comparison is not lost on migrants themselves. In 2015, a photograph circulated on social media showing Central American migrants riding La Bestia and holding a handmade sign reading: "Somos Sirios No Disparen" (We are Syrians Don't Shoot). One of the men in the photograph is holding his fingers in a peace sign over the sign. Through humor, these migrants are making a serious point about the hierarchies of suffering and deservingness that surround mobile and unauthorized populations.

Where Syrians fleeing conditions of civil war might be considered worthy of political asylum, or at least humanitarian attention, Central Americans fleeing a different type of war are most often deemed illegal criminals. The disarticulation of political violence from criminal and gang violence and the erasure of the role of the United States in the political and economic instability of the region serve to characterize Central American migrants as undeserving others. Questions around deservingness and the binary between economic migrants/refugees are very much at the heart of political debates in Europe, Australia, and elsewhere.[2] Such comparisons are important as we consider not only the legal and political ramifications of immigration policies, but at a more immediate and embodied level, the human costs of border securitization.

So-called corridors of death have emerged as a common feature of contemporary global landscapes; boats carrying migrants and asylum seekers capsized off the coasts of Italy, Indonesia, and Miami, and unidentified bodies unearthed in pauper's graves on both sides of the U.S.–Mexico border. Identical chain-link fences enclose asylum seekers in Papua New Guinea and Spanish enclaves in North Africa. The red pimpled maps of migrants' deaths along the U.S.–Mexico borderlands eerily resemble those of the treacherous sea passages surrounding what has become known as "Fortress Europe." The global crisis of migrant death was perhaps crystalized in the haunting and widely circulated image of Alan Kurdi, a three-year-old Syrian boy whose lifeless body washed up on the shore near a resort in Turkey in 2015. The image sparked global outrage and world leaders responded with a mix of lip service and a few concrete efforts couched in humanitarian and human rights discourses. Yet as scholars have argued, it is often the spectacle of tragedy that becomes evidence that such flows must be further contained through increased securitization.[3] Like Mexico, the United States, the European Union, and Australia have all opted for a state security approach that profits from the illegalization of immigrants and asylum seekers.[4]

The United Nations' International Organization for Migration (IOM) has a program called the Missing Migrants Project that tracks the number of missing migrants around the world. Since it began tracking the deaths of migrants through government accounts, media, and academics, the most deadly region has consistently been the Mediterranean, where thousands of Europe-bound migrants traveling on crowded boats that capsize drown off the coasts of Italy and Greece. Corridors of death, like migrant journeys themselves, are not static; they shift over time depending on social, political, and economic conditions. Along the U.S.–Mexico border, the Tucson sector in the heart of the Sonoran desert was long considered the most deadly corridor, based on the number of migrants' remains recovered. In 2014, however, the Rio Grande Valley sector became the most deadly, and the overall number of apprehensions of border crossers in this region, a growing percentage of them Central Americans, also increased.

In 2016, the Missing Migrant Migrants Project documented 7,189 migrant deaths around the world.[5] Of those, 4,812 were people who died while crossing the Mediterranean. The second most deadly crossings were via land routes across the Sahara and northern Africa, where 1,089 deaths were recorded. The U.S.–Mexico border was the site of 409 recorded deaths, and the region called Central America and Mexico recorded 159 deaths. This last figure, while horrific, stands in contrast to the estimates made by human rights groups in Mexico, who claim that as many as twenty thousand Central Americans disappear in Mexico each year. Part of the reason the numbers of missing migrants in Mexico is so underestimated is because no one tracks their deaths. There are no official mechanisms by the Mexican state or NGOs to track or report the kidnappings or deaths of Central American migrants, who in death as in life are selectively treated as invisible by the state. The violence of securitization will not end until there is a world in which human dignity and human life are valued more than national security and global profit.

EL NORTE

I began this book in a migrant shelter in Oaxaca, Mexico. Casa Guadalupe is a space of refuge in a larger matrix of migration and survival. It is also a node in a national and transnational network of solidarity and resistance. The interlocking webs of this network were made clear in early September 2010 at the national conference of Movilidad Humana in the city of Nogales, Mexico, which straddles the U.S.–Mexico border between Sonora and Arizona. Just one week after the Tamaulipas massacre, where 72 migrants were found killed on a ranch, more than 150 delegates from migrant shelters and organizations across Mexico came together to discuss the abuses suffered by Central American migrants in Mexico and concrete strategies to address the issue of migrants' rights.

I had recently returned to Tucson, Arizona, from the summer in Oaxaca, and made the short drive south and across the border to attend the meetings. Araceli was there, as was Padre José. The women from the shelter in Palenque and Las Patronas also had representatives at the meeting. Like many of the shelter workers attending, this was Araceli's first trip to the U.S.-Mexico border. And while we were still in Mexico, she saw the place more as my home than hers. In some ways, that was not surprising, given that we were 3,000 miles from her home but only 75 from mine. It was almost a surreal experience accompanying her to various sites along the border that we had talked so much about both with each other and with migrants, but that she had never seen or experienced herself. After months of joking about it, she finally got to witness the fact that in the north people eat more flour tortillas than corn tortillas and more pinto beans than black beans. As it had been throughout my fieldwork, it was the mundane that often kept us grounded.

On the first day of the conference, we gathered in a large hall at a local hotel. While it was not on the planned schedule, the first matter to be addressed was Tamaulipas. There was still a lot of confusion and skepticism about what had really happened. Was it Los Zetas? Were the local authorities involved? We knew enough to know that there was more to the story than was being reported in the news. But still, we were on guard. We were nervous. This was the first time that many of us had become aware of Central Americans being specifically targeted on the northern border. We knew the ins and outs of the southern border, where violence against Central Americans had become almost normalized and expected. This was different. The northern border was another beast. "No one should leave the hotel by themselves. If you do need to go out, make sure you go along with someone else," one of the organizers warned. Most of those attending the conference did not know the lay of the land here, and who might be watching? Although Mexican nationals, they were outsiders in this borderland.

We boarded a bus and traveled to the site of a future migrant shelter. Local politicians arrived and gave big speeches full of promises. My sense was that this was not much more than a photo op for them. I lingered in the background during one of the speeches, taking note of the state police trucks that surrounded us on the empty dirt lot and men with guns in hand. From our location you could see through the enormous steel wall to the U.S. side of the border and the Border Patrol trucks stationed there. This is what a militarized border looks like.

The next stop on our tour was to a small *comedor* (dining hall) located just a few yards away from the international crossing point on the outskirts of Nogales, Sonora. The long benches were filled with around fifty people eating, mostly men but also a few women. Our group packed into the small space on the perimeter. Many of the migrants did not make eye contact with us, but instead kept their heads down and continued to eat. Several volunteers, both Mexican and American, walked around handing out warm tortillas from plastic shopping bags. One of the nuns who runs the *comedor* stood up in front of the crowd to welcome our group and explained to the migrants that we, the visitors, had each worked in some capacity at migrant shelters throughout Mexico. Her point was that we were not simply there to gawk at their misfortune.

The nun asked the migrants if anyone would like to share their story. One stout man stood up. He came up to the front and took the microphone. He gave us his name, Gabino, and told us he was from Veracruz. A few people smiled and whistled in the audience, perhaps other Veracruzaños. Gabino had lived in the United States for seven years with his wife and two children. Earlier in the year, he had to return to his home in Mexico because his father was sick and it was his responsibility to take care of the family business. On his return to the United States, he was caught by immigration officials. He said that he thought he had a chance to remain in the United States because he was a resident and had family, but the ICE officials gave him a choice. They said that he could argue his case to plead for the opportunity to stay in the United States, but that it was not a guaranteed process and it would take from two to three months for his case to be processed, during which time he would have no communication with his family. Or, he could voluntarily be deported, but be able to speak to his wife and children immediately. He chose to be deported because he could not bear to have them not knowing whether he was dead or alive. He said he would now return to Veracruz and then send for his wife and children to live with him in Mexico.

Another man walked up to the front of the room and took the microphone. He was from the state of Morelos in Central Mexico. He explained that since he had been caught once before for crossing into the United States, in his most recent attempt, he had been sent to a U.S. federal prison. He had just been released after serving six months. His voice cracked as he talked about the hardship of being imprisoned in the United States, and how he would never risk crossing again.

There was a palpable difference between my brief visit to this *comedor* and the feeling at migrant shelters in southern Mexico. In southern Mexico, while people face great risk and danger and are actively crossing some of the most brutal sections of the journey, many still have a great amount of faith and hope that they will successfully reach their destinations. The freshly deported people at this *comedor* now had to decide where to go and what to do next in Mexico's inhospitable, increasingly dangerous northern border zone. This could easily be a place of devastation and uncertainty, void of hope, and for some it is. But as I have learned over the course of my research, migrants are resilient and creative in the strategies and social relations they develop to respond to the state and violence as they forge ahead in their pursuits.

Before we left, Araceli and I spoke to two young women who had come in and sat close to the exit. We asked them where they were from. In hushed voices, they said El Salvador. We exchanged knowing glances and nods. We knew what it meant for these women to be from Central America and to have made it all the way here to the U.S.–Mexico border. They surely must have lied to the U.S. Border Patrol agents and told them that they were Mexican—a strategy used by non-Mexican migrants so that they will not be deported and flown back to their countries of origin. They became animated when we told them that we worked in Oaxaca; they remembered passing through there, they said, but they had not gone to Casa Guadalupe. These two women were not interested in going back home; they would attempt to cross again. They smiled at us and continued to eat their lunch. In that moment, as people ate their flour tortillas, I saw how interconnected these spaces and places that seem so far away really are.

For Central American migrants, the regimes of mobility that shape the possibilities of their movements are interconnected across the arterial border, linking checkpoints like La Arrocera to U.S. Border Patrol checkpoints on the other wide of the wall. Also interconnected are the constellations of care that link the labors of the volunteers inside this *comedor* to the labors of workers in migrant shelters near and far. Finally, through the testimonies of migrants themselves, we see the social and affective ties that link together families across the Americas, in life and in death.

At the end of the day our tour bus took us to the border wall. People snapped photos of border art tacked to the wall that depicted coyotes, skulls, and dollar signs juxtaposed with bone-white crosses with ivy vines growing through them. On the crosses were the faded names of people who have disappeared or died while crossing this border. Their names mirrored the names of the missing persons posters at the bus station in Tapachula and the handmade signs carried by the caravan of mothers as they trekked across the country. They echo the names that migrants had etched into the bark of trees and the concrete washing station on the back patio of Casa Guadalupe. I remember those etchings well: the tiny flag of Guatemala, the names of Roberto Martinez and José Montes from Nicaragua, and the carved words of the Lord's prayer, "Jehova es mi pastor y nada me faltará." In the middle of the etchings were the words, "For Ever Remember" written in English. I often meditated on those names and messages etched into the everyday spaces inside the shelter. These were messages to future migrants. This was a way for people to say, by making their mark, "I was here. Do not forget me."

Mexico is a land where people go missing. And while history often renders invisible the stories and lives of those deemed less worthy, as scholars we have an opportunity to tell some of these stories in ways that humanize those who have been dehumanized by political, economic, and social forces. As political actors and as human beings, one of the most powerful things we can do is not to let those stories be forgotten. The mothers of the caravan do not forget you, the local people whose floors you slept on do not forget you, the shelter workers whose lives you touched do not forget you.

We remember you. We remember you. Forever remember.

Notes

INTRODUCTION

1. Casa Guadalupe and Albergue Nazaret (also a pseudonym) were my two primary field sites, and in order to protect the confidentiality of my interlocutors, the names of these shelters have been changed, as have the names of all shelter workers, priests, local residents, and migrants associated with them.

2. Since this time several compelling monographs written by journalists have been published, notably Sonia Nazario's *Enrique's Journey* (2006) and Óscar Martínez's *The Beast* (2013). Scholarly works that address violence on the journey include Casillas 2007, Brigden 2016, Coutin 2005, Kovic 2008, Castillo 2003, and Izcara Palacios 2016.

3. Kleinman 2000.

4. Klinenberg 2001: 131.

5. Scheper-Hughes and Bourgois 2004.

6. Farmer 2004: 309.

7. De León 2015, Quesada et al. 2011, Holmes 2013.

8. Green 2004: 320.

9. Slack and Whiteford 2011, Izcara Palacios 2016.

10. Crenshaw 2003.

11. Kearney 2004.

12. Brettell 2003.

13. Basch, Glick Schiller, and Blanc-Szanton 1994.

14. Deleuze and Guattari 1987, Canclini 1995, Rouse 1996.

15. Mainwaring and Brigden 2016.

16. Hess 2012, Glick Schiller and Salazar 2013.

17. Coutin 2005.

18. Coutin 2005, Menjivar and Abrego 2012.

19. Collyer et al. 2012, Düvell et al. 2014, Papadopoulou-Kourkoula 2008.

20. See also Mainwaring and Brigden 2016, Brigden 2016, Phillips and Missbach 2017. For a case study on journeys between Indonesia and Australia, see Missbach 2015.

21. Dunn 1996, Nevins 2002, Spener 2009, Heyman 1994.

22. Wilson and Donnan 2012.

23. Parker and Vaughan-Williams 2012, Johnson et al. 2011.

24. Walters 2015: 9.

25. García 2006.

26. Bowling and Sheptycki 2011.

27. Menjívar 2014.

28. Kaiser 2012, Parker and Vaughan-Williams 2012.

29. Hage 2009, Khosravi 2014.

30. Movilidad Humana held its first national conference for the pastoral care of migrants in September 2000.

31. The Scalabrinian Congregation started working in Mexico in 1985 to call attention and bring care to migrants, and in 1999, it officially established the Scalabrini International Migration Network (www.simn-cs.net), which has shelters on both Mexico's southern and northern borders.

32. In Mexico, the influence of liberation theology began with the Second Vatican Council (1962–65) and the subsequent Conference of Latin American Bishops in Medellín, Colombia, in 1968. In 2011, to mark the fiftieth anniversary of Vatican II, a conference on "Hope of Liberation and Theology" in Mexico City was attended by several prominent priests representative of the migrant rights' movement in Mexico.

33. Smugglers of migrants in Mexico are commonly called *coyotes* or *polleros*.

34. Pratt and Rosner 2012, Boris and Parreñas 2010, Wilson 2012, Mountz and Hyndman 2006.

35. Mountz and Hyndman 2006.

36. Boehm 2012, Hirsch 2003, Hondagneu-Sotelo 2001, Hondagneu-Sotelo and Avila 2003, Pessar and Mahler 2003, Menjívar et al. 2016.

37. See, e.g., Boehm 2016 and Abrego 2014.

38. Abrego 2014, Boehm 2012, Yarris 2017, Dreby 2010, Coe 2014, Menjivar 2000.

39. Shah 2011, Luibheid et al. 2018.

40. Boris and Parreñas 2010, Briggs 2010, Brennan 2004, Constable 2009, Ehrenreich and Hochschild 2002, Friedman and Mahdavi 2015.

41. Conlon and Hiemstra 2016.

42. Wilson 2012: 43.

43. My use of the concept of intimate economies is inspired by the work of Ara Wilson in Bangkok (see Wilson 2004).

44. Wilson 2012, 2004.

45. Wilson 2012: 48; Faier 2009.

46. Hastings 2002.

47. Theidon 2016.

48. Merry 2009, Wies and Haldane 2015.

49. Goett 2015.

50. Schiller 2003, Fitzgerald 2006, Smith 2006, Marcus 1995.

51. Clifford 1997, Gupta and Ferguson 1997, Kaplan 1987, Weston 1997.

52. Clifford 1997: 208.

53. These questions become even more complicated as researchers, who are also highly mobile, keep up with their interlocutors through social media like Facebook.

54. Coutin 2007, Lucht 2011, Abrego 2014, Coutin 2005, Terrio 2015.

55. Holmes 2013.

56. Andersson 2014.

57. De León 2015.

58. See ibid., in which Jason De León, who did fieldwork in a migrant shelter in Nogales, discusses the challenges.

59. Fassin 2013: xi.

60. Biehl and Locke 2017.

CHAPTER 1. CIRCULATIONS OF VIOLENCE

1. Rosas 2012.

2. Farmer 2004.

3. The concept of pluralities of violence is from Arias and Goldstein 2010, as discussed later in the chapter.

4. Trouillot 1997.

5. Green 2009.

6. Between 1979 and 1981 an estimated thirty thousand people were killed. In an event known as the El Mozote massacre (Binford 1996), in just three days between December 11 and December 13, 1981, over a thousand people were murdered in six hamlets by the U.S.-trained and equipped Atlacatl Battalion. The conflict officially ended in January 1992 after twelve years of fighting and the signing of a treaty known as the Chapultepec Peace Accords. Over seventy-five thousand people were killed during El Salvador's war, the second highest death toll in Central America after Guatemala.

7. Bellino 2017: 9.

8. Grandin 2004.

9. Meyer et al. 2016.

10. See Gill 2004. The School of the Americas was originally located in Panama at Fort Gulick, but after the Panama Canal Treaty was signed in 1984, it moved to its current location at Fort Benning in Georgia (where it now trains Mexican police for the war on drugs). Despite multiple attempts to shut it down, the School of the Americas, now called the Western Hemisphere Institute for Security Cooperation, continues to operate and train soldiers from Latin America in Fort Benning, Georgia.

11. Kaye 1997.

12. Cohn and Thompson 2004 (1995).

13. In 1981, President Reagan appointed John Negroponte, who was known as strong anti-communist, as the ambassador to Honduras, replacing Jack Binns who had complained about human rights abuses in Honduras. Although Negroponte denied knowing about human rights abuses and unsolved disappearances committed by the Honduran Army, government documents suggest he was aware of them and downplayed their significance. Honduras played an important role in the Central American conflicts and fight against communism as a base for the United States and the Nicaraguan Contras, and between 1981 and 1985, the United States increased military spending in Honduras from $4 million to $77.4 million a year.

14. Grandin 2004:5.

15. According to Title 8, Section 1326, of the United States Code, illegal reentry accounted for nearly half of the criminal immigration prosecutions in 2011. Prosecutions under this statute have continued to rise in the past twenty years, particularly under the Obama administration. For more information including statistics and charts, see http://trac.syr.edu/immigration/reports/251/.

16. See, e.g., Koonings and Krujit 1999, Rotker 2002, Green 1999, Moodie 2010, Burrell and Moodie 2013, Coutin 2007, Pine 2008, Robinson 2003, and Zilberg 2011.

17. According to statistics from the United Nations Office of Drugs and Crime and the World Bank, Honduras and El Salvador have consistently led the world in homicide rates since the early 2000s. In Honduras in 2010, the rate of intentional homicide for every 100,000 people was 82.1. In El Salvador, the rate was 66.0. In Guatemala, the rate was 41.4. In comparison, the homicide rate in Mexico was 18.1 and in the United States was 5.0. El Salvador's homicide rate decreased dramatically in 2012 after a truce was signed between rival gangs. In 2015, however, El Salvador had the highest homicide rate in the world, with 109 homicides for every 100,000 people. Honduras had the second highest rate, with 64 (World Bank 2015, UNODC 2013).

18. Menjívar and Walsh 2017.

19. Coutin 2007, Moodie 2010.

20. Moodie 2010, Burrell 2013, O'Neill and Thomas 2011, Green 1999.

21. Zilberg 2011, Burrell 2013, Menjívar and Walsh 2017.

22. Arias and Goldstein 2010, Burrell and Moodie 2013.

23. Arias and Goldstein 2010, Burrell and Moodie 2013.

24. In the late nineteenth and early twentieth centuries, for example, Guatemala and Honduras were both subject to external political control through their foreign-owned banana industries, earning them the title of "banana republics."

25. Robinson 2003, Moodie 2010.

26. Moodie 2010.

27. Green 2011.

28. Moodie 2010: 41; Klein 2007.

29. Grandin 2006.

30. Robinson 2003, 2008.

31. Green 2003.

32. For research on maquiladoras in Honduras, see Pine 2008.

33. Coutin 2007:175.

34. Bruneau et al. 2011.

35. O'Neill and Thomas 2011.

36. Bellino 2017, O'Neill and Thomas 2011.

37. O'Neill and Thomas 2011.

38. Martinez 2017.

39. Wolseth 2008.

40. Zilberg 2011, Montoya 2011: 107.

41. Coutin 2007, Godoy 2005, Zilberg 2011.

42. Quesada 1998.

CHAPTER 2. THE ARTERIAL BORDER

1. Two notable exceptions are Hernández Castillo 2001 and Galemba 2017

2. De León 2015.

3. Based on their work in Asia, Xiang and Lindquist 2014 have proposed the framework of a "migration infrastructure" to understand the "systematically interlinked technologies, institutions, and actors that facilitate and condition mobility."

4. See also Gilberto Rosas's idea of borders "thickening" (Rosas 2006).

5. Parker and Vaughan-Williams 2012, Kaiser 2012.

6. The Global Detention Project, a nonprofit research center that investigates immigration-related detention, has excellent maps on its web site (www.globaldetentionproject.org) charting detention centers around the world.

7. http://latinalista.com/general/historic-partnership-agreements-signed.

8. https://www.nytimes.com/2017/02/21/business/economy/mexico-immigration-border-wall.html?_r=0.

9. Cruz Burguete 2013.

10. Between 1981 and 1983, an estimated two hundred thousand Guatemalans entered Mexico, and forty-six thousand were officially registered with the UNHCR. Between 1993 and 1999, Mexico organized programs of both voluntary repatriation and settlement of Guatemalan refugees (Castillo 2003). See also García 2006.

11. This name was also later used for the operation that replaced Operation Blockade in the El Paso sector of the U.S.–Mexico border (Frelick 1991, Zucker and Zucker 1996).

12. Frelick 1991, Zucker and Zucker 1996.

13. Frelick 1991, Zucker and Zucker 1996.

14. Ogren 2007, Castillo 2003.

15. Jaramillo 2001, Flynn 2002.

16. Andreas 1998.

17. According to the United Nations Office on Drugs and Crime (UNODC), the estimated value of cocaine shipped from South America to North America in 2008 was U.S. $38 billion.

18. Astorga and Shirk 2010.

19. Zilberg 2011.

20. Stephen 2000: 823.

21. Kovic 2010.

22. Galemba 2017.

23. Frelick 1991: 224.

24. Goett 2015.

25. Stephen 2016.

26. Galemba 2017.

27. Avendaño and Morales 2011.

28. Goett 2015.

29. Aretxaga 2001.

30. Falcón 2007: 44.

31. Stephen 2016.

32. Stephen 2016, Wright 2011.

33. Amnesty International 2011.

34. Brown 1992: 9.

35. An FM3 visa is a temporary visa to stay in Mexico for up to one year.

36. Here I refer to the Zapatista movement and the 2006 social movement in Oaxaca.

37. Brigden 2016.

38. According to Mexico's secretary of the interior, the number of migrants deported in 2014 increased by 35 percent. Mexico deported 80,079 migrants in 2013 and 107,814 in 2014. Most significant is that the number of children deported

increased by 117 percent, from 8,350 in 2013 to 18,169 in 2014 (Boggs 2015). The numbers in 2015 were even higher. In the first three months of 2015, Mexico deported nearly forty thousand Central American migrants, a 79 percent increase over the number of migrants deported in the same months of 2014 (www .theguardian.com/world/2015/jun/11/deportations-mexico-central-america).

39. See, e.g., the Human Rights Watch Mexico report, www.hrw.org/world-report/2017/country-chapters/mexico.

CHAPTER 3. MIGRANT INDUSTRY

1. Maureen Meyer, Washington Office on Latin America, June 3, 2016, www .wola.org/es/analisis/con-mas-de-27000-desaparecidos-el-congreso-de-mexico-retrasa-la-ley-para-enfrentar-esta-crisis.

2. Castles and Miller 2003, Salt and Stein 1997, Kyle 2000.

3. Cranston et al. 2017, Phillips and Missbach 2017.

4. Golash-Boza 2009.

5. Andersson 2014: 8.

6. Andersson 2014.

7. Andreas 2000, Galemba 2017.

8. Coutin 2005: 196, De Genova 2002.

9. Sharp 2000: 293.

10. Harvey 2005: 171.

11. Harvey 2010: 24; Moodie 2006.

12. Grupo Savant 2010, Booth 2011.

13. At some point, "Los Zetas" became a catchall name for all organized criminal groups, and it became unclear which groups were actually Zetas and which were just posing as Zetas. The actual Zetas organization has since undergone several periods of restructuring.

14. It is interesting to reflect on the use of "safe house" to describe the places where migrants are held by shelters, by smugglers, and by kidnappers. The same word is used to describe a place where either people or valuable cargo are being held for safety.

15. Andreas 2000, Galemba 2017.

16. Izcara Palacios 2016.

17. Gibler 2011: 19–23.

CHAPTER 4. EMBODIED MOBILITIES

1. Castañeda et al. 2015, Holmes 2013, Quesada et al. 2011, Willen 2012.

2. For anthropological work on embodiment, see Csordas 1994, Scheper-Hughes and Lock 1987.

3. Weller et al. 2008.

4. Infante et al. 2013.

5. See similar arguments made about the murdered women of Ciudad Juarez in Fregoso and Bejarano 2010, Lagarde y de los Rios 2010, Sanford 2008.

6. Caballero et al. 2002.

7. Weller et al. 2008.

8. Mexico has *jus soli* citizenship laws, meaning that anyone born in Mexican territory has the right to Mexican citizenship. It also has laws that allow parents of Mexican citizens to regularize their unauthorized status.

9. Guttman 1996.

10. See, e.g., Wies and Haldane 2015, Merry 2009.

11. Castañeda 2009, Castañeda et al. 2015, Willen 2007, 2012.

12. Quesada et al. 2011.

13. Willen 2012: 808.

14. Médicos sin Fronteras/Doctors without Borders tracks its treatment of Central American migrants in transit. The project initially worked to improve water and sanitation conditions at several shelters so that overall health conditions within the shelters could be improved. MSF has offered thousands of outpatient consultations with people suffering physical ailments and disease, as well as offering mental health services to migrants who have suffered violence.

15. Redfield 2005:330.

16. Castañeda 2011.

17. Fassin 2011b.

18. See, e.g., James 2010, Ticktin 2011, Fassin 2011a, Bornstein and Redfield 2011.

CHAPTER 5. INTIMATE CROSSINGS

1. Coutin 2005.

2. For recent work on the complexities and nuances of smuggling, see Sanchez 2014, Zhang et al. 2018.

3. For work on intimate economies in Bangkok, see Wilson 2004.

4. For feminist work on the linkages between the global and the intimate, see Pratt and Rosner 2012, Boris and Parreñas 2010, Ehrenreich and Hochschild 2002.

5. See Boehm 2012, Abrego 2014, Hondagneu-Sotelo and Avila 2003, Yarris 2017.

6. For discussion of how intimate ties take many forms beyond the family, see Luibheid et al. 2018.

7. I.e., the 2006 popular uprising against the Mexican state and the violent repression that followed in Oaxaca. For an in-depth ethnography of the movement, see Stephen 2013.

8. Martinez 2013.

9. Eileen Boris and Rhacel Parreñas (2010) conceptualize the "work of intimacy" in the context of everyday forms of work and global economic transformations. They propose "intimate labor" as a useful category to analyze power relations based on race, class, sex, and gender across multiple forms of care work—from nail salons to domestic servitude to sex worker industries—often blurring the lines between social constructions of public/private and productive/unproductive labor.

10. Donaldson 2004.

11. Wilson 2012: 48.

12. Carsten 2000.

13. For more critical discussion on the privileged place of the intimate couple in society, see Povinelli 1999, Berlant 1998.

14. Baldassar and Merla 2014, Yarris 2017.

15. Yarris 2017.

16. Wilson 2012: 48.

CHAPTER 6. (IN)SECURITY AND SAFETY

1. Nazario 2006.

2. Rocha 2005.

3. The linguistic differences between Mexican Spanish and Honduran and Salvadoran Spanish were not immediately apparent to me when I first began fieldwork, though I would learn to distinguish between the accents, cadences, and subtle word differences. In fact, the different words that are used in Mexico and Central America, and especially curse words, often sparked lively conversations at shelters. Central Americans would practice using particular, very Mexican words, such as *pinche* (fucking) and *güey* (mate, pal), in their attempts to pass as Mexican on their travels.

4. While I do not go into this here, transit communities are also spaces where other types of outsiders like international aid workers, student volunteers, journalists, and researchers are increasingly present.

5. Goldstein 2010.

6. Gledhill 2015, Goldstein 2012.

7. Campbell 2009, Muehlmann 2014, Gledhill 2015.

8. O'Neill and Thomas 2011.

9. Burrell 2010; Goldstein 2010, 2012: 5.

10. O'Neill and Thomas 2011.

11. Before the 1970s, when large numbers of Central American refugees began entering Mexico to seek refuge, their status as racialized others or noncitizens was not central to Mexico's national imaginary. Processes of racialization and

the social construction of the illegality and otherness of *los indocumentados* (the undocumented) increased in the mid-1970s, paralleling the legal criminalization of unauthorized foreigners in Mexico under the 1974 Ley de la Población.

12. Kelly 2008.

13. Ibid.

14. The term *cholos* was often used to refer to Chicano gangsters in the United States.

15. Howard Campbell (2009) has described the chronic insecurity and fear in "drug war zones" along the U.S.–Mexico border and certain Mexican cities, which I would argue extend into communities along Central American transit routes, where migrants move alongside criminals, drugs, and weapons. John Gledhill (2015) has examined the historical antecedents of the drug economy and emergence of mafia-style organizations and *autodefensas* in Michoacán.

16. Lind and Williams 2013: 111.

17. Ibid., 112.

18. WOLA report

19. For example, John Gledhill (2015) has analyzed the ways local people in Michoacán create their own armed self-defense forces (*autodefensas*) rather than rely on state institutions for justice and protection. See also, www.insightcrime.org/news-briefs/rise-in-mexico-lynchings-reflects-regional-trend

20. Goldstein 2010:498.

21. Goldstein 2003, Burrell 2013.

22. Chávez 2013.

23. "IACHR Urges the State to Guarantee Conditions of Security in Shelter for Migrants in Mexico, August 2, 2012," www.oas.org/en/iachr/media_center/preleases/2012/098.asp.

24. Stephen 2002.

25. Turner 1967.

26. Goldstein 2010.

27. Bauman 2004: 56–57.

CHAPTER 7. CONSTELLATIONS OF CARE

1. Schirmer 1993, Stephen 1995, Bejarano 2002.

2. Lamphere 2016.

3. Boss 2004.

4. www.versobooks.com/blogs/3025-trump-fascism-and-the-construction-of-the-people-an-interview-with-judith-butler.

5. Mueller et al. 2009.

6. Stephen 1995, Schirmer 1993, Bejarano 2002.

7. Briggs 2012.

8. Bejarano 2002.

9. Green 2011b: 22.

10. "Las Patroñas: 20 años después," https://lapatrona.wordpress.com/2015/02/20/20-anos-de-las-patronas.

11. Bruzzone 2017.

12. Ibid.

13. Stephen 1995.

CONCLUSION

1. www.theguardian.com/global-development/2016/sep/06/mexico-african-asian-migration-us-exit-permit.

2. See Holmes and Castañeda 2016.

3. Mountz 2010, Andersson 2014.

4. Andersson 2014.

5. https://missingmigrants.iom.int/migrant-deaths-worldwide-top-7100-over-half-mediterranean.

References

Abrego, Leisy J. 2014. *Sacrificing Families: Navigating Laws, Labor, and Love across Borders*. Stanford: Stanford University Press.

Amnesty International. 2010. *Invisible Victims: Migrants on the Move in Mexico*. London : Amnesty International.

Andersson, Ruben. 2014. *Illegality Inc.: Clandestine Migration and the Business of Bordering Europe* Berkeley: University of California Press.

Andreas, Peter. 1998. "The Political Economy of Narco-Corruption in Mexico." *Current History* (April): 160–65.

———. 2000. *Border Games: Policing the U.S.-Mexico Divide*. Ithaca, NY: Cornell University Press.

Aretxaga, Begoña. 2001. "The Sexual Games of the Body Politic: Fantasy and State Sexual Violence in Northern Ireland." *Culture, Medicine and Psychiatry* 25: 1–27.

Arias, Enrique Desmond, and Daniel Goldstein, eds. 2010. *Violent Democracies in Latin America*. Durham, NC: Duke University Press.

Astorga, Luis, and David A. Shirk. 2010. "Drug Trafficking Organizations and Counter-Drug Strategies in the U.S.-Mexican Context." UC San Diego: Center for U.S.-Mexican Studies. https://escholarship.org/uc/item/8j647429.

Avendaño, Olga Rosario, and Alberto Morales. 2011. "Migrante pierde pierna durante operativo en Oaxaca." *El Universal*, January 24, Estados. http://www.eluniversal.com.mx/notas/739569.html.

Baldassar, Loretta, and Laura Merla, eds. 2014. *Transnational Families, Migration and the Circulation of Care: Understanding Mobility and Absence in Family Life*. New York: Routledge.

Basch, Linda, Nina Glick Schiller, and Cristina Blanc-Szanton. 1994. *Nations Unbound: Transnational Projects, Postcolonial Predicaments and Deterritorialized Nation-States*. London: Routledge.

Bauman, Zygmunt. 2004. *Wasted Lives: Modernity and Its Outcasts*. Cambridge: Polity Press.

Bejarano, Cynthia. 2002. "Las Super Madres de Latino America: Transforming Motherhood by Challenging Violence in Mexico, Argentina, and El Salvador." *Frontiers: A Journal of Women Studies* 23 (1): 126–50.

Bellino, Michelle. 2017. *Youth in Postwar Guatemala: Education and Civic Identity in Transition*. New Brunswick, NJ: Rutgers University Press.

Berlant, Lauren. 1998. "Intimacy: A Special Issue." *Critical Inquiry* 24 (2): 281–88.

Biehl, João, and Peter Locke, eds. 2017. *Unfinished: The Anthropology of Becoming*. Durham, NC: Duke University Press.

Binford, Leigh. 1996. *The El Mozote Massacre: Anthropology and Human Rights*. Tucson: University of Arizona Press.

Boehm, Deborah. 2012. *Intimate Migrations: Gender, Family, and Illegality among Transnational Mexicans*. New York: New York University Press.

———. 2016. *Returned: Going and Coming in an Age of Deportation*. Berkeley: University of California Press.

Boggs, Clay. 2015. "Mexico's Southern Border Plan: More Deportations and Widespread Human Rights Violations." Washington Office on Latin America.www.wola.org/analysis/mexicos-southern-border-plan-more-deportations-and-widespread-human-rights-violations.

Booth, William, and Nick Miroff. 2011. "Mexican Drug Cartels Draws [sic] Guatemalan Army to Jungles Where It Fought Civil War." *Washington Post*, February 9.

Boris, Eileen, and Rhacel Salazar Parreñas, eds. 2010. *Intimate Labors: Cultures, Technologies and the Politics of Care*. Stanford: Stanford University Press.

Bornstein, Erica, and Peter Redfield, eds. 2011. *Forces of Compassion: Humanitarianism between Ethics and Politics*. Santa Fe, NM: School for Advanced Research Press.

Boss, Pauline. 2004. "Ambiguous Loss Research, Theory, and Practice: Reflections After 9/11." *Journal of Marriage and Family* 66 (554).

Bowling, Benjamin, and James W. E. Sheptycki. 2011. *Global Policing*. Los Angeles : Sage.

Brennan, Denise. 2004. *What's Love Got to Do With It? Transnational Desires and Sex Tourism in the Dominican Republic*. Durham, NC: Duke University Press.

Brettell, Caroline. 2003. *Anthropology and Migration: Essays on Transnationalism, Ethnicity and Identity*. Walnut Creek, CA: Alta Mira Press.

Brigden, Noelle. 2016. "Improvised Transnationalism: Clandestine Migration at the Border of Anthropology and International Relations." *International Studies Quarterly*. doi: http://dx.doi.org/10.1093/isq/sqw010.

Briggs, Laura. 2010. "Foreign and Domestic: Adoption, Immigration and Privatization." In *Intimate Labors: Cultures, Technologies, and the Politics of Care*, ed. Eileen Boris and Rhacel Salazar Parreñas. Stanford: Stanford University Press.

———. 2012. *Somebody's Children: The Politics of Transracial and Transnational Adoption*. Durham, NC: Duke University Press.

Brown, Wendy. 1992. "Finding the Man in the State." *Feminist Studies* 18 (1): 7–34.

Bruneau, Thomas, Lucía Dammert, and Elizabeth Skinner. 2011. *Maras: Gang Violence and Security in Central America*. Austin: University of Texas Press.

Bruzzone, Mario. 2017. "Respatializing the Domestic: Gender, Extensive Domesticity, and Activist Kitchenspace in Mexican Migration Politics." *Cultural Geographies* 24 (2): 247–63.

Burrell, Jennifer. 2010. "In and Out of Rights: Security, Migration, and Human Rights Talk in Postwar Guatemala." *Journal of Latin American and Caribbean Anthropology* 15 (1): 90–115.

———. 2013. *Maya after War: Conflict, Power, and Politics in Guatemala*. Austin: University of Texas Press.

Burrell, Jennifer, and Ellen Moodie, eds. 2013. *Central America in the New Millenium: Living Transition and Reimagining Democracy*. New York: Berghahn.

Caballero, M., A. Dreser, R. Leyva, C. Rueda, and M. Brofman. 2002. "Migration, Gender and HIV/AIDS in Central America and Mexico." Proceedings of Social Science XIV AIDS International Conference, 263–67. Barcelona: Monduzzi Editore.

Campbell, Howard. 2009. *Drug War Zone: Frontline Dispatches from the Streets of El Paso and Juárez*. Austin: University of Texas Press.

Canclini, Nestor Garcia. 1995. *Hybrid Cultures: Strategies for Entering and Leaving Modernity*. Minneapolis: University of Minnesota Press.

Carsten, Janet. 2000. *Cultures of Relatedness: New Approaches to the Study of Kinship*. Cambridge: Cambridge University Press.

Casillas, Rodolfo. 2007. *Una vida discreta, fugaz y anónima: Los Centroamericanos transmigrantes en México*. México: Comisión Nacional de los Derechos Humanos.

Castañeda, Heide. 2009. "Illegality as Risk Factor: A Survey of Unauthorized Migrant Patients in a Berlin Clinic." *Social Science and Medicine* 68 (8): 1552–60.

———. 2011. "Medical Humanitarianism and Physicians' Organized Efforts to Provide Aid to Unauthorized Migrants in Germany." *Human Organization* 70 (1): 1–10.

Castañeda, Heide, Seth Holmes, Daniel Madrigal, Maria-Elena DeTrinidad Young, Naomi Beyeler, and James Quesada. 2015. "Immigration as a Social Determinant of Health." *Annual Review of Public Health* 36: 375–92.

Castillo, Manuel Angel. 2003a. "The Mexico-Guatemala Border: New Controls on Transborder Migrations in View of Recent Integration Schemes?" *Frontera Norte* 15 (29): 35–64.

———. 2003b. "Los desafíos de la emigración centroamericana en el Siglo XXI." *Amérique Latine Histoire et Mémoire* 7.

Castles, Stephen, and Mark J. Miller. 2003. *The Age of Migration.* New York: Guilford Press.

Chávez, Mariana. 2013. "Querétaro: Protectora de migrantes pide apoyo para seguir ayudándolos." *La Jornada,* August 12.

Clifford, James. 1997. "Spatial Practices: Fieldwork, Travel and the Disciplining of Anthropology." In *Anthropological Locations,* ed. Akhil Gupta and James Ferguson. Berkeley: University of California Press.

Coe, Cati. 2014. *The Scattered Family: Parenting, African Migrants, and Global Inequality.* Chicago: University of Chicago Press.

Cohn, Gary, and Ginger Thompson. 2004 (1995). "Torture at CIA Battalion 316: The Record of Washington's New 'Ambassador' to Iraq." http://globalresearch .ca/articles/COH405A.html.

Collyer, Michael, Franck Duvell, and Hein de Haas. 2012. "Critical Approaches to Transit Migration." *Population, Space and Place* 18 (4): 407–14.

Conlon, Deirdre, and Nancy Hiemstra, eds. 2016. *Intimate Economies of Immigrant Detention.* London: Routledge.

Constable, Nicole. 2009. "The Commodification of Intimacy: Marriage, Sex, and Reproductive Labor." *Annual Review of Anthropology* 38: 49–64.

Coutin, Susan Bibler. 2005. "Being en route." *American Anthrolpologist* 107 (2): 195–206.

———. 2007. *Nations of Emigrants: Shifting Boundaries of Citizenship in El Salvador and the United States.* Ithaca, NY: Cornell University Press.

Cranston, Sophie, Joris Schapendonk, and Ernst Spaan. 2017. "New Directions in Exploring Migration Industries: Introduction to Special Issue." *Journal of Ethnic and Migration Studies* 44 (4): 543–57. DOI: 10.1080/1369183X.2017 .1315504.

Crenshaw, Kimberlé. 1991. "Mapping the Margins: Intersectionality, Identity Politics, and Violence against Women of Color." *Stanford Law Review* 43, no. 6: 1241–99.

Cruz Burguete, Jorge Luis. 2013. "Diferenciación social e identidad étnica en la frontera sur de México." *Boletín Científico Sapiens Research* 3 (1): 8–13.

Csordas, Thomas. 1994. "Introduction: The Body as Representation and Being-in-the-World." In *Embodiment and Experience: The Existential Ground of Culture and Self,* ed. Csordas. Cambridge: Cambridge University Press.

De Genova, Nicholas. 2002. "Migrant 'illegality' and Deportability in Everyday Life." *Annual Review of Anthropology* 31: 419–47.

De León, Jason. 2015. *The Land of Open Graves: Living and Dying on the Migrant Trail.* Berkeley: University of California Press.

Deleuze, Gilles, and Felix Guattari. 1987. *A Thousand Plateaus: Capitalism and Schizophrenia.* Minnneapolis: University of Minnesota Press.

Donaldson, Stephen. 2004. "Hooking Up: Protective Pairing for Punks." In *Violence in War and Peace: An Anthology,* ed. Nancy Scheper-Hughes and Philippe Bourgois. Oxford: Blackwell.

Dreby, Joanna. 2010. *Divided by Borders: Mexican Migrants and their Children.* Berkeley: University of California Press.

Dunn, Timothy. 1996. *The Militarization of the U.S.-Mexico Border 1978–1992: Low-Intensity Doctrine Conflict Comes Home.* Austin: Center for Mexican American Studies, University of Texas at Austin.

Düvell, Franck, Irina Molodikova, and Michael Collyer. 2014. *Transit Migration in Europe.* Amsterdam: Amsterdam University Press.

Ehrenreich, Barbara, and Arlie Hochschild. 2002. *Global Woman: Nannies, Maids, and Sex Workers in the New Economy.* New York: Metropolitan Books.

Faier, Lieba. 2009. *Intimate Encounters: Filipina Women and the Remaking of Rural Japan.* Berkeley: University of California Press.

Falcón, Sylvanna. 2007. "Rape as a Weapon of War: Militarized Rape at the U.S.-Mexico Border." In *Women and Migration in the U.S.-Mexico Borderlands,* ed. Denise A. Segura and Patricia Zavella. Durham, NC: Duke University Press.

Farmer, Paul. 2004. "An Anthropology of Structural Violence." *Current Anthropology* 45 (3): 305–25.

Fassin, Didier. 2011a. *Humanitarian Reason: A Moral History of the Present.* Berkeley: University of California Press.

———. 2011b. "Noli Me Tangere: The Moral Untouchability of Humanitarianism." In *Forces of Compassion: Humanitarianism between Ethics and Politics,* ed. Erica Bornstein and Peter Redfield. Santa Fe, NM: School of Advanced Research Press.

————. 2013. *Enforcing Order: Ethnography of Urban Policing*. Cambridge: Polity Press.

Fitzgerald, David. 2006. "Towards a Theoretical Ethnography of Migration." *Qualitative Sociology* 29 (1): 1–24.

Flynn, Michael. 2002. "U.S. Anti-Migration Efforts Move South." *CIP Americas online journal, July 3*, www.cipamericas.org/archives/1066.

Fregoso, Rosa-Linda, and Cynthia Bejarano. 2010. *Terrorizing Women: Feminicide in the Américas*. Durham, NC: Duke University Press.

Frelick, Bill. 1991. "Running the Gauntlet: the Central American Journey in Mexico." *International Journal of Refugee Law* 3 (2): 208–42.

Friedman, Sara, and Pardis Mahdavi, eds. 2015. *Migrant Encounters: Intimate Labor, the State, and Mobility across Asia*. Philadelphia: University of Pennsylvania Press.

Galemba, Rebecca. 2017. *Contraband Corridor: Making a Living at the Mexico-Guatemala Border*. Stanford: Stanford University Press.

García, María Cristina. 2006. *Seeking Refuge: Central American Migration to Mexico, the United States, and Canada*. Berkeley: University of California Press.

Gibler, John. 2011. *To Die in Mexico: Dispatches from Inside the Drug War*. San Francisco: City Lights Books.

Gill, Lesley. 2004. *The School of the Americas: Military Training and Political Violence in the Americas*. Durham, NC: Duke University Press.

Gledhill, John. 2015. *The New War on the Poor: The Production of Insecurity in Latin America*. London: Zed Books.

Glick Schiller, Nina. 2003. "The Centrality of Ethnography in the Study of Transnational Migration: Seeing the Wetlands instead of the Swamp." In *American Arrivals: Anthropology Engages the New Immigration*, ed. Nancy Foner. Santa Fe, NM: School of American Research Press.

Glick Schiller, Nina, and Noel B. Salazar. 2013. "Regimes of Mobility across the Globe." *Journal of Ethnic and Migration Studies* 39 (2).

Godoy, Angelina Snodgrass. 2005. "Democracy, 'Mano Dura,' and the Criminalization of Politics." In *(Un)Civil Societies: Human Rights and Demicratic Transitions in Eastern Europe and Latin America*, ed. Rachel May and Andrew Milton. Lanham, MD: Lexington Books.

Goett, Jennifer. 2015. "Securing Social Difference: Militarization and Sexual Violence in an Afro-Nicaraguan Community." *American Ethnologist* 42 (3): 475–89.

Golash-Boza, Tanya. 2009. "The Immigration Industrial Complex: Why We Enforce Immigration Policies Destined to Fail." *Sociology Compass* 3 (2): 295–309.

Goldstein, Daniel. 2003. "'In Our Own Hands': Lynching, Justice, and the Law in Bolivia." *American Ethnologist* 30 (1): 22–43.

———. 2010. "Toward a Critical Anthropology of Security." *Current Anthropology* 51 (4): 487–517.

———. 2012. *Outlawed: Between Security and Rights in a Bolivian City.* Durham, NC: Duke University Press.

Grandin, Greg. 2004. *The Last Colonial Massacre: Latin America in the Cold War.* Chicago: University of Chicago Press.

———. 2006. *Empire's Workshop: Latin America, the United States, and the Rise of the New Imperialism.* New York: Metropolitan Books.

Green, Linda. 1999. *Fear as a Way of Life: Mayan Widows in Rural Guatemala.* New York: Columbia University Press.

———. 2003. "Notes on Mayan Youth and Rural Industrialization in Guatemala." *Critique of Anthropology* 23 (1): 51–73.

———. 2004. Comments on "An Anthropology of Structural Violence" by Paul Farmer. *Current Anthropology* 45 (3).

———. 2009. "The Fear of No Future: Guatemalan Migrants, Dispossession and Dislocation." *Anthropologica* 51 (9): 327–42.

———. 2011a. "The Nobodies: Neoliberalism, Violence, and Migration." *Medical Anthropology* 30 (4): 366–85.

———. 2011b. "The Utter Normalization of Violence: Silence, Memory and Impunity among the Yup'ik People of Southwestern Alaska." In *Violence Expressed: An Anthropological Approach*, ed. Nina Six-Hohenbalken and Nerina Weiss. Surrey, England: Ashgate.

Grupo Savant. 2010. "Los Zetas Threaten a Nation-State: An Indications and Warning Analysis." Washington, DC. www.gruposavant.com/Report_Zetas_Threaten_a_Nation-State_30DEC10.pdf.

Gupta, Akhil, and James Ferguson, eds. 1997. *Anthropological Locations.* Berkeley: University of California Press.

Guttman, Matthew. 1996. *The Meanings of Macho: Being a Man in Mexico City.* Berkeley: University of California Press.

Hage, Ghassan. 2009. *Waiting.* Carlton South, Victoria: Melbourne University Press.

Harvey, David. 2005. *A Brief History of Neoliberalism.* Oxford: Oxford University Press.

———. 2010. *A Companion to Marx's Capital.* London: Verso.

Hastings, Julie. 2002. "Silencing State-Sponsored Rape: In and Beyond a Transnational Guatemalan Community." *Violence against Women* 8 (10): 1153–81.

Hernández Castillo, Rosalva Aída. 2001. *La otra frontera : identidades múltiples en el Chiapas poscolonial.* México: CIESAS : Miguel Angel Porrúa.

Hess, Sabine. 2012. "De-naturalising Transit Migration: Theory and Methods of an Ethnographic Regime Analysis." *Population, Space and Place* 18: 428–40.

Heyman, Josiah McC. 1994. "The Mexico–United States Border in Anthropology: A Critique and Reformulation." *Journal of Political Ecology* 1.

Hirsch, Jennifer. 2003. *A Courtship after Marriage: Sexuality and Love in Mexican Transnational Families.* Berkeley: University of California Press.

Holmes, Seth. 2013. *Fresh Fruit, Broken Bodies: Migrant Farmworkers in the United States.* Berkeley: University of California Press.

Holmes, Seth, and Heide Castañeda. 2016. "Representing the 'European refugee crisis' in Germany and Beyond: Deservingness and Difference, Life and Death." *American Ethnologist* 43 (1): 12–24.

Hondagneu-Sotelo, Pierrette. 2001. *Doméstica: Immigrant Workers Cleaning and Caring in the Shadows of Affluence.* Berkeley: University of California Press.

Hondagneu-Sotelo, Pierette, and Ernestine Avila. 2003. "'I'm here, but I'm there': The Meanings of Latina Transnational Motherhood." In *Gender and U.S. Immigration: Contemporary Trends,* ed. Hondagneu-Sotelo. Berkeley: University of California Press.

Infante, César, Rubén Silván, Marta Caballero, and Lourdes Campero. 2013. "Sexualidad del migrante: Experiencias y derechos sexuales de centroamericanos en tránsito a los Estados Unidos." *Salud Pública de México* 55: 58–64.

Izcara Palacios, Simón Pedro. 2016. "Violencia postestructural: Migrantes centroamericanos y cárteles de la droga en México." *Revista de Estudios Sociales* 56: 12–25.

James, Erica. 2010. *Democratic Insecurities: Violence, Trauma, and Intervention.* Berkeley: University of California Press.

Jaramillo, Velia. 2001. "Mexico's 'Southern Plan': The Facts." *World Press Review* 48 (9).

Johnson, Corey, Reece Jones, Anssi Paasi, Louise Amoore, Alison Mountz, Mark Salter, and Chris Rumford. 2011. "Interventions on Rethinking 'the border' in Border Studies." *Political Geography* 30: 61–69.

Kaiser, Robert. 2012. "Performativity and the Eventfulness of Bordering Practices." In *A Companion to Border Studies,* ed. Thomas Wilson and Hastings Donnan. Hoboken : WileyBlackwell.

Kaplan, Caren. 1987. "Deterritorializations: The Rewriting of Home and Exile in Western Feminist Discourse." *Cultural Critique* 6 (Spring): 187–98.

Kaye, Mike. 1997. "The Role of Truth Commissions in the Search for Justice, Reconciliation and Democratisation: the Salvadoran and Honduran Cases." *Journal of Latin American Studies* 29 (3): 693–716.

Kearney, Michael. 2004. *Changing Fields of Anthropology: From Local to Global.* Lanham, MD: Rowman & Littlefield.

Kelly, Patty. 2008. *Lydia's Open Door: Inside Mexico's Most Modern Brothel.* Berkeley: University of California Press.

Khosravi, Shahram. 2014. "Waiting." In *Migration: A COMPAS Anthology,* ed. B. Anderson and M. Keith. Oxford: COMPAS.

Klein, Naomi. 2007. *The Shock Doctrine: The Rise of Disaster Capitalism*. New York: Metropolitan Books.

Kleinman, Arthur. 2000. "The Violences of Everyday Life: The Multiple Forms and Dynamics of Social Violence." In *Violence and Subjectivity*, ed Veena Das, Arthur Kleinman, Mamphela Ramphele, and Pamela Reynolds. Berkeley: University of California Press.

Klinenberg, Eric. 2001. "Bodies That Don't Matter: Death and Dereliction in Chicago." In *Commodifying Bodies*, ed. Nancy Scheper-Hughes and Loic Wacquant. Thousand Oaks, CA: Sage.

Koonings, Kees, and Dirk Krujit, eds. 1999. *Societies of Fear: the Legacy of Civil War, Violene and Terror in Latin America*. London: Zed Books.

Kovic, Christine. 2008. "Jumping from a Moving Train: Risk, Migration and Rights at NAFTA's southern Border." *Practicing Anthropology* 30 (2): 32–36.

———. 2010. "The Violence of Security: Central American Migrants Crossing Mexico's Southern Border (photo essay)." *Anthropology Now* 2 (1): 87–97.

Kyle, David. 2000. *Transnational Peasants: Migrations, Networks, and Ethnicity in Andean Ecuador*. Baltimore: John Hopkins University Press.

Lagarde y de los Rios, Marcela. 2010. "Preface: Feminist Keys for Understanding Feminicide: Theoretical, Political and Legal Construction." In *Terrorizing Women: Feminicide in the Américas*, ed. Rosa-Linda Fregoso and Cynthia Bejarano. Durham, NC: Duke University Press.

Lamphere, Louise. 2016. "Feminist Anthropology Engages Social Movements: Theory, Ethnography, and Activism." In *Mapping Feminist Anthropology in the Twenty-First Century*, ed. Leni Silverstein and Ellen Lewin. New Brunswick, NJ: Rutgers University Press.

Lind, Amy, and Jill Williams. 2013. "Engendering Violence in De/Hyper-Nationalized Spaces: Border Militarization, State Territorialization, and Embodied Politics at the U.S.–Mexico Border." In *Feminisms in North America: Identities, Citizenship, Human Rights*, ed. Anne Sisson Runyan, Marianne Marchand, Patricia McDermott, and Amy Lind. New York: Ashgate.

Lucht, Hans. 2011. *Darkness before Daybreak: African Migrants Living on the Margins in Southern Italy Today*. Berkeley: University of California Press.

Luibheid, Eithne, Rosi Andrade, and Sally Stevens. 2018. "Intimate Attachments and Migrant Deportability: Lessons from Undocumented Mothers Seeking Benefits for Citizen Children." *Ethnic and Racial Studies* 41 (1): 17–35.

Mainwaring, Cetta, and Noelle Brigden. 2016. "Beyond the Border: Clandestine Migration Journeys." *Geopolitics* 21 (2): 243–62.

Marcus, George E. 1995. "Ethnography in/of the World System: The Emergence of Multi-Sited Ethnography." *Annual Review of Anthropology* 24: 95–117.

Martínez, Óscar. 2013. *The Beast: Riding the Rails and Dodging Narcos on the Migrant Trail*. London: Verso.

———. 2017. *A History of Violence: Living and Dying in Central America.* New York: Verso.

Menjívar, Cecilia. 2000. *Fragmented Ties: Salvadoran Immigrant Ties in America.* Berkeley: University of California Press.

———. 2014. "Immigration Law beyond Borders: Externalizing and Internalizing Border Controls in an Era of Securitization." *Annual Review of Law and Social Science* 10: 353–69.

Menjívar, Cecilia, and Leisy J. Abrego. 2012. "Legal Violence: Immigration Law and the Lives of Central American Immigrants." *American Journal of Sociology* 117 (5): 1380–1421.

Menjívar, Cecilia, Leisy Abrego, and Leah Schmalzbauer. 2016. *Immigrant Families:* Wiley.

Menjívar, Cecilia, and Shannon Drysdale Walsh. 2017. "The Architecture of Feminicide: The State, Inequalities, and Everyday Gender Violence in Honduras." *Latin American Research Review* 52 (2): 221–40.

Merry, Sally Engle. 2009. *Gender Violence: A Cultural Perspective.* Chichester, England: Wiley-Blackwell.

Meyer, Peter, Rhoda Margesson, Clare Seelke, and Maureen Taft-Morales. 2016. "Unaccompanied Children from Central America: Foreign Policy Considerations." Congressional Research Service.

Missbach, Antje. 2015. *Troubled Transit: Asylum Seekers Stuck in Indonesia.* Singapore: ISEAS-Yusof Ishak Institute.

Montoya, Ainhoa. 2011. "'Neither War nor Peace': Violence and Democracy in Post-War El Salvador." PhD diss., University of Manchester School of Social Sciences.

Moodie, Ellen. 2006. "Microbus Crashes and Coca-Cola Cash: The Value of Death in 'free-market' El Salvador." *American Ethnologist* 32 (1): 62–80.

———. 2010. *El Salvador in the Aftermath of Peace: Crime, Uncertainty, and the Transition to Democracy.* Philadelphia: University of Pennsylvania Press.

Mountz, Alison. 2010. *Seeking Asylum: Human Smuggling and Bureaucracy at the Border.* Minneapolis: University of Minnesota Press.

Mountz, Alison, and Jennifer Hyndman. 2006. "Feminist Approaches to the Global Intimate." *Women's Studies Quarterly* 34 (1/2).

Muehlmann, Shaylih. 2014. *When I Wear my Alligator Boots: Narco-Culture in the U.S.-Mexico Borderlands.* Berkeley: University of California Press.

Mueller, Carol, Michelle Hansen, and Karen Qualtire. 2009. "Femicide on the Border and New Forms of Protest: The International Caravan for Justice." In *Human Rights Along the U.S.-Mexico Border: Gendered Violence and Insecurity,* ed. Kathleen Staudt, Tony Payan, and Anthony Kruszewski. Tucson: University of Arizona Press.

Nazario, Sonia. 2006. *Enrique's Journey: The Story of a Boy's Dangerous Odyssey to Reunite with his Mother.* New York: Random House.

Nevins, Joseph. 2002. *Operation Gatekeeper: The Rise of the "Illegal Alien" and the Making of the U.S.-Mexico Boundary.* New York: Routledge.

O'Neill, Kevin Lewis, and Kedron Thomas, eds. 2011. *Securing the City: Neoliberalism, Space and Insecurity in Postwar Guatemala.* Durham, NC: Duke University Press.

Ogren, Cassandra. 2007. "Migration and Human Rights on the Mexico-Guatemala Border." *International Migration* 45 (4).

Papadopoulou-Kourkoula, Aspasia. 2008. *Transit Migration: The Missing Link between Emigration and Settlement.* Houndsmills, Hants, England: Palgrave Macmillan.

Parker, Noel, and Nick Vaughan-Williams. 2012. "Critical Border Studies: Broadening and Deepening the 'Lines in the Sand' Agenda." *Geopolitics* 17: 727–33.

Pessar, Patricia, and Sarah Mahler. 2003. "Transnational Migration: Bringing Gender In." *International Migration Review* 37 (3): 812–46.

Phillips, Melissa, and Antje Missbach. 2017. "Introduction. Special Issue on Transit Migration: Renewing the Focus on a Global Phenomenon." *International Journal of Migration and Border Studies* 3 (2–3): 113–20.

Pine, Adrienne. 2008. *Working Hard, Drinking Hard: On Violence and Survival in Honduras.* Berkeley: University of California Press.

Povinelli, E., and G. Chauncey. 1999. "Thinking Sexuality Transnationally." *GLQ* 5 (4): 439–49.

Pratt, Geraldine, and Victoria Rosner, eds. 2012. *The Global and the Intimate: Feminism in Our Time.* New York: Columbia University Press.

Quesada, James. 1998. "Suffering Child: An Embodiment of War and Its Aftermath in Post-Sandinista Nicaragua." *Medical Anthropology Quarterly* 12 (1): 51–73.

Quesada, James, Laurie Kain Hart, and Philippe Bourgois. 2011. "Structural Vulnerability and Health: Latino Migrant Laborers in the United States." *Medical Anthropology* 30 (4).

Redfield, Peter. 2005. "Doctors, Borders, and Life in Crisis." *Cultural Anthropology* 20 (3): 328–61.

Robinson, William. 2003. *Transnational Conflicts: Central America, Social Change, and Globalization.* London: Verso.

———. 2008. *Latin America and Global Capitalism.* Baltimore: Johns Hopkins University Press.

Rocha, Ramon C. 2005 "Casa del migrante Ricardo Zapata: Migrantes centroamericanos en su paso por Veracruz." http://studylib.es/doc/7102278/casa-del-migrante-ricardo-zapata—migrantes.

Rosas, Gilberto. 2006. "The Thickening Borderlands: Diffused Exceptionality and 'Immigrant' Social Struggles during the 'War on Terror.'" *Cultural Dynamics* 18 (3): 335–49.

———. 2012. *Barrio Libre: Criminalizing States and Delinquent Refusals of the New Frontier.* Durham, NC: Duke University Press.

Rotker, Susana, ed. 2002. *Citizens of Fear: Urban Violence in Latin America* New Brunswick, NJ: Rutgers University Press.

Rouse, Roger. 1996. "Mexican Migration and the Social Space of Postmodernism." In *Between Two Worlds: Mexican Immigrants in the United States,* ed. David G. Gutiérrez. Wilmington, DE: Scholarly Resources.

Salt, John, and Jeremy Stein. 1997. "Migration as a Business: the Case of Trafficking." *International Migration* 35 (4): 467–94.

Sanchez, Gabriella. 2014. *Human Smuggling and Border Crossings.* New York: Routledge.

Sanford, Victoria. 2008. "From Genocide to Feminicide: Impunity and Human Rights in Twenty-First Century Guatemala." *Journal of Human Rights* 7: 104–22.

Scheper-Hughes, Nancy, and Philippe Bourgois, eds. 2004. *Violence in War and Peace: An Anthology.* Oxford: Blackwell.

Scheper-Hughes, Nancy, and Margaret Lock. 1987. "The Mindful Body: A Prolegomenon to Future Work in Medical Anthropology." *Medical Anthropology Quarterly* 1 (1): 6–41.

Schirmer, Jennifer. 1993. "The Seeking of Truth and the Gendering of Consciousness: The CoMadres of El Salvador and the Conavigua Widows of Guatemala." In *Viva: Women and Popular Protest in Latin America,* ed. Sarah Radcliffe and Sallie Westwood. London: Routledge.

Shah, Nayan. 2011. *Stranger Intimacy: Contesting Race, Sexuality, and the Law in the North American West.* Berkeley: University of California Press.

Sharp, Lesley. 2000. "The Commodification of the Body and Its Parts." *Annual Review of Anthropology* 29: 287–328.

Slack, Jeremy, and Scott Whiteford. 2011. "Violence and Migration on the Arizona-Sonora Border." *Human Organization* 70 (1): 11–21.

Smith, Robert Courtney. 2006. *Mexican New York: Transnational Lives of New Immigrants* Berkeley: University of California Press.

Spener, David. 2009. *Clandestine Crossings: Migrants and Coyotes on the Texas-Mexico Border.* Ithaca, NY: Cornell University Press.

Stephen, Lynn. 1995. "Women's Rights Are Human Rights: The Merging of Feminine and Feminist Interests among El Salvador's Mothers of the Disappeared (CO-MADRES)." *American Ethnologist* 22 (4): 807–27.

———. 2000. "The Construction of Indigenous Suspects: Militarization and the Gendered and Ethnic Dynamics of Human Rights Abuses in Southern Mexico." *American Ethnologist* 26 (4): 822–42.

———. 2002. "Sexualities and Genders in Zapotec Oaxaca." *Latin American Perspectives* 29 (123): 41–59.

———. 2013. *We Are the Face of Oaxaca: Testimony and Social Movements.* Durham, NC: Duke University Press.

———. 2016. "Gendered Transborder Violence in the Expanded United States–Mexico Borderlands." *Human Organization* 75 (2): 159–67.

Terrio, Susan. 2015. *Whose Child Am I? Unaccompanied, Undocumented Children in U.S. Immigration Custody.* Berkeley: University of California Press.

Theidon, Kimberly. 2016. "A Greater Measure of Justice: Gender, Violence, and Reparations." In *Mapping Feminist Anthropology in the Twenty-First Century,* ed. Ellen Lewin and Leni Silverstein. New Brunswick, NJ: Rutgers University Press.

Ticktin, Miriam. 2011. *Casualties of Care: Immigration and the Politics of Humanitarianism in France.* Berkeley: University of California Press.

Trouillot, Michel-Rolph. 1997. *Silencing the Past: Power and the Production of History.* Boston: Beacon Press.

Turner, Victor. 1967. *The Forest of Symbols: Aspects of Ndembu Ritual.* Ithaca, NY: Cornell University Press.

United Nations Office on Drugs and Crime. 2013. *Global Study on Homicide: Trends, Contexts, Data.* Vienna: UNODC.

Walters, William 2015. "Reflections on Migration and Governmentality." *Movements: Journal for Critical Migration and Border Regime Studies* 1 (1): 1–25.

Weller, Susan, Roberta Baer, Javier Garcia de Alba Garcia, and Ana Salcedo Rocha. 2008. "*Susto* and *Nervios*: Expressions for Stress and Depression." *Culture, Medicine and Psychiatry* 32 (3): 406–20.

Weston, Kath. 1997. "The Virtual Anthropologist." In *Anthropological Locations,* ed. Akhil Gupta and James Ferguson. Berkeley: University of California Press.

Wies, Jennifer, and Hillary Haldane, eds. 2015. *Applying Anthropology to Gender-Based Violence: Global Responses, Local Practices.* Lanham, MD: Lexington Books.

Willen, Sarah. 2007. "Toward a Critical Phenomonology of 'Illegality': State Power, Criminalization, and Abjectivity among Undocumented Migrant Workers in Tel Aviv, Israel." *International Migration* 45 (2).

———. 2012. "Migration, 'illegality,' and Health: Mapping Embodied Vulnerability and Debating Health Related Deservingness." *Social Science and Medicine* 74: 805–11.

Wilson, Ara. 2004. *The Intimate Economies of Bangkok: Tomboys, Tycoons, and Avon Ladies in the Global City.* Berkeley: University of California Press.

———. 2012. "Intimacy: A Useful Category of Transnational Analysis." In *The Global and the Intimate: Feminism in Our Time,* ed. Geraldine Pratt and Victoria Rosner. New York: Columbia University Press.

Wilson, Thomas, and Hastings Donnan, eds. 2012. *A Companion to Border Studies*. Hoboken, NJ : John Wiley & Sons.

Wolseth, Jon. 2008. "Everyday Violence and the Persistence of Grief: Wandering and Loss among Honduran Youths." *Journal of Latin American and Caribbean Anthropology* 13 (2): 311–35.

World Bank. 2015. Intentional Homicides. https://data.worldbank.org/indicator /VC.IHR.PSRC.P5?locations=GT.

Wright, Melissa 2011. "Necropolitics, Narcopolitics, and Femicide: Gendered Violence on the Mexico–U.S. Border." *Signs* 36 (3): 707–31.

Xiang, Biao, and Johan Lindquist. 2014. "Migration Infrastructure." *International Migration Review* 48 (1): 122–48.

Yarris, Kristin. 2017. *Care across Generations: Solidarity and Sacrifice in Transnational Families*. Stanford: Stanford University Press.

Zhang, Sheldon, Gabriella Sanchez, and Luigi Achilli. 2018. "Crimes of Solidarity in Mobility: Alternative Views on Migrant Smuggling." *ANNALS of the American Academy of Political and Social Science* 676 (1): 6–15.

Zilberg, Elana. 2011. *Spaces of Detention: The Making of a Transnational Gang Crisis between Los Angeles and San Salvador*. Durham, NC: Duke University Press.

Zucker, Norman, and Naomi Zucker. 1996. *Desperate Crossings: Seeking Refuge in America*. New York: M. E. Sharpe.

Index

People who help them along the way
→ Shelters /homes etc

CPSIA information can be obtained
at www.ICGtesting.com
Printed in the USA
LVHW032345081218
599806LV00001B/31/P